Lyndon B. Johnson School of Public Affairs
Policy Research Project Report
Number 60

The Use of Public Services by Undocumented Aliens in Texas: A Study of State Costs and Revenues

A report by
The Undocumented Workers Policy Research Project
The University of Texas at Austin
1984

Final report to the Governor's Budget and Planning Office pursuant to interagency contract No. IAC-82-83-1554-GBPO, between the GBPO and the University of Texas at Austin

Library of Congress Card Number: 84-80044
ISBN: 0-89940-662-9

Printed in the U.S.A.
Cover design by Barbara Jezek

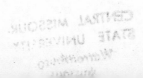

POLICY RESEARCH PROJECT PARTICIPANTS

Sheng-Ih Chang
Scott C. Cleland
Michael P. Cohen
Julia E. R. Curry
Pamela J. Dixon
David A. Dominey
Adela I. Flores
Jesus M. Garcia
Diego J. Gonzalez
Teresa E. Griffin
Kimberly A. Jenkins
Margaret C. Mendez
Arthur D. Pedersen, Jr.
Norman C. Plotkin
Willie H. Pruitt, Jr.
Anne D. Rader
Marc Techner
Martha A. Van Haitsma
Diane J. Vigil

Project Directors

Sidney Weintraub, Dean Rusk Chair, Lyndon B. Johnson School of
  Public Affairs

Gilberto Cardenas, Assistant Professor of Sociology, The University
  of Texas at Austin

TABLE OF CONTENTS

LIST OF TABLES

LIST OF TABLES, Continued

LIST OF TABLES, Continued

LIST OF TABLES, Continued

LIST OF TABLES, Continued

LIST OF FIGURES

LIST OF ANNEXES

Foreword

The Lyndon B. Johnson School of Public Affairs has established inter-disciplinary research on policy problems as the core of its educational program. A major part of this program is the nine-month policy research project, in the course of which two or three faculty members from different disciplines direct the research of ten to twenty graduate students of diverse backgrounds on a policy issue of concern to a government agency. This "client orientation" brings the students face to face with admini-strators, legislators, and other officials active in the policy process, and demonstrates that research in a policy environment demands special talents. It also illuminates the occasional difficulties of relating research findings to the world of political realities.

This report on the costs and revenues generated by undocumented aliens in Texas is the product of a policy research project conducted at the LBJ School in 1982-83. The publication was primarily funded by the Governor's Budget and Planning Office, with support from the Lyndon B. Johnson Foundation.

The curriculum of the LBJ School is intended not only to develop effective public servants but also to produce research that will enlighten and inform those already engaged in the policy process. The project that resulted in this report has helped to accomplish the first task; it is our hope and expectation that the report itself will contribute to the second.

Finally, it should be noted that neither the LBJ School nor The Uni-versity of Texas at Austin necessarily endorses the views or findings of this study.

Max Sherman
Dean

ACKNOWLEDGEMENTS

This study of public service utilization and taxes paid by undocumented aliens in the State of Texas was made possible by interagency contract No. IAC-82-83-1554-GPBO between the Governor's Planning and Budget Office and The University of Texas at Austin.

The vehicle of research was a Policy Research Project of the LBJ School of Public Affairs directed by two faculty members (Sidney Weintraub, LBJ School, and Gilbert Cardenas, Department of Sociology) and twenty graduate students from the LBJ School, the Institute of Latin American Studies, and the Department of Sociology.

Several members of the LBJ School staff provided assistance above and beyond their required duties. Among them were Carl Ratliff and Michael Donovan of the School's Computer Center, and Linda Borchardt, secretary to Professor Sidney Weintraub. Mrs. Borchardt is owed a special word of thanks for her careful production of numerous drafts of the report, including this final draft, on the School's computer text-processing system.

The United States Immigration and Naturalization Service, and its affiliate agency, the U.S. Border Patrol, allowed the project's interviewers to speak to aliens detained in several locations in the state. In San Antonio, special mention goes to the District Director, Ricardo Casillas, and Investigator Steve Fuentes. In South Texas, Cecilio Ruiz, Assistant Deportation Officer, permitted access to the Port Isabel (Los Fresnos) INS Detention Center. U.S. Border Patrol Chief Alan Eliason and Officer Jim Herman, El Paso sector, and Chief Jack Richardson, Del Rio sector, permitted interviewers to talk to aliens prior to their voluntary return to Mexico. (In all cases it was made clear to interviewees that they were under no compulsion to grant the interview.)

The graduate students who traveled to the field for interviews received the hospitality of several persons. Acting hosts were: Mike and Barbara Flores in Dallas; Alice Petry in El Paso; Maria Angela Flores in Houston; and Raul Solis, Professor of Social Work, Pan American University, in McAllen.

Numerous individuals assisted by providing guidance from their personal experiences. This was especially valuable to the project's researchers who administered surveys to undocumented aliens in the six cities targeted in the study. The following is a listing of these individuals by location:

AUSTIN

Paul Parsons, Esq.; Abraham Torres, Institute of Latin American Studies; Cindy Schaefer, Our Lady of Guadalupe Catholic Church; Dan Nieto, Linda Phillips, Stella Fiori, Julius Corpus and Carmen Rodriguez, staff of the

Community Action Program; and Robbie Davis, Information Resource Program at the School of Social Work, The University of Texas.

DALLAS

Nancy Boye, Proyecto Adelante; Father Uriel Osnaya, St. Matthew's Cathedral's Hispanic Ministeries; Ed Purcell and Pam Merrifield, Catholic Migration and Refugee Services, Diocese of Dallas; David Moreno and M. Anita Cerda, Dallas Concilio of Hispanic Service Organizations; Sister Mary Walz, Director, Marillac Social Center; Josefina Torres, and Rosa Urretia.

EL PASO

L. A. Velarde, Director, United States Catholic Conference; and Miguel Angel Nunez.

HOUSTON

Father Roberto Flores, El Centro para Inmigrantes; Diane Perez, Ripley House Community Center; Jose Medina, Esq.; Maria Martinez; and Susan McMarms, Associate Professor of Political Science at the University of Houston.

MCALLEN AND SOUTH TEXAS

Chadd Richardson, Professor of Sociology, Pan American University; Gilbert Cardenas, Professor of Economics, Pan American University; Juanita Valdez-Cox, United Farm Workers; Jose Acosta, General Counsel, Border Association for Refugees from Central America (BARCA); Laurier McDonald, Esq.; Lisa Brodyaga, Director, Proyecto Libertad; Alfredo de Avila, Texas Farm Workers; Rev. Ralph Baumgartner, Pastor, First Lutheran Church; and Rose Ann Renteria.

SAN ANTONIO

Alma Lopez, Esq., Catholic Family Services; Dr. Norma Carreon, San Antonio Independent School District.

In gathering information about the undocumented school population, several public officials provided special assistance. They are: John Kennedy, Research Analyst, Texas Research League; Charles Nixon, Associate Commissioner for Planning and Research, Texas Education Agency (TEA); Thomas Patton,

Director of State Funding, TEA; the Superintendents of the Independent School Districts in Dallas, El Paso, Brownsville, Houston, McAllen and San Antonio, as well as the Assistant Superintendent for Instruction of the Austin I.S.D., Gonzalo Garza.

Several law enforcement agencies provided information and cooperated in a survey administered to patrolmen in various locations. In Austin, mention goes to Robert Chapman, Director, and Kim Peterson, Planner, of the Research and Planning Division; Police Chief Frank Dyson; and Lt. Neal, Criminal Investigation Bureau, of the Austin Police Department. Also, the Research and Planning Bureaus of the Dallas, El Paso, and Houston Police Departments, and to Captain Peter Casias and Lt. Dale B. Jacobs in San Antonio. Our thanks also go to the McAllen Police Department's Division of Support and Services and the many police officers in Texas who voluntarily completed questionnaires for the project.

Local agencies and members of their staffs throughout the state cooperated with the project's researchers by supplying information. Following is a list of some of them:

AUSTIN

Carlos Herrera and Sue Soffer, Department of Human Resources, City of Austin; Caritas; The Urban League; Rape Crisis Center; Center for Battered Women; South Austin Neighborhood Council Youth Bureau; Youth Advocacy; and Youth Employment Services.

DALLAS

Assistant Director John Wood and Callie Foster, Department of Human Resources, City of Dallas; Ron Skopek, Community Development Program; Carol Ann Blackburn, Director, Department of Human Resources; Rape Crisis Center; Dallas County Community Action Committee, Inc.; Family Outreach; Big Brothers/Big Sisters; Community Council of Greater Dallas; Dallas Child Guidance; The United Way; The Family Place; Catholic Charities of Dallas; and the staff of Martin Luther King, Jr. Community Center.

EL PASO

Norm Haley, Vice-President, Private Industry Council; Henry Neil, Director, Department of Community Development, El Paso County; Charles Taylor, Department of Parks and Recreation, El Paso County; Office of the Comptroller, El Paso County; Henry Nava, Director, El Paso County General Assistance Program; The Boys Clubs; Transitional Living Center, Inc.; Aliviane, Inc.; Women's Resources Center; Child Guidance Center; Youth Assistance Program; Rape Crisis Center; and Richard C. Hagerty, The United Way.

SAN ANTONIO

Leslie Schockner and other staff members, San Antonio Department of Human Services and Resources; R. Bahaghe, Ella Austin Youth Advocacy Guidance Program, Ella Austin Community Center; Domingo Bueno, Vice President for Human Resources, Mexican American Unity Council; Pedro Roque, Director of Program Operations, Centro Del Barrio; Richard Brown, Director of Multi-Service Centers of San Antonio; Ben Butler, Eastside Multi-Service Center; Bill Wallace, West End Multi-Service Center; Sergio G. Soto, Director of City of San Antonio Youth Services Project.

MCALLEN

Willie Seguin, Budget Director, City of McAllen Budget Office.

HOUSTON

Comptroller's Office, City of Houston.

Several state-wide agencies, and their personnel, assisted in gathering information on the usage of their services by undocumented aliens. They are:

TEXAS COMMISSION FOR THE DEAF

Phil Roch, Business Manager

TEXAS STATE COMMISSION FOR THE BLIND

Rolando Garza and Lorenzo Garcia

TEXAS EMPLOYMENT COMMISSION (TEC)

Peter Acosta, Monitor/Advocate

TEC offices in Brownsville, Dallas, Edinburg, El Paso, Austin, Houston, San Antonio and McAllen

TEXAS REHABILITATION COMMISSION (TRC)

John Wylie, Program and Facility Services

TRC offices in Austin, Dallas, Harlingen and San Antonio

TEXAS DEPARTMENT OF COMMUNITY AFFAIRS

Dr. John Guzman, Migrant Workers' Advocate; Roy Fewell, Housing and Community Development Division; Mary S. Tijerina, Drug Abuse Prevention Division; Richard H. Ross, Children and Youth Services Division; and John Clay, Local Governmental Services Division.

TEXAS DEPARTMENT OF HUMAN RESOURCES

The Family Self-Support Branch, Protective Services Division, the Income Assistance Division, and the Management and Budget Division.

COUNTY AGENCIES

The Child Welfare Departments of Bexar, Dallas, El Paso, Harris, and Hidalgo Counties, and the Harris County Social Services Department.

Demographic information was supplied by the Planning Departments of the Cities of Austin, El Paso, McAllen and San Antonio; the Houston Chamber of Commerce; the North Central Texas Council of Governments; and Jerry Olson of the Bureau of Business Research, The University of Texas at Austin.

Health-related information came from a variety of sources, both state and local.

TEXAS DEPARTMENT OF HEALTH

Dr. Ralph Norris, Director, Local Health Services; Dr. John Bradley, Director, Region 3; Dr. Earl Gorby, Deputy Director, and Director, Tuberculosis Control, Region 3; Mike Young, Tuberculosis Program Manager, Region 3; and Louise Fisher, Administrator, Region 3.

CLINICS AND LOCAL HEALTH AGENCIES

Austin

South Austin, Montopolis and East Austin Clinics; and Mike Candelas, Assistant Administrator, Austin-Travis County Health Department.

Dallas

West Dallas, North Dallas, Martin Luther King, Jr., Oak Cliff and Juanita Craft Clinics; and D.H. Howell, Director, Dallas Human Health Services.

El Paso

Dr. Lea Hutchinson, Director, El Paso City-County Health Department; and Bill Brown, Director, Personal Health Services, El Paso City-County Health Department.

Harris County

Curtis Baker, Assistant Fiscal Administrator, Harris County Hospital District.

South Texas

Region 8 Clinics in Donna, Edinburg, Hidalgo, McAllen, Mercedes, Mission, Pharr, and Weslaco; and Sister Mary Vincelli, Director of Nursing, Hidalgo County Health Department.

PUBLIC HOSPITALS

Brackenridge Public Hospital (Austin)

Robert Spurck, Hospital Administrator; Nicolas Overby, Assistant Administrator; Robert Hueffmeier, Business Office Manager; Josie Hernandez, Admissions Supervisor; and Marie Cruz, Billing Supervisor.

Bexar County Hospital (San Antonio)

John J. Walsh, Controller; John Guest, Administrator; and Ferdinand Ginzle, Associate Executive Director for Fiscal Services.

Parkland Memorial Hospital (Dallas)

Steve Nathan, Assistant Administrator; and Tom Cox, Hospital Attorney.

R. E. Thomasen General Hospital (El Paso)

Bill Kenedy, Assistant Administrator; Bob Bridgehour, Director of Admitting; Alice Martinez, Shift Leader, Emergency Room; and Mrs. Orozco, Supervisor, Out-Patient Registration.

The foregoing is not a complete history. Many persons preferred not to be named.

Finally, perhaps the most important acknowledgements should go to the several hundred undocumented aliens from various countries who answered many questions about their lifestyles and personal histories. Without them, the data provided by the agencies and individuals mentioned above would have been incomplete.

EXECUTIVE SUMMARY

The purpose of the study was to compare the cost to provide public services to undocumented persons with the revenue received from taxes and fees paid by them. The comparisons were made at two levels, one covering the State of Texas and the other six urban areas of the state, namely, Austin, Dallas, Houston, San Antonio, El Paso, and the Rio Grande Valley region centering on McAllen. Two techniques were used to gather data. The first was to obtain information from state and local agencies providing public services, using published and unpublished material as well as personal interviews for this purpose. The second was to interview, in Spanish, undocumented aliens directly. Most of the undocumented individuals questioned were living at home, but some were interviewed in detention or holding centers of the Immigration and Naturalization Service in order to have a test population for comparison.

The following summary recapitulates the findings by chapter. The material in the seven chapters making up the body of the study is amplified and documented in the nine appendices. The techniques used to estimate costs of services and revenues received are set forth in detail at each appropriate point in the study.

As explained in the opening chapter, the study focused on four major public service areas--health, social services, education, and criminal justice--as being the most significant in terms of usage and cost. The choice of cities and sectors of cities on which to concentrate was based on census data showing residence patterns of the state's Hispanic population. The questionnaire (in English and Spanish) used to interview undocumented persons included questions on birth and migration patterns, family characteristics, demographic and income data, and the use of specific publicly funded services.

As detailed in Chapter Two, a total of 253 undocumented persons were interviewed for the study; 214 were undetained and 39 persons were interviewed in detention centers. The households of the interviewees, that is, the total sample population, numbered 868. Of these, 805 persons resided in undetained households while 63 lived in "detained" households. Over 60 percent of the persons in the sample were born in Mexico and 18.5 percent were born in Central or South American countries. There were twenty Mexican states and the Federal District represented in the sample. Three states (Chihuahua, Michoacan, and Tamaulipas) were the former residence of almost one-half of the Mexican respondents. Almost 20 percent of the sample consisted of persons born in the U.S., primarily spouses and children of undocumented aliens. Over 30 percent of all 253 households included U.S.-born children.

Comparisons of various characteristics were made between the detained and undetained populations in order to make judgments about the differences between the two populations. Background information on origin and patterns of migration indicated that the two sample groups differed in several key aspects. For example, there were striking differences in the length of stay in the U.S. between the detained and undetained undocumented. While almost one-half of the detainees had been in the U.S. less than a year, only 16 percent of the nondetainees had been here less than a year. While the average length of stay for the detained undocumented alien was seven months, the average for the undetained was more than four years. The undetained population in our sample did not exhibit the characteristics of single, male migrant workers coming to the U.S. for only short periods of time. The detained and undetained varied also in the number of repeat entries with almost 68 percent of the detained coming to the U.S. more than once compared to less than 40 percent for the undetained. Our evidence indicates that the two populations are distinct and that valid conclusions about one population cannot be made from evidence about the other.

The principal reason given for coming to the U.S. was to look for work; 65 percent of the respondents gave this reason. The other main reason given by Mexicans was family reunification. Undocumented persons from Central and South American countries often stated that their reason for coming was to escape political oppression.

Males and females were equally represented in the undetained sample while the detained sample was primarily male. The largest age group in the undetained sample was children up to four years old, with 30 percent of the sample being under ten years of age. Persons from 20 to 24 and from 25 to 29 were the second and third largest age groups in the undetained population. There were only three persons in the detained population under age 14 while over 70 percent were from 15 to 29 years old. The detained sample population was primarily male and under 30 years, while the undetained population was comprised of younger persons and was evenly divided between males and females. The age and sex characteristics of the undetained population suggest a present and future need for health services such as maternity, family planning, and child health programs.

The undetained respondents are more likely to be married and living with nuclear families and other relatives than the detained population--63 percent of the undetained were married and more than 70 percent were living with family members while only 25 percent of the detained sample were married and 90 percent were not living with relatives. Educational attainment for both sample groups was mixed. Undetained persons tended to have more years of schooling than did the detained, while fewer of the detained had no education at all.

The employment characteristics of both detained and undetained respondents were similar. Most persons were employed in the service area, primarily hotel and restaurant positions. Of the rest, 22 percent were employed in construction; most of these were in Houston. In addition, 24 percent of the respondents were employed as domestics or in factories. There was little unemployment among respondents--only 1.3 percent were without jobs.

As shown in Chapter Three, the detained and undetained populations differed considerably in their use of public services in Texas. The detained population used almost no public services while the undetained reported use of services in all of the public areas surveyed. Over one-fourth of the

undetained population used some kind of publicly supported health service.
Most of these were children using the services of public health clinics,
especially immunization services. Adults also used public health clinics to
some extent, but their usage of publicly supported hospitals and emergency
rooms was more significant. There was little reported use of family planning
and maternity services. Most emergency room and hospital admissions were for
the treatment of accidents and for childbirth. Less than 5 percent of the
sample used public dental services. The undocumented population paid for
their health services primarily on a cash basis, although hospitalization
costs often required payment by a contract arrangement. Only 21 percent paid
for medical bills with health insurance.

There was little use of social services in any of the regions surveyed.
Fewer than 5 percent of the respondents reported that they used such general
assistance services as AFDC, food stamps, rent and utility bill aid,
transportation, WIC, counseling services, workman's compensation, and
unemployment benefits. Most households receiving food stamps and WIC had
legal U.S. residents living in the household, mostly U.S.-born children.

Among the households questioned, 79 had 202 children enrolled in U.S.
schools, 188 were enrolled in public schools and 71 percent of these were
undocumented children. Most children used special programs in the public
schools, including bilingual education, school breakfast, and school lunch
programs.

Almost one-half of the households received some kind of legal assistance.
In the last year, more than 70 percent of this assistance was for immigration
matters. Over one-fourth used private practitioners, but public and church-
sponsored legal aid were also important. Almost one-half of the households
had persons using public transit services. Public recreation facilities were
used by over 40 percent of the sample population.

Chapter Four contains the estimate of income earned and taxes paid by
undocumented aliens. The figures are based on an independent estimate of the
size of the undocumented population in Texas (the estimate made in 1982 by
Frank D. Bean, Allan G. King, and others of the Texas Population Research
Center), U.S. Census data on the Hispanic population in Texas, and data
obtained in our surveys. The revenue estimates are given in ranges, based on
an undocumented population equal to that estimated by Bean and King (X), a
population half that size (X/2), or twice that size (2X). We assumed that the
undocumented population was distributed across the state in the same ratio as
the Hispanic population. Under this assumption, the six cities surveyed
contained 54.9 percent of the state's undocumented population. The midpoint
of the undocumented population in the state in 1980 was 918,400.

Whenever a choice had to be made in estimating tax revenue received from
undocumented aliens, the lowest viable figure was selected in order to be
conservative. The taxes estimated are social security, income, sales, and
various excises. The estimates can be recapitulated as follows:

Taxes Paid by Undocumented Persons
(millions of dollars)

	Low Estimate	High Estimate
Social Security	122	197
Income	175	282
Sales	48	78
Excises	14	23

Chapter Five contains estimates of the costs to the state and the six regions to provide public services. The estimates are based on information from providers of public services and the survey of the undocumented aliens. Whenever a choice had to be made among estimates, the highest viable cost figure was used, that is, the reverse of the revenue technique. Our methodology, therefore, was to bias downward revenue estimates and bias upward cost estimates. The motivation for this was to arrive at conservative estimates.

The cost estimates were made separately for the localities and for the state. Different localities do not provide the same range of services; for example, not all have public hospitals. The most significant services in terms of cost are hospitalization, other health care, education, and the administration of criminal justice. The use of social services (AFDC, food stamps, WIC, etc.) is less costly since these services are not used as much by undocumented aliens. When they are used, there is often a legal resident in the household; that is, the cost is not to provide a service to an undocumented alien.

The estimates on costs to provide public services are combined in Chapter Six. The totals are then contrasted with the revenues received from taxes paid by undocumented aliens. The key comparisons are the following:

Costs and Revenues to the State
(millions of dollars)

	Low Estimate	High Estimate
Cost	50	97
Revenue	157	277

Costs and Revenues to the Six Localities
(millions of dollars)

	Low Estimate	High Estimate
Cost	13	35
Revenue	5	9

What is apparent from the two foregoing tables is that state revenue from undocumented persons far exceeds cost to provide services to them, but that localities bear significantly greater cost to provide services than direct revenue received. Taken together, state and local revenues far exceed costs. Some of the excess revenue received by the state is returned to localities, but the amounts are not easily specified.

Chapter Seven summarizes the conclusions and recommendations of the study. They can be further summarized here as follows:

- Despite our biasing the costs upward and the revenues downward, tax revenues from undocumented aliens clearly exceed costs to provide public services to them.

- In this revenue/cost comparison, the state comes out well but the localities come out badly.

- At the individual level it is possible to talk of documented and undocumented aliens, but this clear demarcation disappears at the household level where legal and illegal aliens live together.

- It is impossible to reach any substantial conclusion about the undetained undocumented population from an examination of persons in Immigration and Naturalization Service (INS) detention or holding centers.

- The most costly services used by undocumented persons—hospitals, immunization, education—are somewhat beneficial to U.S. society generally as well as being valuable to the undocumented persons using these services.

CHAPTER 1

INTRODUCTION

For the past several years the issue of illegal immigration has received a great deal of attention from American policymakers and the general public. This is apparent from the study commissions, public hearings, and debates at the state and national levels, and by the many proposals which have been introduced to reform U.S. immigration laws. One salient aspect of this debate has been the question of the economic impact of the undocumented population on the nation as a whole and on the particular states and localities in which this population is concentrated. More specifically, the question of net cost for providing publicly funded social services to undocumented persons has been a concern at all jurisdictional levels. This question is the main focus of the present research.

Before discussing the specifics of our research project, an explanation of the language used to describe the population under investigation is in order. The label "illegal alien" is used in much of the literature, but this term may carry a negative connotation. Therefore, in this study the term "undocumented person" or "undocumented alien" is utilized instead. The Immigration and Nationality Act (INA) defines an alien as "any person not a citizen or national of the United States." Our study is concerned with those aliens who, because they do not possess the proper documents required by the Immigration and Naturalization Service (INS), are residing in the United States unlawfully. An undocumented person may be one who entered the country illegally (without papers), or one who after legal entry (with papers) violated the terms of admission. In the two border communities studied (El Paso and the Rio Grande Valley), there is a large population of individuals who do not reside in the United States at all, but who commute from the bordering Mexican communities. Some of these persons have legal documents while others do not. While we did not target these individuals for our sample, their presence may be reflected in the figures supplied by service providers regarding the use of public services by undocumented persons in these border areas. Our study does not target those aliens who may be legally residing in the United States, but who, because of their engagement in some activity not authorized by their visa, may also be in violation of U.S. immigration laws.

In this study we attempt to estimate what costs are incurred by the State of Texas for the provision of public services—such as welfare, education, health care, police, fire protection, and others—to undocumented persons residing in the state, and to contrast these costs with the direct and indirect contributions made by this population to the taxes and other revenues which fund these programs. The study focuses on six localities—Austin, Dallas, El Paso, Houston, San Antonio, and the McAllen-Rio Grande Valley area—and the State of Texas as a whole. Because the costs for providing services often fall on a jurisdiction different from that receiving revenues paid by the undocumented aliens, it is necessary to examine separately local, state and federal taxes paid by these persons. It is also necessary that the funding sources for each service-providing agency be broken down into the same categories.

ORGANIZATION OF RESEARCH

The research team of twenty graduate students and two faculty supervisors took a dual approach to the research problem. Information was obtained from agencies charged with providing the public services in question, as well as from a sample of the undocumented population in these six areas. Taking both perspectives into account made it possible to have a cross check on the data. The methodology for data collection is detailed in Appendix A, but is briefly described below.

From the standpoint of the providing agencies, the investigation was organized according to four general types of service--health, education, welfare/social services, and law enforcement. Although research techniques varied according to the particular circumstances of each service, the basic approach was similar. The researchers began by examining official publications, local and state budgets, and organizational charts to learn about the types of services available, eligibility requirements, and jurisdictional responsibilities for provision of each service. We used census data to familiarize ourselves with the demography of each locality to be studied. It was necessary not only to target certain neighborhoods where undocumented persons were believed to reside, but also to focus on the types of services these aliens were most likely to utilize. Questions regarding the use of services by the undocumented were then developed for service providers from the management to the caseworker level.

For gathering information about the use of educational and law enforcement services by the undocumented, we relied heavily on questionnaires. Formulated inquiries about undocumented children's school attendance were sent to superintendents of school districts within each of the areas under investigation. In the case of law enforcement, questionnaires were distributed to hundreds of police officers in the target cities asking them about the extent and nature of police contact with undocumented persons. For information about health care and social service usage by the undocumented, we relied primarily on personal and telephone interviews with administrators, supervisors, caseworkers, and intake and billing personnel from the various service-providing agencies. These individuals often do not know the immigration status of their clients, particularly if this information is not part of the eligibility criteria. However, many of these persons, based on their experience, did supply useful estimates and valuable qualitative information on the use of health care and social services by the undocumented.

The second broad aspect of the research involved the collection of empirical data from a sample of the undocumented population regarding their use of public services and their contributions to government revenues. This required the development and testing of a survey instrument, establishment of a sample, administration of the questionnaires, and statistical analysis of the data. The survey instrument, a questionnaire, the English and Spanish versions of which appear in Appendices C and D, was administered in Spanish to individuals in the six localities. A total of 214 usable completed forms were collected with information about a total of 805 household members. The questionnaire consisted of three types of questions. First, demographic questions were asked about the respondent and each member of his/her household. Second, questions were asked about income, direct payment into tax funds, and expenditures which contribute indirectly to revenues at all jurisdictional levels. Third, the questionnaire inquired about the use of all public services, including welfare-type programs with strict eligibility standards as well as community services available to all residents, such as police and fire protection.

Because of the clandestine lifestyles of many of the undocumented, it is difficult to establish contact with individual members of the population and impossible to establish a perfectly representative sample for study. Our sample was generated with the cooperation of individuals and institutions having direct contact with undocumented persons within each of the six areas. Unlike many of the earlier studies on undocumented aliens, we targeted undetained individuals. However, for a control group, we did interview 39 undocumented persons being held in INS detention centers. Strict confidentiality was maintained in all interviews with undocumented persons, as well as with those service providers who so requested.

ORGANIZATION OF STUDY

The following chapters present the findings of our study based on analysis of the data collected from our survey of the undocumented population and the representatives of the service-providing agencies.

Chapter Two describes the population interviewed in our sample. The chapter includes the population's demographic characteristics and information regarding household composition and use of public services.

Chapter Three contains a brief summary of the use of public services by the sample population.

Chapter Four presents estimates of the income levels and tax payments of Texas' undocumented population. We based our population estimates on the Bean and King (1982) study of the number of undocumented persons residing in Texas. For purposes of our calculations we used their low estimate of 568,900 and their high estimate of 918,400 as our range. For some purposes, we also examined data based on half their low estimate and twice their high estimate, which gives a wide range of undocumented persons in Texas between 284,450 and 1,836,500. We applied the information obtained from the responses of our sample to these figures in order to estimate the overall income and taxation levels for this population. To the extent possible we broke down the tax payments into state and federal revenues.

In Chapter Five we estimate the costs to provide public services to the undocumented population in Texas. Here, too, we use the estimation formula described for Chapter Four. The estimates based on data obtained from the service providers were uniformly higher than estimates based on survey responses from the undocumented. Again, we attempted to break down the costs according to jurisdictional level.

In Chapter Six we compare the findings presented in the two previous chapters; that is, the estimate of taxes paid by undocumented persons with the estimate of cost of services provided to this population. Here we present estimates of the net economic impact of the undocumented population on the State of Texas. The chapter also provides conclusions from our study.

Nine appendices, attached to this report, contain a detailed description of the methodology employed in the study, copies of the questionnaires used, information obtained from service providers in each of the four general categories noted above, and a brief annotated bibliography of other studies which address questions similar to those treated here.

There are limitations inherent in our study which should be acknowledged. These apply to our sources of information as well as to our estimation methods. Many of the estimates on the use of services by undocumented aliens are necessarily based on judgments on the part of the providers. Unless citizenship or legal residency is a requirement for eligibility, service providers do not always inquire about a client's immigration status. Sometimes the client volunteers this information, at other times the caseworkers know the person's immigration status from another source, and sometimes caseworkers just suspect the person to be undocumented. Consequently, there is room for error in the information gathered from the providers of social services. Gathering comparable information from undocumented persons directly provided some cross check on data obtained from service providers.

There are limitations with our sample. First, because in dealing almost entirely with organizations catering to Hispanics for help in obtaining interviews, our sample population necessarily consisted of a majority of people of Hispanic origin. There are undoubtedly non-Hispanic undocumented persons in Texas. Second, since we worked through organizations to get many of our contacts, our sample may not include members of the undocumented population who have no formal contact with the community, and who, instead, rely entirely on self-help and personal networks for assistance. Also, since the interviews were conducted in urban centers, our sample may not reflect that segment of the undocumented population which resides in rural communities.

Our estimates of the total revenues paid by undocumented aliens and of the costs to the state incurred by these persons are also subject to limitations. Because our study relies on the Bean and King estimates, our conclusions will reflect the problems inherent in that study. Another possible error may have entered the study due to our assumption that the undocumented population is distributed in the state in the same proportion as the Hispanic population.

Error in our estimates cannot be directly determined through statistical procedures because of the limitations mentioned above. However, confidence in the estimates can, in part, be indirectly assessed to the extent that measures from similarly constructed non-probability sample designs yield similar, though not necessarily identical, results. All the familiar efforts to minimize error in survey research, such as standardization of the survey measure, interviewing practices, and so forth, were adhered to in this study.

Despite its limitations, we believe this study contributes a great deal of useful information to the body of research which exists on the undocumented population. Because of the underground existence of undocumented immigrants, we cannot know with certainty the characteristics of that population or measure precisely its impact on the economy of the nation or the localities in which they reside. Thus, in order to obtain a composite sketch of the undocumented population, we had to piece together information obtained from various studies, each using different nonrandom samples. The data from the present study will, we believe, bring us one step closer to understanding the financial issues created by the presence of these migrants. Although our study was primarily aimed at fiscal questions, it also yielded general demographic and behavioral information about the undocumented population. Used in conjunction with existing information, this study should help policy makers in effectively evaluating legislative and administrative proposals regarding undocumented persons.

The present study is particularly valuable because data were obtained from two diverse sources, permitting a comparison of the responses of providers as well as of users regarding public services. Furthermore, it is one of the few studies in which both detained and undetained undocumented individuals were interviewed, making it possible to examine the differences that exist between the two populations.

CHAPTER 2

CHARACTERISTICS OF THE SAMPLE POPULATION

In order to understand the need for and the use of public services by a population group, it is first necessary to identify the characteristics which influence and determine the demand for public services. A profile of the sample undocumented alien population is presented in this chapter. Specific attention is given to those characteristics which allow us to predict the use by this population of publicly funded health, education, and social services. Particular attention is also given to similarities and dissimilarities in characteristics between detained and undetained undocumented aliens. Past studies have generally focused on persons detained in Immigration and Naturalization Service (INS) holding centers. In our sample, detained aliens represent only 15 percent of the interviewees. The other 85 percent are undocumented aliens residing in six urban areas in Texas. There are striking differences between these two population groups which help explain the differences in their use of public services. Evaluation of public policy affecting the provision of services for undocumented aliens in Texas must take these differences into account. This chapter presents background data and demographic and socio-economic characteristics of the sample populations obtained from the survey. It should be noted that in many instances the population totals presented in the tables will differ because of varying response rates to individual questions.

BACKGROUND: ORIGIN AND PATTERNS OF MIGRATION

The sample population totaled 368 persons, including 305 from undetained and 63 from detained households. Information on the place of birth for 836 persons in the sample population is provided in Table 2.1. Over 60 percent of the sample population were born in Mexico and 18 percent were born in Central or South American countries. Three-fourths of the persons in the detained population group were born in Mexico, while less than 13 percent were from Central or South America. Almost 20 percent of the total sample population are comprised of U.S.-born persons, primarily spouses and children of undocumented aliens. Of 253 total households, 87 (or 34.4 percent) included U.S.-born children. There was an average of two U.S.-born children in the 87 households. The percentage of persons born in Mexico in the undetained group was smaller (60.3 percent) because of the larger number of Central and South American and U.S.-born in this group (see Table 2.1).

Twenty states and the Federal District are represented when Mexican respondents identified their former state of residence (see Table 2.2). Two of the Mexican border states, Chihuahua and Tamaulipas, were the former

Table 2.1

Place of Birth

Where Born	Totals		Non-Detainees		Detainees	
	N	%	N	%	N	%
Mexico	513	61.4	466	60.3	47	74.6
Central or South America	155	18.5	147	19.0	8	12.7
United States	159	19.0	156	20.2	3	4.8
Other[1]	9	.5	4	.5	5	7.9
Totals	836[2]	100.0	773[3]	100.0	63	100.0

Source: Texas Undocumented Survey.

Percentages may not total 100 because of rounding.

[1]Unspecified African countries.

[2]Total sample size is 868; missing data on 32 persons.

[3]Non-detainee sample size is 805; missing data on 32 persons.

Table 2.2

Respondents' Former Residence States
(Mexican Immigrants)

State	Totals		Non-Detainees		Detainees	
	N	%	N	%	N	%
Chihuahua	36	18.7	34	20.8	2	6.7
Coahuila	15	7.8	14	8.6	1	3.3
Federal District	7	3.6	5	3.1	2	6.7
Durango	7	3.6	6	3.7	1	3.3
Guanajuato	14	7.3	8	4.9	6	20.0
Jalisco	13	7.0	12	7.4	1	3.3
Mexico	9	4.7	8	4.9	1	3.3
Michoacan	24	12.4	20	12.3	4	13.3
Morelos	3	1.6	3	1.8	0	–
Nuevo Leon	6	3.1	6	3.7	0	–
San Luis Potosi	14	7.3	13	8.0	1	3.3
Tamaulipas	28	14.5	24	14.8	4	13.3
Zacatecas	7	3.6	2	1.2	5	16.6
Other[1]	10	5.2	8	4.9	2	6.6
Totals	193	100.0	163	100.0	30	100.0

Source: Texas Undocumented Survey.

Percentages may not total 100 because of rounding.

[1]Other = Baja California Sur, Colima, Guerrerro, Hidalgo, Nayarit, Oaxaca, Puebla, and Quintana Roo.

residence for one-third of the Mexican respondents.* A total of 24 (or 12 percent) of the Mexican respondents formerly lived in Michoacan, a more southern Mexican state. The three states mentioned account for 45 percent of all Mexicans in the sample, but the proportions vary between detainees and non-detainees. Figure 2.1 illustrates the wide dispersion in the former residences of the Mexican respondents. Information on the former country of residence of the non-Mexicans is presented in Table 2.3. Eight Central and South American countries are represented in the survey with the majority of respondents from El Salvador.

Of those interviewed, 630 persons provided information on their length of stay in the U.S. There are striking differences between the detained and undetained undocumented aliens in terms of their time in the United States (see Table 2.4). Almost half the detainees have been here less than one year, while fewer than 15 percent of the non-detainees have been here less than one year. Over one-third of the non-detainees came to the U.S. five or more years ago, whereas only about 22 percent of the detainees have been here that long. The average length of stay for the detained sample is seven months. The average length of stay for the undetained population is 4.3 years. This suggests that a large proportion of the sample population has established permanent residence in the U.S. The undetained sample does not exhibit the characteristics of "classic" single, temporary migrants coming to the U.S. for only short periods of time.

As is indicated in Table 2.5, a large proportion of the respondents have been in the U.S. prior to their current stay. In part, this may be explained by the border crossing activity in the two border cities in this sample (El Paso and McAllen), but the high rate of repeat entries by the detainee population (68.6 percent) is an additional influence. In contrast, less than 36 percent of the undetained respondents have had repeat entry experience. More than two-thirds of the undetained respondents who had been to the U.S. prior to their current stay are male. Most of the female respondents (75 percent) are in the U.S. for the first time.

Although most of the respondents are in the U.S. illegally,** 13 percent or 32 persons entered the country with legal documents (see Table 2.6.) The legal documents were primarily temporary work permits and border crossing cards. Of the respondents, 87 percent entered the U.S. (this time) without papers.

The principal reason given by respondents for coming to the U.S. was for economic purposes. Because of financial and employment conditions in their countries, 65 percent of the respondents came to the U.S. to look for work.

---

*Respondents were asked for their former state of residence. Higher rates of representation, such as from the northern Mexican states, may therefore be influenced by internal migration from southern or eastern states.

**Four respondents were here legally but were married to undocumented aliens.

FIGURE 2.1   Mexican States Represented in the Undocumented Alien Sample

o Dallas

o Austin   o Houston

o San Antonio

Quintana
Roo

Tamaulipas
28

Puebla

Hidalgo

San Luis Potosi Guanajuato

o McAllen   2

Oaxaca
1

Nue
Leon   9
6

Morelos
3

Coahuila
15

Zacatecas   Guerrero
14   2

Distrito
Federal 7

El Paso
o

Durango
7   Jalisco
13

Chihuahua
36   1

Michoacan.   Mexico
24

Nayarit   Colima
1

Baja
California
Sur

States represented
in the population
sample

Table 2.3

Respondents' Former Residences
(non-Mexican respondents)

Country	Totals		Non-Detainees		Detainees	
	N	%	N	%	N	%
Colombia	2	4.5	2	5.0	0	-
El Salvador	31	70.5	31	77.5	0	-
Guatemala	3	6.8	3	7.5	0	-
Other[1]	8	18.2	4	10.0	4	100.0
Totals	44	100.0	40	100.0	4	100.0

Source: Texas Undocumented Survey.

[1]Other = Argentina, Ecuador, Honduras, Peru, and Venezuela.

Table 2.4

Length of Stay in United States
(excluding U.S. born)

Time in U.S.	Totals		Non-Detainees		Detainees	
	N	%	N	%	N	%
Less than 1 year	101	16.0	81	13.8	20	47.6
1 - 2 years	161	25.5	153	26.0	8	19.0
3 - 4 years	137	21.7	132	22.4	5	12.0
5+ years	231	36.6	222	37.8	9	21.4
Totals	630	100.0	588	100.0	42	100.0

Source: Texas Undocumented Survey.

Percentages may not total 100 because of rounding.

Table 2.5

First or Repeat Entry
(respondents only)

| | Non-Detainees | | | Detainees |
	Total	Male	Female	(Males)[1]
First Entry	64.1%	54.8%	75.5%	31.4%
	(N=134)	(N=63)	(N=71)	(N=11)
Repeat Entry	35.9%	45.2%	24.5%	68.6%
	(N=75)	(N=52)	(N=23)	(N=24)
Totals	100%	100%	100%	100%
	(N=209)	(N=115)	(N=94)	(N=35)

Source: Texas Undocumented Survey.

[1] No female detainees were interviewed.

Table 2.6

Entry With or Without Papers
(respondents only)

| | Non-Detainees | | | Detainees |
Form of Entry	Total	Male	Female	(Males)
With Papers	(N=30)	(N=14)	(N=16)	(N=2)
Without Papers	(N=180)	(N=99)	(N=81)	(N=32)
Totals	100.0	100.0	100.0	100.0
	(N=210)	(N=113)	(N=97)	(N=34)

Source: Texas Undocumented Survey.

Percentages may not total 100 because of rounding.

Twenty-eight (28) of the 35 detained respondents came to the U.S. for economic reasons. The majority of persons giving other reasons for coming to the U.S. were undetained respondents. Of the 30 respondents identifying family reunification as the reason for coming to the U.S., 27 were from Mexico. Particularly interesting is the large number of Central and South Americans giving political reasons for coming to the U.S.; these totaled 24 of the 26 persons in this category (see Table 2.7).

We can summarize the foregoing characteristics:

For both the detained and undetained groups, most of the sample population is Hispanic and primarily Mexican. Twenty percent of the sample is comprised of U.S.-born persons, including spouses and children. Of the Mexican respondents, a large proportion formerly resided in two northern Mexican states, although two-thirds of the Mexican states (and the Federal District) are represented in the sample population. Differences between the detained and undetained population groups are most evident in length of stay, repeated entry, entry with papers, and reasons for coming to the U.S. Relatively more of the non-detainees (1) have been here for more than three years, (2) have fewer repeat entries and came with legal documents for entry, and (3) were more likely to cite both economic and reunification reasons for coming to the U.S. than their detained counterparts.

DEMOGRAPHIC CHARACTERISTICS AND SOCIO-ECONOMIC INDICATORS

Certain characteristics of a population group make it possible to estimate the kinds and levels of services that will be needed by members of the group. Some of these characteristics, such as age, sex, education, income, and household data in particular, allow us to explain the current use of public services and to some extent to project the continued need for certain kinds of services.
This section presents a demographic and socio-economic profile of the sample population. Special attention is given to those indicators which are typically related to the use of health, education, and social services. Further consideration is given to differences between the detainee and non-detainee sample population so as to determine any major variation in the use of public services.

Demographic Characteristics

Age and Sex. The undetained sample population consists of 214 households and totals 805 persons. As is indicated in Figure 2.2, the total number of males and females is fairly equal, with males comprising 51 percent and females 49 percent of the population. The largest group by age is children under 4 years. Adding the 5 to 9 years age group, about 30 percent of the sample population is under 10 years of age. As might be expected, given the importance of economic reasons for migration, persons between 20 to 24 and from 25 to 29 years of age represent the second and third largest groups,

Table 2.7

Respondents' Reasons for Coming to the U.S.

Reason Given	Total		Mexican Origin		Central or South American Origin	
	N	%	N	%	N	%
Economic Reason	158	64.5	143	71.9	15	34.1
Reunite With Family	30	12.2	27	13.6	3	6.8
Political Reason	26	10.6	2	1.0	24	54.5
Other[1]	31	12.7	27	13.6	2	4.5
Totals	245	100.0	199	100.0	44	100.0

Source: Texas Undocumented Survey.

Percentages may not total 100 because of rounding.

[1] Other reasons include miscellaneous responses such as wanting to see the U.S.

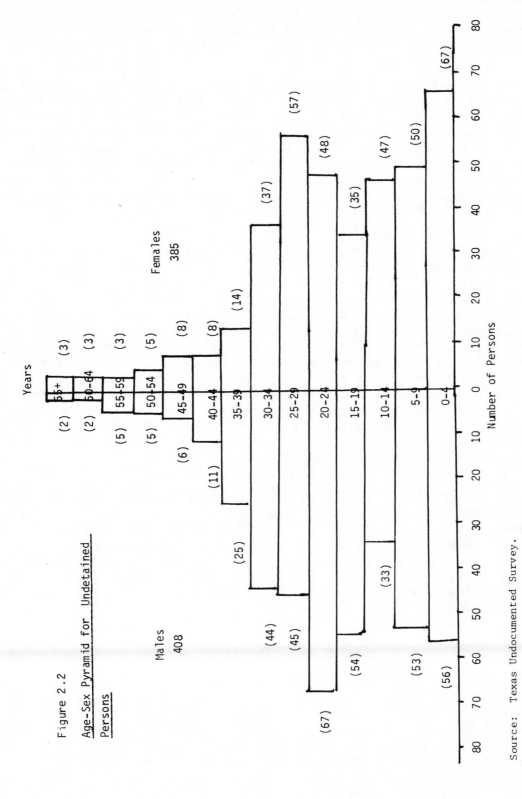

Figure 2.2

Age-Sex Pyramid for Undetained
Persons

Source: Texas Undocumented Survey.

(N) = Number of persons in that age group.
Pyramid reflects a population total of 793 because of missing information on 12 persons.

respectively. These two age groups are typically the most mobile. After age 34 the number of persons in each group drops for both males and females. The average age for the undetained population is 19.7 years, while that of the detained population is 24.3 years. The younger average age for the undetained group is influenced by the large number of children in this population.

The detainee population totaled 63 persons in 39 households. Figure 2.3 includes all members of the detainees' households. Therefore, although all detainee respondents were male, there were some females in their households. Some of the respondents in holding centers had been living in multiperson households including women and children before apprehension. There are only three persons under 14 years of age in this population, whereas 50 percent are between the ages of 20 and 29 years. Over 70 percent are from 15 to 29 years of age. Thus, the detainee population is primarily male and under 30 years of age.

Simply considering age and sex, we get a distinct picture of some of the services these two groups may need. Typically, young children and women demand a high level of health services. Females of child-bearing age (15 to 44 years) comprise about 25 percent (N=199) of the non-detainee population. This suggests that about one-fourth of the non-detainee group requires, or may at some time require, maternity and/or family planning services. Furthermore, the present and future children of the females in this group will need basic child health and education services. Finally, the large number of child-bearing females should be noted, since future children will be U.S. citizens and may potentially entitle the household to a variety of services and benefits. The detainee group, on the other hand, does not suggest a great present or future need for these public services. This predominantly male and over-school-age population does not presage an increase in the demand for health, social, and education services.

Marital Status. The marital status of respondents in detention centers varies considerably from that of those who were not detained. As is shown in Tables 2.8 and 2.9, while only 25 percent of the detained respondents were married, over 60 percent of those in the larger, non-detainee sample were married. And, while some past studies characterize the undocumented alien as a single male, almost two-thirds of the undetained male respondents in our sample are married. A majority of the female respondents in this group are also married.

Socio-economic Indicators

While age and sex characteristics can identify the levels and demand for certain kinds of services, social and economic characteristics are better indicators of the need for other services, and particularly of the extent to which the population is able to provide for its own needs.

Household Characteristics. These can be regarded from two aspects:

Figure 2.3

Age-Sex Pyramid for the Detained

Sample Population

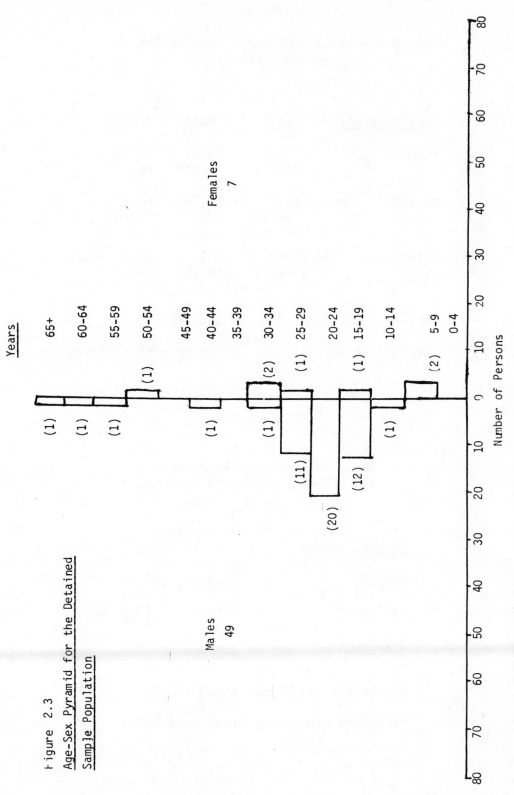

Source: Texas Undocumented Survey.

(N) = Number of persons in that age group.
Pyramid reflects a population total of 56 because of missing information on 7 persons.

Table 2.8

Respondents' Marital Status by Sex
(non-detainees only)

Marital Status	Total	Sex	
		Male	Female
Single	36.6% (N=78)	35.3% (N=41)	38.1% (N=37)
Married	63.4% (N=135)	64.7% (N=75)	61.9% (N=60)
Totals	100.0 (N=213)	100.0 (N=116)	100.0 (N=97)

Source: Texas Undocumented Survey.

Percentages do not total 100 because of rounding.

Table 2.9

Respondents' Marital Status
(detainees only)

Marital Status	Detainee[1]	
	N	%
Single	26	75.0
Married	9	25.0
Totals	35	100.0

Source: Texas Undocumented Survey.

[1]All detainees interviewed were male.

1. Household Size. Of all the households in the undetained group, over 75 percent had five persons or less living within the household. Twenty percent were single-member households and primarily included respondents living in boarding houses. Almost one-third of the households had only two to three persons (see Table 2.10). The detained respondents presented a different picture from the undetained group. As illustrated in Table 2.10, over 60 percent (or 24) of the detained respondents lived in single-member households with over 80 percent (or 32) living in households with less than three persons. The average household size for the detained population is 1.7 persons compared to the average size of the undetained population household of 3.8 persons.

2. Type of Household. The households in the two population groups are further characterized by the relationships among household members. Table 2.11 reinforces the predominant picture of the single-male household in the detained group, while less than 20 percent in the undetained group appear to be in this category. In the undetained population, 50 percent of the households are nuclear families. Also, while less than 10 percent of the households in the undetained group consist of unrelated persons, almost one-quarter of the detainee households are composed of unrelated persons living together.

The differences between detainee and non-detainee households are again accentuated in considering the legal and illegal status of the household members. Table 2.12 shows that almost 75 percent of the households in the detained group are comprised only of undocumented persons. On the other hand, over 50 percent of the households in the undetained group included both undocumented and legal residents. Legal residents include citizen spouses and/or children and legal immigrants. Furthermore, 100 (47 percent) of the households in the undetained sample population had individuals born in the U.S. as household members. Only three (8 percent) of the detained population households had U.S.-born persons living in the households. Of the 200 persons born in the U.S., 169 are children under 19 years of age. Thus 85 percent of the U.S.-born population are children. Of the total sample population, almost one-fourth are persons born in the U.S. (see Table 2.13). This characteristic may be an important factor in qualifying households for government services through the legal household members. Moreover, the presence of legal residents in the household suggests additional incentives for the undocumented alien to remain in the United States. It also complicates the usual demarcation of legal or illegal as descriptive words for immigrants, since families are frequently a mixture of both.

Although the various household characteristics of the detainee population support the typical picture of a young and single male, the characteristics of the undetained group suggest a wide variety of household arrangements. The existence of both nuclear and extended family member households implies that the undocumented alien in the undetained sample functions in a more supportive environment and certainly with a more permanent base than does the detained alien. A family or support group may diminish the need for public aid by providing other alternatives. At the same time, such an extended group may need more public assistance, but it will also be in a better position to pay for these through taxes.

Table 2.10

Size of Households

# of Household Members	Totals		Austin		San Antonio		City El Paso		McAllen		Dallas		Houston	
	N	%	Det.[1]	Undet.	Det.	Undet.	Det.	Undet.	Det.	Undet.	Det.[1]	Undet.	Det.	Undet.
Single	67	26.6	–	3	4	7	4	0	5	9	–	8	11	16
2-3	75	30.0	–	6	1	6	0	13	1	9	–	22	6	11
4-5	54	21.4	–	6	2	12	0	12	0	3	–	12	0	7
6-7	32	12.7	–	3	1	5	0	9	0	0	–	10	0	4
8-9	11	4.4	–	2	0	2	0	2	0	0	–	4	0	1
10 or more	13	5.2	–	3	0	2	0	2	0	0	–	1	4	1
Totals	252	100.0	–	23	8	34	4	38	6	21	–	57	21	40

Source: Texas Undocumented Survey.

[1]There were no Austin or Dallas detainees.

Percentages may not total 100 because of rounding.

Table 2.11

Type of Households

			# of Households			
	Totals		Non-Detainees		Detainees	
Household Type	N	%	N	%	N	%
Single	62	25.6	40	19.1	22	66.7
Nuclear	105	43.4	104	50.0	1	3.0
Nuclear & Others	23	9.5	23	11.0	0	0
Multi-family	6	2.5	5	2.4	1	3.0
Misc. Relatives	18	7.4	17	8.1	1	3.0
Misc. Non-Relatives	28	11.6	20	9.6	8	24.2
Totals	242	100.0	209	100.0	33	100.0

Source: Texas Undocumented Survey.

Percentages may not total 100 because of rounding.

Table 2.12

Household Composition
(by legality)

			# of Households			
	Totals		Non-Detainees		Detainees	
	N	%	N	%	N	%
Undocumented Only	127	50.2	98	45.8	29	74.4
Mixed Legal & Illegal	126	49.8	116	54.2	10	25.6
Totals	253	100.0	214	100.0	39	100.0

Source: Texas Undocumented Survey.

Percentages may not total 100 because of rounding.

Table 2.13

Households With U.S.-Born Persons

# of U.S.-Born Per Household	Total Households N	%
none	146	58.6
1	30	20.1
2	26	10.4
3	17	6.8
4	6	2.4
5	3	1.2
6	0	0.0
7	1	.4
Totals	249	100.0

Source: Texas Undocumented Survey.

Percentages may not total 100 because of rounding.

Education and Employment. The educational level of a recipient population is a critical factor in the design and development of public service programs. In the area of health services, low educational levels typically indicate a lower level of knowledge of good health practices, which often leads to a higher incidence of preventable health problems. In addition, lower educational levels generally limit individuals to lower-paying jobs* and possibly an increased need for financial and social service assistance. For the undocumented alien, a low educational level, illegal status, and the inability to speak English further limit employment opportunities and suggest an increased need for public assistance. Let us look at the educational levels and employment history of our sample in detail.

1. Education. In the undetained undocumented population only 24 percent of the adult members of this group have completed six years of school, with 10 percent not even completing one year of school. The undocumented aliens who were detained have a higher percentage of persons finishing at least six years (42 percent) and fewer with no years completed at all (5.5 percent). Almost 30 percent of the undetained group have completed between seven to eleven years of school, while less than 20 percent have reached this level in the detained group (see Table 2.14). A higher percentage of undetained persons (12.7 percent) had completed more than twelve years of school than did the members of the detained population sample (8.3 percent).

2. Employment. Over 40 percent of all the respondents were employed in service jobs, which generally included a variety of positions in restaurants and hotels. Almost one-quarter (22 percent) were employed in construction with half of these jobs located in Houston. Almost one-half of the factory workers in the sample (12 percent of all respondents) were employed in Dallas. The respondents in detention centers were employed in all categories with the exception of retail services. Although agriculture is only a minor employment area in this sample, one-half of the agricultural workers were detainees. Most of the detainees in Houston were employed in construction (see Table 2.15). Similar information is presented in Table 2.16, which includes a further breakdown of non-detainee employment by sex. The high 12 percent "not in labor force" rate is influenced by the number of females (23 persons) who work primarily as homemakers.

Over 6 percent of all male and female respondents reported having second jobs (Table 2.17). Only two respondents in the detainee population had second jobs. In Table 2.18 the picture of the undocumented alien employed in lower-paying jobs is further supported. Fewer than 5 percent are occupied in skilled or white-collar positions. About 10 percent of the respondents work primarily as homemakers. Almost 70 percent are employed in mining (oil and gas) or in unskilled positions. However, the unemployment rate for all respondents is very low, numbering only 1.3 percent (three persons) of the respondent population.

---

*A discussion of income for the sample is presented in Chapter Four.

Table 2.14

Years of School Completed
(adults only)

(# of Adults)

Age	Non-Detainees N=408 Years Completed					Detainees N=36 Years Completed				
	0	1-5	6	7-11	12+	0	1-5	6	7-11	12+
18-29	18	39	66	77	37	2	8	14	6	3
30-39	14	39	25	22	10	0	0	1	1	0
40-49	4	13	5	16	1	0	0	0	0	0
50-59	4	8	2	0	0	0	1	0	0	0
60+	1	2	1	0	4	0	0	0	0	0
Totals										
N	41	101	99	115	52	2	9	15	7	3
Percentages	10.0	24.8	24.3	28.2	12.7	5.5	25.0	42.0	19.4	8.3

Source: Texas Undocumented Survey.

Percentages may not total 100 because of rounding.

25

Table 2.15

Respondents' Jobs by City

City	Respondent	Totals N	%	Domestic	Service	Factory	Construction	Agri.	Other	Retail
Austin	Undetained	17	8.5	0	16	0	1	0	0	0
San Antonio	Detained	33	16.5	0	1	1	2	3	0	0
	Undetained			3	13	0	6	1	2	1
El Paso	Detained	29	14.5	0	1	0	0	3	0	0
	Undetained			6	13	3	1	0	1	1
McAllen	Detained	26	13.0	0	2	1	1	0	1	0
	Undetained			5	3	1	4	5	2	1
Houston	Detained	51	25.5	1	3	0	11	0	0	0
	Undetained			3	12	7	11	0	1	2
Dallas	Undetained	44	22.0	6	17	11	7	0	3	0
Totals	N	200		24	81	24	44	12	10	5
	%		100.0	12%	41%	12%	22%	6%	5%	2.5%

Source: Texas Undocumented Survey.

There were no Austin or Dallas detainees interviewed.

Table 2.16

Respondents' Sectors of Employment (Main Jobs)

Sector	Totals		Non-Detainees				Detainees		
			Male	Female	N	%	Male	N	%
Not in Labor Force	28	12.0	2	23	25	12.5	3	3	8.8
Agri. & Fish	12	5.1	5	1	6	3.0	6	6	17.6
Mining [1]	2	.9	2	0	2	1.0	0	0	0
Manufacturing	28	12.0	18	8	26	13.0	2	2	5.9
Construction	45	19.2	31	0	31	15.5	14	14	41.2
Commerce	10	4.3	8	1	9	4.5	1	1	2.9
Collective Services	77	33.0	41	30	71	35.5	6	6	17.6
Other Personal Svcs. [2]	32	13.7	6	24	30	15.0	2	2	5.9
Totals	234	100.0	113	87	200	100.0	34	34	100.0

Source: Texas Undocumented Survey.

[1] Mining = oil and gas; job categories from Codebook for Assimilation of Latin American Immigrant Minorities Study, 1978, Principal Investigator: Alejandro Portes.

[2] Other = Self-employed in personal services such as a live-in domestic, a gardener/yardwork person, taking in sewing jobs, etc.

Table 2.17

Respondents' Second Jobs

Job	Non-Detainees Male 116	Female 97	Totals	Detainees Male 39	Totals
Domestic	0	3	3	0	0
Service	5	2	7	1	1
Factory	2	0	2	0	0
Construction	1	1	2	1	1
Totals	8	6	14	2	2
% of Population (by sex)	6.9	6.2		5.13	

Source: Texas Undocumented Survey.

Table 2.18

Respondents' Main Occupations

Occupation	Totals		Detainees		Non-Detainees	
	N	%	N	%	N	%
Homemaker	24	10.3	1	2.9	23	11.5
Not in Labor Force	3	1.3	2	5.9	1	.5
Agriculture	12	5.1	6	17.6	6	3.0
Minor Urban Service	96	41.0	7	20.6	89	44.5
Unskilled	66	28.2	14	41.2	52	26.0
Semi-Skilled	22	9.4	3	8.8	19	9.5
Skilled	4	1.7	0	0	4	2.0
White-Collar (Profess.)	5	2.1	1	2.9	4	2.0
Other[1]	2	.85	0	0	2	1.0
Totals	234	100.0	34	100.0	200	100.0

Sources: Texas Undocumented Survey. Job categories from Alejandro Portes, Latin American Immigrant Minorities in the United States, Codebooks for Mexican Sample (Department of Sociology, Duke University, October 1978).

Percentages may not total 100 because of rounding.

[1]Other = Self-employed.

SUMMARY

The detained and undetained population samples differ considerably in several areas--most notably in those which influence the demand for certain public services. Males and females are equally represented in the undetained sample, while most of the detainees are male. The undetained respondents are more often married and living with nuclear families and other relatives than the detained respondents. A large proportion of the households in the undetained sample includes legal residents and U.S. citizens, while most of the detainees live alone or with unrelated, illegal residents, and persons not born in the United States. Educational attainment for both the detained and undetained populations is mixed. In both groups most of the respondents have attended school for at least several years, but the non-detainees tend to have more years of schooling than do the detainees, although this is not uniform. Employment characteristics of the detained and undetained population are similar, with the majority employed in service and unskilled positions. The unemployment rate for both sample populations is very low.

After comparing the detained and undetained populations, it is clear that using either population to extrapolate to the other would be very misleading. This is particularly true when attempting to study tax revenues and the cost of providing social services, because the two groups have different needs and different service utilization rates. For example, by using the undetained population for our cost estimates, we are biasing costs and service utilization rates upward. Non-detainees represent the high service user portion of the total undocumented population.

CHAPTER 3

THE USE OF PUBLIC SERVICES BY THE SAMPLE POPULATION

As discussed in the preceding chapter, the undetained population may be expected to demand a higher level of public services than the detained population. A review of the utilization data from the surveys supports this and in fact shows that persons interviewed in detention centers use very few of the services provided by public agencies. What follows is a description of the use of publicly funded services, including health, social, education, legal, and other general services by the undetained sample.

HEALTH

Respondents were asked about the use of certain kinds of publicly funded health services by members of the household in the last year. Table 3.1 reports the use of health services by the sample population. Over one-fourth of the sample used some kind of public health service.* About 70 percent of these users were children. The major kinds of services used were those in public health clinics, including immunization services. The high use of public clinic services was expected, as these clinics typically have fewer eligibility requirements than non-public clinics, are often free, and are generally located in areas where they are accessible to target populations. Almost 85 percent of the adults in the sample using health services were for emergency room, hospital, and clinic services. Few persons used dental or ambulance services; only 16 percent of the health service users and about 4 percent of the sample population made use of these services.

The persons in this sample requesting assistance received treatment for a variety of conditions. Most persons treated in emergency rooms were seen for accidents and illnesses (40 cases), 7 for childbirth, and 1 for a violent wound. Almost 40 percent of the hospital admissions were for childbirth (17 cases), with 18 others admitted for surgery and medical treatment. Services received in public health clinics varied, with 24 percent of the users utilizing adult health clinics and 23 percent child health clinics. Of the clinic users, 22 percent received immunizations, while 8.4 percent received maternity services. Only 1 person indicated receipt of family planning services at a public health clinic.

The low usage rates of family planning and maternity services corroborates information from surveyed health providers (see Appendix E) that

---

*Some of these services may be double counted, e.g., an adult using first the emergency room and then being admitted to the hospital in this period is counted as two cases rather than as one.

Table 3.1

Use of Health Services (Undetained Sample)

Provider	# Adults Attended	# Children Attended	Total # Times Attended (or Days)	Total Persons Attended	% of Sample Population (N=805)
Emergency Room	37	22	74	59	7.3
Hospital	35	8	at least 75[2]	43	5.3
Public Clinic	39	42	at least 181[3]	81	10.1
Dental Clinic[1]	14	14	at least 45	28	3.5
Ambulance	6	1	7	7	.9
Totals	131	87	at least 382	218	27

Source: Texas Undocumented Survey.

[1] These were services provided only by state or local health departments.

[2] Information on the number of days hospitalized was given in ranges (other than 1 day). "2-5 days" was counted as 3, "6-9" as 7, "10 or more" as 10.

[3] Information for dental and public clinics was given on the number of visits, except for the last category, which was for "more than 5" visits. For calculation this response was counted as 6.

undocumented women receive either no or inadequate prenatal care, leading to a higher incidence of pregnancy and birth complications. These low rates for public health maternity care suggest that undocumented women may be using other health providers for this kind of health care, such as private practitioners, private and nonprofit clinics, midwives, and local folk healers. In this sample a large number of women had already given birth to children in the U.S., yet few were currently using public family planning and maternity services. Demands from undocumented persons for these and child health related services may grow in the future, given the considerable need among this population for these services.

Two problems were encountered in interviewing respondents about health service usage. First, in some instances respondents were not sure if they had used a public or private facility, since in most instances patients were required to pay for services rendered. Secondly, a fair proportion of the users of health services, especially children identified as users, may be legal residents and eligible for care. With 20 percent of the sample consisting of U.S.-born children, it is reasonable to assume that undocumented parents would be less hesitant to request needed health services for their legal children as opposed to undocumented children. Given these considerations it is felt that the data on the use of public health services by the undocumented population is somewhat overstated as presented in Table 3.1. Many of the users are documented.

The primary method of payment for the health services received by the undocumented in the sample was an "out of pocket" payment (67.4 percent). Another 10 percent paid with insurance from their job, while 11 percent paid with other kinds of health insurance (private and government-provided). A final category of 8 percent paid their health bills by contract, and most of these were for hospital services (see Table 3.2).

SOCIAL SERVICES

The use of social services by the undocumented sample was quite low given the generally low income status of this population. For most programs and services the user rate was 5 percent or less, with the largest number of households receiving aid from food stamps, counseling, and the Women, Infants, and Children (WIC) nutrition programs (see Table 3.3). The rates vary due to the different eligibility requirements for each program and the varying demand for certain kinds of services. Only 24 households received counseling services (family, drug-alcohol, financial, etc.), while 23 received food stamps. In each of the households receiving food stamps there was at least one legal household member. As might be expected, the program with the largest number of (household) recipients was the WIC program. WIC is a federal program with eligibility based on a financial and physical evaluation of pregnant and lactating women and children under five years of age. In most cases the determination of a patient as being at "nutritional risk" automatically qualifies him/her for this service. As already stated, factors such as inadequate health care, low income, and low educational levels increase the health risk factors for undocumented women and qualify them for

Table 3.2

Method of Payment for Health Services

Provider	Responses	Out of Pocket	Private Ins.	Job Ins.	Govt. Ins.	Employer Paid	Contract
Emergency Room	38	18	3	8	5	2	2
Hospital	30	11	4	6	1	0	8
Public Clinic	50	46	0	1	0	2	1
Dental Clinic	22	19	1	0	2	0	0
Ambulance	4	3	0	0	0	0	1
Totals N	144	97	8	15	8	4	12
%	100	67.4	5.6	10.4	5.6	3.0	8.3

Source: Texas Undocumented Survey.

Percentages may not total 100 because of rounding.

Table 3.3

Use of Social Services (Undetained Sample)

Program/Aid Received	# Responses	# Households Receiving Services	% Households Receiving Services
AFDC	197	9	4.6
Utilities Payment	194	9	4.6
Rent Payment	199	10	5.0
Food Stamps	186	23	12.4
WIC	197	34	17.3
Unemployment	198	6	3.0
Worker's Compensation	199	9	4.5
Senior Citizens Services	196	5	2.6
Counseling Services	204	24	11.8

Source: Texas Undocumented Survey.

this kind of nutrition program.

Utility and rent assistance is most often available through local emergency assistance agencies. The strict residency requirements of agencies for this kind of aid (with the exception of the Travis County Office--see Appendix F) accounts for the low user rate for these services. Such assistance is generally available only in extreme cases and on a one-time basis. Among the respondents, 6 households reported that a member received unemployment benefits, while 9 reported that a household member received Worker's Compensation. While both programs are state administered, benefits are provided on the basis of the employer's contribution to the programs.

In addition to questions about the use of specific services, respondents were asked a series of questions about where or to whom they had gone in the past to meet certain needs (temporary housing, help finding work, etc.). These questions were designed to elicit general help-seeking patterns. The results are summarized in Tables 3.4 and 3.5. Clearly, most undocumented persons seek out friends and relatives more readily than professionals or agencies when they need assistance. It should be noted that the category "agencies or professionals" includes many privately funded services, especially those provided by clergy or church organizations. Table 3.4 gives a breakdown of responses--not individuals. Responses indicate that a person used a formal or informal resource at least once, not the number of times such resources were used. Table 3.5 indicates the number of respondents who said they had sought aid from formal or informal sources. These are not mutually exclusive categories. In fact, none of the respondents who reported asking for aid went only to an agency or a professional. A number of respondents did, however, go only to friends and relatives.

EDUCATION

With the large number of children included in the sample population it was expected that many children would be enrolled in school. In this sample, 202 children were enrolled in school (see Table 3.6), with 188 attending public schools and 14 children enrolled in private schools. Almost 40 percent of households (N=79) had children enrolled in a U.S. school. Of the 188 in public schools, 143 or 71 percent were undocumented children. This is explained by the fact that most of the undocumented aliens in the sample have been in the U.S. less that five years and many of the U.S.-born offspring are not yet of school age. Given the generally low income status of the sample population and its inability to speak English fluently, it was anticipated that many of these undocumented children would participate in a variety of special programs. Table 3.7 presents information on the use of special programs by school children in the sample. Although it was not possible to determine the number of legal children also receiving these services, it can be reasonably assumed that most of the undocumented children were receiving bilingual instruction and participated in the school breakfast and lunch programs.

The sample included 31 households with adults who were participating in

Table 3.4

Source of Support Services by Type of Aid
(number of responses, nonexclusive categories)

Type of Aid	Agency or Professional[1]	Friend or Relative	Agency or Professional[1]	Friend or Relative
Find Work	10	88	0	14
Food/Lodging	19	49	0	13
Translation	16	70	1	8
Transportation	5	41	0	8
Information	22	42	0	2
Totals	72	290	1	45

Source: Texas Undocumented Survey.

[1]Includes private agencies and privately paid professionals.

Table 3.5

Where Undocumented Persons Sought Aid
(number of respondents, nonexclusive categories)

Aid Source	Non-Detainees	Detainees
Agency or Professional[1]	49	1
Friend or Relative	137	22
Totals	186	23

Source: Texas Undocumented Survey.

[1]Includes private agencies and privately paid professionals.

Table 3.6

Number of Children Attending U.S. Schools

# of Children per Household in School	# of Children Totals	Number of Households City					
		Austin	San Antonio	El Paso	McAllen	Houston	Dallas
0	0	4	5	5	1	7	6
1	27	5	6	8	1	3	4
2	40	3	3	7	1	1	5
3	39	0	5	5	0	1	2
4	32	1	1	2	0	0	4
5	35	3	2	0	0	0	2
6-9	29	0	1	3	0	0	0
	202[1]						

Source: Texas Undocumented Survey.

[1]Of this total, 188 attended public schools and 14 attended private schools.

Table 3.7

Use of Public School Programs

Program/Service	# of Children	% of School-Enrolled Children (N=202)
Bilingual Program	139	68.8
School Lunch	163	80.7
School Breakfast	152	75.2
Special Education	23	11.4
Ride the Bus	82	40.6
Drivers' Education	8	4.0

Source: Texas Undocumented Survey.

adult education programs; the majority were receiving some kind of instruction in English. Most of these programs were community or church sponsored.

LEGAL SERVICES

Almost one-half of the respondents reported that someone in the household had received legal assistance in the last year: 26 percent were assisted by private practitioners (56 cases), almost 12 percent got help from church-sponsored legal aid programs, and 13 households went to public agencies for legal aid (see Table 3.8). Over 70 percent of those receiving legal aid requested help with immigration matters. As indicated in Table 3.9, most of the people with legal problems paid fees for these legal services, although many of the fees were modest. Consequently, those who seek legal aid are not likely, given these sample results, to obtain free, publicly funded services.

Members of the sample were involved with the legal system in other ways: 47 persons received traffic tickets, with 43 of these paying a fine; 24 persons were arrested in the last year, while 1 person was placed on probation; 16 persons were detained in jail, with 11 of these staying for only one day.

OTHER PUBLIC SERVICES

Respondents indicated that they and other household members used other publicly provided services. Of the respondents, 49 percent stated someone in the household used the public transit system, while over 43 percent used public recreation services (see Table 3.10).

SUMMARY

About one-fourth of the population made use of some type of public health service, with public clinics and hospitals being used the most. Persons were treated primarily for illness and childbirth in hospitals, while clinics offering adult health, child health, and immunization services were the most often used by the sample population. Social service programs were not widely used, except for food stamps and the WIC program, with 12.4 percent and 17.3 percent respectively of the households receiving this sort of aid in the last year. In most cases legal residents were living in the households receiving this aid. A total of 188 children were enrolled in public schools, and over 70 percent of these were undocumented. Most of these children participated in special school programs, including bilingual education and the school lunch and school breakfast programs. Legal services were used primarily for immigration problems. Other public services were also utilized, especially recreation facilities and the public transit system, the latter being used by almost one-half of the households in the sample.

Table 3.8

Type of Legal Agency

Agency	# of Households	% of Total Households (N=214)
Private	56	26.2
Church Sponsored	25	11.7
Public[1]	13	6.1
Other	1	.5
Don't Know	3	1.4
Totals	98	45.9

Source: Texas Undocumented Survey.

[1]Public legal services included those provided by city social service agencies.

Table 3.9

Payments for Legal Services by the Undocumented
(from surveys)

Type of Agency	Total	None (services free)	$5-$25 (nominal)	$26-$99	$100-$499	$500-$999	$1,000-$1,500
				Fees Paid (#s of people)			
Private Legal/ Law Firm	46	5	11	8	9	11	2
Church-Sponsored Agency	21	8	5	5	2	1	0
Legal Aid (Publicly Funded)	8	1	2	0	3	1	1
City Official (Publicly Funded)	4	0	0	3	0	1	0
Other (Self, Friend, etc.)	2	0	0	1	0	0	1
Total	81	14	18	17	14	14	4

Source: Texas Undocumented Survey.

Table 3.10

Other Public Services Used

Service	# Households Used Service	# Responses	Percent
Public Transit	101	206	49.0
Recreation	90	207	43.5
Fire Protection	9	207	4.4
Subsidized Housing	7	203	3.5

Source: Texas Undocumented Survey.

CHAPTER 4

UNDOCUMENTED INCOME RECEIVED AND TAXES PAID

In this chapter, we will estimate the total income of the undocumented alien population in Texas and the total taxes paid by this population. The estimates are built up from three sources:

1. estimates of the total population of undocumented aliens by Bean and King;*

2. 1980 population figures for the State of Texas from the U.S. Bureau of the Census; and

3. labor force participation rates and income and tax data from surveys of the sample population.

ESTIMATING THE NUMBER OF UNDOCUMENTED ALIENS IN TEXAS

The Bean and King figures are used as the basis for our estimates of undocumented aliens. We have taken their estimates, doubled them and then halved them, in order to consider a range of possible numbers of undocumented aliens in Texas (see Table 4.1).

Table 4.1

Undocumented Aliens in Texas

	Low	High
X/2	284,450	459,200
X	568,900	918,400
2X	1,137,800	1,836,800

Source: Bean and King, 1980. The Bean and King estimates are X in this table.

---

*Frank D. Bean, Allan G. King, Robert D. Benford, and Laura B. Perkinson, Estimates of the Number of Illegal Migrants in the State of Texas, Texas Population Research Center Paper No. 4.001 (Austin: University of Texas, 1982).

From Table 4.1, our low estimate of the number of undocumented aliens in Texas is 284,450; our high estimate is 1,836,800.

The sample population for this study consists of 585 nondetained,* undocumented aliens living in Austin, Dallas, El Paso, Houston, the McAllen area, and San Antonio. The Hispanic population of these cities represents 54.9 percent of the Hispanic population of the State of Texas. Assuming that the undocumented population is distributed across the state in approximately the same fashion as the Hispanic population,** 54.9 percent of the undocumented population resides in the sampled cities. Using the percentage of Hispanics in an area as a proxy for the percentage of undocumented in an area, and using the estimates of total number of undocumented in the state from Table 4.1, it is possible to estimate the number of undocumented in each sampled city. These data are summarized in Table 4.2.

ESTIMATING THE INCOME OF THE UNDOCUMENTED POPULATION IN TEXAS

In order to estimate the income of the undocumented population in Texas, questions regarding household income and taxes were asked of a sample of 214 persons in households where either the respondent or the respondent's spouse was undocumented. The responses of this sample were used to estimate labor force participation rates, hourly wages, and gross income. Below is a description of the steps that were taken to arrive at the final estimates of taxes paid by the undocumented population in Texas and the results of the analysis.

Description of the Sampled Population

A total of 214 adults in 6 cities in the total sample provided enough information for use in our estimates. Only 4 of the respondents were legal residents of the state.

Of the respondents, 135 were married. There were 104 spouses living in

---

*Although a small sample of detainees were interviewed for comparison purposes, only non-detainees are used for estimations of costs and revenues. This is the more relevant population on the use of public services.

**This is a commonly used assumption first advanced by David North and Marion Houstoun (1976). Referred to as the "cluster hypothesis," this assumption is based on the behavior of undocumented persons who, because of demographic factors, economic constraints, and preferences, tend to cluster in community areas where other linguistically/ethnically similar immigrants reside.

Table 4.2

Estimated Number of Undocumented Aliens in Sampled Cities in Texas

SMSA[1]	% of Undocumented in City	X/2	X	2X
Austin[2]	3.16	8,989-14,511	17,977-29,021	35,954-58,043
Dallas[2]	3.72	10,582-17,082	21,163-34,164	42,326-68,329
El Paso	9.95	28,303-45,690	56,605-91,381	112,211-182,762
Houston	14.23	40,477-65,344	80,954-130,688	161,909-261,377
McAllen	7.71	21,931-35,404	43,862-70,809	87,724-141,617
San Antonio	16.13	45,882-74,069	91,764-148,138	183,527-296,276
TOTAL	54.9	156,163-252,101	312,326-504,202	624,652-1,008,403

Source: Bean and King, 1980; U.S. Bureau of the Census, Population Data for 1980 for the State of Texas.

[1] Standard Metropolitan Statistical Area--includes urbanized counties contiguous to city.

[2] These estimates are for the city of Dallas rather than for the Dallas-Fort Worth SMSA, since the undocumented population in Fort Worth was not sampled.

the United States in the same household as the respondents; 78 of these spouses were undocumented and 26 were legal residents. There were 129 other persons over the age of 18 in the respondents' households; 112 of these did not have legal status. Moreover, there were 358 children, of which 185 were undocumented and 173 citizens or legal residents. A total of 805 persons lived in the households of the respondents; unrelated and related adults and children within the household are included in this total. Table 4.3 describes the sampled households.

Table 4.3

Description of the Sampled Population

	Total	%	Undoc.	%	Legal	%
Respondents	214	26.6	210	35.9	4	1.8
Children[1]	358	44.5	185	31.6	173	78.6
Spouses	104	12.9	78	13.3	26	11.8
Other Adults	129	16.1	112	19.2	17	7.7
	805	100.0	585	100.0	220	100.0

Source: Texas Undocumented Survey.

[1] Those under age 18.

Labor Force Participation Rates of Sampled Population

The labor force participation rates of the sampled population can be used
to construct estimates of income and social security taxes paid by the
undocumented population in Texas. First, the participation rates of the
undocumented population are estimated; then the taxes paid are estimated.

Table 4.4 shows the work force patterns of the sampled households. Of
the 214 total respondents surveyed, 167 were in the work force; 164 of the
working respondents did not have legal papers. Also in the work force were 53
undocumented spouses, 87 other undocumented adults living in the households,
and 12 undocumented persons under the age of 18.

Table 4.4

Work Force Status

	All Workers	%	Undoc.	%	Legal	%
Respondents	167	47.6	164	51.9	3	8.6
Spouses	69	19.7	53	16.8	16	45.7
Other Adults	100	28.5	87	27.5	13	37.1
Children under 18	15	4.3	12	3.8	3	8.6
Total	351	100.0	316	100.0	35	100.0

Source: Texas Undocumented Survey.

Table 4.5 converts the numbers of those working into the percentages of
those in the sample who are in the work force.

Table 4.5

Percent Labor Force Participation in Sample

	All Workers	Undoc.	Legal
Respondents	78.0	78.1	75.0
Spouses	66.3	68.0	61.6
Other Adults	77.5	77.7	76.5
All Adults	75.2	76.0	68.1
Total Population	43.6	54.0	15.9

Source: Texas Undocumented Survey and previous tables.

Labor Force Participation of Undocumented Aliens in Texas

　　　Using the high and low estimates of the undocumented population from the Bean and King survey and the labor force participation rates of the sampled population, we can estimate the undocumented work force in the State of Texas. Two approaches can be used. First, we can assume that the undocumented adults represent 68.4 percent of the total undocumented population, as in our sample; and also, that 76 percent of the adult undocumented population is in the work force—again, the same distribution as in our sample. The labor force participation rate for undocumented males should be higher than for undocumented females and the total undocumented population probably has a higher proportion of males. The high and low estimates are shown below:

Table 4.6

Estimates of Undocumented Work Force in Texas

	Low Estimate	High Estimate
Total Undocumented Population	568,900	918,400
	X .684	X .684
Adult Undocumented Population	389,128	628,186
	X .76	X .76
Working Undocumented Population	295,737	477,421

Source: Bean and King, 1980; Texas Undocumented Survey
　　　　　and previous tables.

In the second approach, we can assume that 54 percent of the total undocumented population is in the work force, since 54 percent of the undocumented in our sample were working. These calculations are shown below:

Table 4.7

Alternative Estimates of Undocumented Work Force in Texas

	Low Estimate	High Estimate
Total Undocumented Population	568,900	918,400
	X .54	X 3.54
Working Undocumented Population	307,206	495,936

Source: Bean and King, 1980; Texas Undocumented Survey and previous tables.

The first estimates will be used in the estimation of taxes paid, since these figures represent a more conservative estimate of work force participation and consequent tax payments.*

Estimating Social Security Tax Payments by Undocumented Aliens

In order to estimate taxes paid, it is necessary to determine the number of undocumented aliens paying social security taxes, the wages of those who are paying these taxes, and the hours worked. The standard deduction of 6.7 percent of income withheld for social security taxes** can then be applied to an estimate of annual income of the undocumented population.

According to the above estimates (see Table 4.6), the working undocumented population in Texas is between 295,737 and 477,421 persons. In our sample, 71.8 percent of the respondents said that they paid social security taxes. (The respondents were also asked whether their spouses, if working, paid social security taxes; however, because of the possible error factor when asking one person about another's income and taxes, spouse payment of these taxes was not included in the estimate.) Therefore, we can estimate that between 212,339 and 342,783 undocumented persons in Texas pay social security taxes.

---

*Throughout the study we have given the most conservative estimates of taxes paid and the most generous estimates of the costs to provide services. If there is to be a bias, we prefer to overstate the costs and understate the revenues.

**Circular E and Supplement Reprint of the IRS, July 1982.

In our sample, the average hourly wage of the respondents was $4.13; this average was derived from the hourly wage of the 141 respondents who provided information on their wages. Again, only the respondent's hourly wage was used as a base for this average because of the error inherent in asking one person about another's income. Within our samples, the average hours worked per week for respondents was 39.1; for the purpose of estimation, it is assumed that individuals work 40 hours per week and 52 weeks per year. At $4.13 an hour, the average gross income of an undocumented alien is $8,590 per year.

The social security tax rate is .067 of gross annual income, or an average of $575.53 annual taxes deducted per person surveyed.

Applying the taxes paid per person to the number of undocumented persons paying social security taxes, it can be estimated that $122,207,465 to $197,284,778 in taxes are paid annually into the social security system by the undocumented in Texas (see Table 4.8).

Table 4.8

Social Security Contributions by Undocumented Workers

	Low Estimate	High Estimate
Number of Undocumented Contributing	212,339	342,788
Average Annual Contribution	X 575.53	X 575.53
Total Social Security Taxes Paid	$122,207,464.67	$197,284,777.64

Source: Texas Undocumented Survey and previous tables.

Estimating Income Tax Payments by Undocumented Aliens

Income tax payments are estimated in the same fashion as social security tax payments. In our sample, 65.3 percent of the respondents who were working had income taxes withheld from their income.

If the undocumented population in the work force in Texas is between 295,737 and 477,421, and 65.3 percent have income taxes withheld from their pay, then between 193,116 and 311,756 undocumented persons in Texas contribute income taxes to the United States Treasury.

In order to estimate the amount of taxes paid by each undocumented alien, the withholding rate for single taxpayers* can be applied to the average annual wage of the respondents, computed at $8,590 earlier. At this rate, the weekly tax withheld is $17.40 and the average annual income tax withheld for an undocumented worker in Texas is $904.80.

The high and low estimates of total taxes withheld for undocumented workers are shown below in Table 4.9.

Table 4.9

Income Taxes Paid by Undocumented Workers in Texas

	Low Estimate	High Estimate
Number of Undocumented Taxpayers	193,116	311,756
Average Tax Paid	904.80	904.80
Total Taxes Paid	$174,731,356.80	$282,076,828.80

Source: Texas Undocumented Survey and previous tables.

Estimating Net Annual Income of Undocumented Workers

The average gross annual income of undocumented workers is estimated to be $8,590.40. This figure is derived from our sample, in which respondents reported their hourly wage. The calculation is as follows: $4.13/hr X 40 hrs/wk X 52 wks/yr.

The average social security deduction is $575.53, but only 71.8 percent of the working population in the sample had social security taxes deducted. Therefore, the average social security deduction for the entire population is $575.653 X .718 = $413.23. Likewise, the average annual income tax withheld for the sample working population is $904.80, but only 65.3 percent of the

---

*The rate for single taxpayers is used because the Internal Revenue Service instructs employers to use that rate: (1) if the employee does not give the employer a completed Form W-4, or (2) if the employee is a nonresident alien or married to a nonresident alien. More than half of our respondents were unmarried, and it can be assumed that a large portion of the remainder had taxes withheld at the single taxpayer rate for one of the above reasons. The resulting estimate may be slightly high, if some of the undocumented aliens fill out the W-4 form and have taxes withheld at the rates for taxpayers who have dependents.

population has taxes withheld. Thus, the average income tax withheld for the undocumented population is $904.80 X .653 = $590.83.

Given these estimates, the net annual income of the undocumented worker is estimated as follows:

Table 4.10

Average Net Income of Undocumented Workers

Average Gross Income	$8,590.40
Average Social Security Tax Withheld	− 413.30
Average Income Tax Withheld	− 590.83
Average Net Annual Income	$7,586.27

Source: Texas Undocumented Survey and previous tables.

It is possible to verify this estimate, since the sampled population was specifically asked what their net take-home pay was. Of the 167 working respondents, 142 answered this question. This sample had an average take-home pay of $7,599. There is a difference of only $12.80 between our point estimate of their net annual income and the respondent's actual average take-home pay.

Estimating Sales Taxes Paid by Undocumented Aliens

Income subject to state sales tax is the net income minus all income not subject to the sales tax, which includes rent, food, utilities, remittances and savings. Rent and utilities are subject to other taxes. The data collected on expenditure patterns are arranged by household. To accurately estimate the sales tax paid by the total undocumented population, the expenditure patterns of households must be converted to individual estimates. This task is complicated by the fact that the household data include expenditures of individuals with legal status in the country. However, since there is no reason to believe that these persons have different expenditure patterns from the undocumented individuals in our sample, we have not attempted to disaggregate the expenditures of the legal persons in the households.

The average net income of undocumented workers has been estimated to be $7,586 (see Table 4.10). There is no significant difference between the income of the spouses and the income of the respondents.* We know the income of 167 respondents plus 69 spouses, or 236 of the 351 workers in our sample. We will further assume that all 351 workers have an average net income of $7,586. This is reasonable, since although some members of the respondents' households may earn considerably more than the respondents, the sample also includes part-time workers within the households. The aggregate net income for the total sample population is shown in Table 4.11.

Table 4.11

Aggregate Net Income of Sample

Average Net Income for Sample	$7,596
Undocumented Workers in Sample	X 351
Aggregate Net Income for Sample	$2,693,030

Source: Texas Undocumented Survey and previous tables.

The 214 households in the sample reported nontaxable expenses totaling $1,327,382. Thus the income subject to sales tax is $1,365,648. For the 805 individuals in our sample, the average income per capita that can be spent on taxable goods is $1,696. Assuming that this amount is spent on taxable items, at a tax rate of 5 percent, the sales tax remitted to the state per person in our sample is $84.80 per year.

Based on the earlier estimates of the undocumented population, the estimated sales taxes that accrue to the state from expenditures of undocumented aliens statewide are shown in Table 4.12.

Table 4.12

Sales Taxes Accruing to Texas from Expenditures
by Undocumented Aliens
(Assuming $84.80 per capita)

	Low Estimate	High Estimate
X/2	$24,121,360	$38,940,160
X	48,242,720	77,880,320
2X	96,485,440	155,760,000

Source: Texas Undocumented Survey; text; previous
tables.

---

*Respondents' average hourly wage is $4.13/hr; spouses' average wage is $4.24/hr. A test of difference between two means proved them to be equal at p< .01.

Division of the sales taxes into what stays with the state and what goes to the cities will be discussed in Chapter 6.

Estimating Excise Taxes Paid by Undocumented Aliens in Texas

Excise taxes are charged against expenditures for certain items specified by the State legislature. In order for us to estimate these taxes, respondents provided information about their purchases of cigarettes, beer, wine, liquor bought by the bottle, mixed drinks, gasoline, electricity and water, telephone, telegraph, gasoline, vehicle registration, license places, and inspection stickers. Of these items, mixed beverages, wine, liquor by the bottle, and telegraph expenditures were dropped because the number of respondents was very low. The expenditures of the sample population for the remaining items are as given in Table 4.13.

Table 4.13

Selected Expenditure Pattern of Undocumented Aliens

Item	Total Monthly Expenditures	Per Capita Yearly Expenditures (N=805)
Gas	$ 37,292	$ 46.33
Electricity and Water	52,964	65.79
Telephone	37,668	46.79
Cigarettes	22,424	27.86
Beer	41,623	51.71
Gasoline	141,984	176.38
Vehicle Registration	1,357	1.69
Driver's License	878	1.09
Inspection Stickers	1,559	1.93
Total Per Capita		$419.57

Source: Texas Undocumented Survey.

As with other expenditures, some respondents did not provide information on their expenditures in these categories. Therefore, the true expenditure pattern for these items is probably higher than the reported expenditures.

The total excise taxes paid by the undocumented aliens in Texas are estimated in Table 4.14. Using the low and high estimates of the undocumented population in Texas, the excise taxes paid total $14,034,763 to $22,656,928.

The data in this chapter will be summarized in Chapter Six together with data on the costs to provide public services.

Table 4.14

Excise Taxes Paid by the Undocumented Population in Texas

Item	Per Capita Expenditures	Tax Rate	Tax Per Capita (N=805)
Gas	$ 46.33	2.247%	$ 1.04
Electricity and Water	65.79	2.163%	1.42
Telephone	46.79	2.5025%	1.17
Cigarettes	27.86	$.185/pack	6.87
Beer	51.71	$.09/six-pack	1.89
Gasoline	176.38	$.05/gallon	8.82
Vehicle Registration	1.69	-	1.69
Driver's License	1.09	-	1.09
Inspection Stickers	1.93	35%	.68
Total			$24.67

Source: 1982 Annual Financial Report from the Texas Comptroller of
           Public Accounts.

Explanatory Notes: (1) Gasoline expenditures were figured at $1.00
per gallon and $.05 tax per gallon. (2) Cigarette expenditures were
figured at $.75 per pack of 20 cigarettes with a tax of $.185 per pack.
(3) Gas is taxed at 1.997% utility tax and .25% gas utility
administrative tax.   (4) Electricity and water are taxed at 1.997%
utility tax and .166% for Public Utility Commission. (5) The tax on
beer is $5.00 per barrel. One barrel = 31 gallons or 55.11 six-packs;
hence, a six-pack has a tax of $.09. The per capita expenditures of
$51.71 represent about 21 six-packs at $2.50 a six-pack; therefore,
the tax per capita is $1.89. (6) Vehicle inspection is $5.00 per car
per year; 35% of this is state tax.

CHAPTER 5

COSTS OF PUBLIC SERVICES PROVIDED
TO UNDOCUMENTED ALIENS

Undocumented aliens residing in Texas use a variety of public services funded by tax revenues. These include education for undocumented children, subsidized public transportation, social services, and public health services. This chapter will attempt to estimate the cost of public services to state and local governments.

Undocumented aliens may receive public services in several ways: (1) simply by living within the state borders, as in the case of police protection; (2) because providers have determined that it is in the public interest for all residents to receive the service, as in the case of immunizations; or (3) they may request certain services that they need or qualify for as individuals. Not all services are included in this study, because it would be virtually impossible to identify all the public services used by any specific population. However, this study does include the major cost areas for services provided by state and local governments. The survey of undocumented aliens verifies that the services most used by this population are included.

The services covered in this chapter are public education, criminal justice, health care, and social services.

The primary sources of information on usage of these services by undocumented aliens were the administrators and staff of the programs providing the services and the undocumented aliens questioned in our survey. Most of the estimates of the costs of providing services come from information received from the providers. We used the Bean and King estimates of undocumented alien residents (see Chapter 4) as the basis for estimating the number of undocumented in the state or in a region.

We gained valuable information about use of services from the survey of undocumented persons residing in Texas. However, the information from providers of services is more generally reliable for purposes of estimation for two reasons. First, when estimating usage of services provided by local governments, such as clinic-based health care, the numbers of undocumented persons in our survey using the specific service were too small to provide a basis for estimating usage rates and costs. Second, the sampling techniques used in our study probably resulted in a sample population with large numbers of users of public services, since access to the undocumented population in most cities was through community agencies that either provide services or refer persons to public services. Information from the questionnaires was used to verify the use of public services but not to estimate usage rates, except in the important case of education, where it was felt that our sample provided more reliable information than the provider estimates.

Each area of public services will be examined separately to determine the usage rates of undocumented aliens and the costs to state and local governments of providing these services. The costs to the local governments will be separated from the costs to the state government. Many public services are funded and/or provided by state agencies. These state agencies and their regional offices provided estimates of use rates and costs that are used to estimate statewide costs where appropriate. Since service providers and undocumented persons were surveyed in six specific regions of the state, usage rates and costs in these areas are described for each public service. Where appropriate, information gained in the six areas is also used to estimate statewide usage rates and costs. The estimates in this report are based on per person (not marginal) average costs for a service; however, it should be kept in mind that even if the undocumented alien population were reduced, the cost of providing the service would not necessarily be reduced by the average costs.

ESTIMATING THE COST OF HEALTH CARE FOR UNDOCUMENTED ALIENS

Costs of health care for undocumented aliens have been estimated using information from surveys of providers of hospital and health clinic services. The clinics researched were administered by city and county health departments and included child health services and immunization programs, family planning clinics, tuberculosis control clinics, venereal disease treatment programs, and maternal health clinics. These were the clinics identified by administrators as most often used by the undocumented. Costs of hospital care were derived from information from the public hospitals in our six surveyed regions. Health care areas not researched include dental services, mental health services, mental retardation programs, drug abuse and alcoholism treatment programs, and government-sponsored health insurance programs.

Information from the providers of health services was used rather than the information from the survey of undocumented aliens for reasons already stated. In addition, health service use among our sampled population varied substantially from region to region, and the provider surveys yielded a more consistent utilization pattern in the regions studied. Many of the undocumented interviewed were unable to specify whether the health services they used were public or private.

The estimates of costs will be separated into state and regional costs. Where possible, costs are separated on the basis of funding source. Estimates of costs to the state are thought to be overstated in this chapter since the state receives federal grants for health care; however, in the next chapter some accounting will be made of federal revenues received by the state.

Locally Provided Health Services

Local funds are used to support public hospitals and health departments. Costs for hospital care will be examined first.

Hospitals and Emergency Room Care. The cost to local governments for hospital and emergency care of the undocumented population derives from the treatment of "bad debt," or the portion of hospital bills that is not paid by the patient or by third-party payers, e.g. insurance. All providers surveyed stated that the majority of undocumented aliens served pay or attempt to pay their bills; their bad debt usually results from some form of catastrophic illness or injury. Any public hospital by law must admit anyone in need of hospitalization, regardless of ability to pay.

The majority of hospitals surveyed financed their operating budgets by a mix of patient fees and tax receipts. In these instances, bad debt resulting from hospitalization costs of undocumented aliens is covered by tax revenues. The one exception found was Brackenridge Hospital, the city hospital for Austin and Travis County. Brackenridge Hospital attempts to cover its estimated bad debt in advance through higher fees for private patients. If the estimate of the uncollectible bills is too low, the City of Austin covers the difference at the end of the fiscal year. In 1982, bad debt from undocumented aliens at Brackenridge was estimated to be approximately $500,000; the cost to the City of Austin could be anywhere from zero to $500,000.

Clinics and Health Centers. Local health departments offer clinics and services to 75 percent of the population in Texas. In fiscal year 1982, these services and clinics were provided without charge on the basis of proof of residency within the pertinent area. These health departments receive some funding assistance from the state, although a high proportion of these "state" funds are from federal health grants and contracts. Furthermore, the amount of state assistance varies by program, with the state providing more support for some programs, such as immunization and tuberculosis control, than for others.

The state provides direct services to the remaining 25 percent of the Texas population without local health departments through its regional health programs. However, budget information for state provision of these direct services was not available and direct estimates could not be made. Therefore, the cost to the state of clinic services has been estimated only in terms of the state contribution to the operation of the local health departments in the regions surveyed.

The estimated totals in Table 5.1 are based on information from Appendix E. Local health departments receive federal and state funding assistance through the Texas Health Department; however, the cost of services often cannot be traced back to a specific funding source because funds are mixed at the local level. State funding is accounted for in these estimates, either on the basis of the actual state contribution for the specific services identified, or on the basis of the average state contribution to the particular health department, as illustrated in Table E.1 in Appendix E.

It must be reiterated that the estimated total costs of providing public health services shown in Table 5.2 reflect the costs associated with public health clinics which are most often used by the undocumented population as

Table 5.1

Costs of Hospital Care for Undocumented Aliens

Region	Estimated Total Cost to Hospital (Bad Debt Only)	% of Operating Budget Paid by Taxes	Amount Paid by Taxes
Austin-Travis County Brackenridge Hosp.	500,000	Unknown	0-500,000
Dallas-Dallas Co. Parkland Hosp.	1,630,980	57	929,659
El Paso-El Paso Co. R. E. Thomason	750,000	40	300,000
Houston-Harris Co. Jeff Davis Hosp. Ben Taub Hosp.	3,054,795	85	2,596,576
McAllen-Hidalgo Co. McAllen Hosp. Mission Hosp. Edinburg Hosp.	(no estimates available from providers and no information on budgets available)		
San Antonio-Bexar Co. Bexar County Hosp.	1,000,000	34	340,000

Cost to local governments in surveyed areas: $4,166,235 to $4,666,235

Source: Provider estimates.

Table 5.2

Costs for Local Health Department Programs for the Undocumented
(Selected Programs)

Health Dept.	Estimated Total Clinic Costs for Undoc.		State Contribution[1]		Local Contribution	
	Low 315,208	High 448,930	Low 116,969	High 176,013	Low 198,197	High 272,225
Austin	4,518	76,814	2,494	42,401	2,824	33,721
Dallas	36,205	36,205	1,702	1,702	34,503	34,503
El Paso	89,223	98,823	89,223	98,823	0	0
Houston-Harris	107,523	107,523	9,247	9,247	98,276	98,276
San Antonio	(no estimates available)					
McAllen	77,739	129,565	14,304	23,840	63,435	105,725

Source: All estimates were based on provider information on the use of specific programs by the undocumented, or calculated on the basis of the Hispanic population in the city (Houston-Harris County) (see Appendix E).

[1]Includes federal grant and contract monies.

identified by health department administrators. The El Paso costs, for example, are for the tuberculosis and immunization clinics only. The Houston costs are for three clinics which were thought to be used most often by the undocumented in that area.

The state contribution estimate is highly influenced by the El Paso City-County clinic costs for tuberculosis and immunization programs which are totally state funded in this health department. The local contributions to public health clinic services for undocumented persons are more than twice the estimated state costs. Clearly, local governments (city and county) are bearing the bulk of the costs for providing health care for the undocumented in their localities. The secondary role of the state is further accentuated by the fact that most of the costs attributed to the state health department may be federal monies funded through that agency.

Table 5.3 shows the estimated totals for hospital and public clinic costs in the regions surveyed. As would be expected, Dallas and Houston have the highest costs for providing health care to the undocumented population. For each city the high costs of hospitalization and emergency care are the most significant parts of the public health expenses for the undocumented.

ESTIMATING THE COST OF SOCIAL SERVICES FOR UNDOCUMENTED ALIENS

As in the estimation of costs for health services, estimation of costs of social services is based primarily on information from providers of the services. In this case, our survey of the undocumented did provide information on receipt of several categories of social services, but not all. For example, day care and protective services data were available only from provider interviews. Estimates of costs are, thus, derived from information from providers about the cost of services, total numbers of persons served in the state, and estimates of usage by undocumented aliens. Where providers were unable to estimate usage rates of undocumented aliens, these rates were estimated based on data from the survey of the undocumented population and on usage rate estimates in other parts of the state for similar services. State costs will be estimated first, then costs in the six regions surveyed.

State Costs

Texas Department of Human Resources (TDHR).

1. Aid to Families with Dependent Children (AFDC). Estimates of usage of this program by undocumented persons were based on a TDHR study done in 1981 and 1982. Usage estimates were then applied to monthly average of families on AFDC to get the monthly average of undocumented families receiving AFDC. The usage rate for the undocumented is estimated to be 0.1 percent of

Table 5.3

Total Estimated Health Care Costs for Undocumented, 1982

Region	Total		Hospital-ER Costs		Clinic Costs	
	Low	High	Low	High	Low	High
Austin	4,518	576,814	0	500,000	4,518	76,814
Dallas	965,864	965,864	929,659	929,659	36,205	36,205
El Paso	389,223	398,823	300,000	300,000	89,223	98,823
Houston	2,704,099	2,704,099	2,596,576	2,596,576	107,523	107,523
McAllen "Valley"	77,739	129,565	(no estimates available)		77,739	129,565
San Antonio	340,000	340,000	340,000	340,000	(no estimates available)	
Totals	$4,481,443 -	5,115,165	$4,166,235 -	$4,666,235	$315,208 -	$448,930

Source: Provider estimates.

the total, or 93 families per year.

AFDC is funded by a mix of federal and state monies. The state pays 45.87 percent of the total program cost. The average household receiving AFDC grants had 3 or 4 persons. The AFDC payment per person is $34.52 per month; a 3-person family receives $103.56 per month and a 4-person family receives $138.08 per month. The calculations of cost to the state are shown in Table 5.4.*

Table 5.4

Estimated State Cost for AFDC for Undocumented Aliens

Low Estimate   High Estimate

(93 families) X ($103.56) = $9,631.08   (93) X ($138.08) = $12,841,44

($9,631.08) X (12 months) = $115,573   ($12,841.44) X (12) = $154,098

(45.87%) X ($115,573) = $53,013   (45.87%) X ($154,098) = $70,634

Range of state costs is $53,013 to $70,684 per year.

Source: Provider estimates.

Additional benefits, including medical assistance (Medicaid) and general social services, for example, are provided with AFDC eligibility, but are not included in this range.

2. Ongoing Services. Use of ongoing services varied on a regional basis. Estimates given were supplied by regional administrators. The state covers 35 percent of the entire program cost.

The regions surveyed are estimated to represent 54.9 percent of the population of undocumented persons in Texas. Therefore, applying this to the data in Table 5.5, the total cost of on-going services to the state is estimated as follows:

---

*In order to remain conservative, these estimates are left as is, with the assumption that there are no legal children in the household. We know from our sample, however, that families receiving aid such as AFDC are extremely likely to have citizen children present in the home. While a case might be made that money "received by" legal children of undocumented families is actually used for all family/household members, some of whom are undocumented, it is important to note that this money is most likely to be obtained by entitlement, not fraud.

Table 5.5

Use of Ongoing Services by the Undocumented in the Regions Surveyed

Region	% Undoc. (Est.)	# Undoc. Seen	Per Client Cost	Total Client Cost (Undoc.)	Cost for Undoc. (@ 35%) State Contrib.	Cost for Undoc. (@ 65%) Local Contrib.
Austin-Travis Co.	0	0	-	-	-	-
Dallas-Dallas Co.	3	20	1,772	35,440	12,404	23,036
El Paso-El Paso Co.	1-5	16-79	2,399	37,424-189,520	13,434-66,332	23,990-123,188
Houston-Harris Co.	1	86	1,343	115,498	40,424	75,074
McAllen-Hidalgo Co.	8	128	4,014	513,792	179,827	333,965
San Antonio-Bexar Co.	0	0	-	-	-	-
Totals				$702,154-$854,250	$246,089-$298,987	$456,065-$555,263

Source: Provider estimates, supplemented by Texas Undocumented Survey data.

Low estimate: $448,250

High estimate: $544,603

These statewide totals are based on the assumption that usage of ongoing services in the rest of the state by the undocumented is similar to that estimated by administrators in the six surveyed areas. This is probably an overestimation of the costs to the state, again in the interest of giving a "worst case" estimate of state costs for providing public services.

3. Day Care. Estimates of costs for publicly funded day care for undocumented children were based on interviews with TDHR administrators and day care center personnel. Average length of stay varied, so a range based on a 6-month and 12-month stay was calculated. The total estimates given in summary Table 5.6 may be high, as eligibility is based on income and fees are imposed on a sliding scale arrangement. Some undocumented families may pay the day care center between 2 and 4 percent of their gross monthly income per week. These fees are not reflected in the estimates presented in the table.

4. Family Violence Programs. TDHR is the major funding source for regional and local family violence centers. Estimates of usage given by program administrators and intake workers ranged from 1 to 5 percent for undocumented women and children. This range was applied to each agency's caseload to establish a base for estimating statewide usage. Regional costs are defined in Appendix F and are counted as part of the regional cost estimations. The total statewide estimate for family violence services for the undocumented is $4,836 to $21,698, based on the method described for "Ongoing Services." Family violence centers tend to be concentrated in urban centers; hence, this extended estimate is felt to overstate costs.

Other State Agencies.

No estimation of cost to the state was calculated for the Texas Commission for the Deaf, Texas State Commission for the Blind, Texas Rehabilitation Commission, and the Texas Employment Commission. Administrative personnel for these state agencies maintained that use of services by undocumented aliens was almost zero. Strict eligibility requirements for the programs of these agencies insure that virtually no undocumented persons receive agency services. Other state-supported costs for programs used by the undocumented are discussed below and also shown in Table 5.6.

1. Texas Department of Community Affairs (TDCA). TDCA provides state and federal monies to establish contracts with agencies for service provision. The following two divisions provide funding assistance for services known to be used by undocumented persons:

a. Drug Abuse Programs. Provider surveys showed that from 1 to 5 percent

Table 5.6

State Social Service Costs for the Undocumented

		Low	High
TDHR:	AFDC	$ 53,013	$ 70,684[1]
	Ongoing Services for Child Welfare	448,250	544,603[1]
	Day Care	263,787[2]	544,323[2]
	Family Violence Ctrs.	5,464[1]	27,322[1]
TDCA:	Drug Abuse Programs	1,500	7,500
	Child and Youth Services	7,880[1]	7,880[1]
State Support for Regional Svcs.		35,312	47,142[1]
	STATE TOTALS	$815,206	$1,249,454

Source: Provider interviews.

[1]Extended estimate for the state based on a population estimate
for the undocumented of 54.9 percent.

[2]Extended estimate for the state based on a 6 percent estimate of
undocumented use and 30 percent state cost.

of these clients were possibly undocumented. Given this estimate of service
usage, we can estimate a cost to the state of providing this service to
undocumented clients of between $1,500 and $7,500 for fiscal year 1982.

b. Child and Youth Services. This program was also estimated to have an
undocumented clientele of between 1 and 5 percent. Based on the 1 to 5
percent service usage range, there is an estimated $2,163 to $10,815 cost to
the state of Texas for providing these services to undocumented clients.

2. State Support of Regional and Local Services. State funds were a
source of support to numerous regional and local agencies in the six areas
surveyed. For some programs receiving state funds the cost of coverage was de
minimis and therefore not estimated. The level of state support varied from 1
percent to 17.5 percent for these programs with the total cost to the state
for providing services to undocumented persons estimated to be from $19,332 to
$25,881 in the six surveyed regions (see Appendix F). Extending this level of
state support on a statewide basis, the total estimated cost to the state
could be $35,213 to $47,142 to serve undocumented persons for these kinds of
programs. A problem with this approach, however, is that these particular
kinds of services depend on local circumstances and local needs. Funding for
these kinds of services is varied and, as is indicated by the low levels of

state support, these programs are often more dependent on private funding sources. It is likely that the cost of state support of these regional programs for the undocumented population is greatly overestimated in the extended projections.

Costs of Local and Regional Social Services

Local and regional departments provide a variety of social services for local and county residents. There is a major difficulty in specifying the costs to local governments for providing support services for undocumented persons. Services are by no means uniform but are, instead, developed locally to meet the particular needs of the community served. Consequently, funding arrangements for these services and their eligibility requirements will vary considerably, making it difficult to disaggregate the costs to county and city government for serving the undocumented and to estimate these costs on a statewide basis.

Most locally funded social services are provided by the city or county through a contracting arrangement with a private, non-profit organization. Following is a breakdown of general social services provided to the undocumented by local and county governments in Texas. Use of services by the undocumented and funding estimates are based entirely on figures given by providers in the six surveyed cities. Statewide estimates are consequently based on the funding patterns found in these cities.

City Costs for Direct Services for the Undocumented. Most of the cities surveyed provided general social services of a type shown in Table 5.7 to local residents through neighborhood, multi-purpose, and community centers. Centers located in predominantly Hispanic neighborhoods are most likely to serve undocumented aliens, although none of the providers interviewed indicated this population had an impact on marginal service costs. An estimate was made, however, for one San Antonio project which offered services to young people. Almost $35,000 in city funds were expended for undocumented youth in San Antonio.

County Costs for Direct Services to the Undocumented. Texas counties have the authority to provide general welfare programs for residents. Thus many of the larger Texas counties allocate welfare funds for indigents living within the county. While some counties provide emergency funds for indigents on a demand basis, the counties surveyed provided services through both county departments and local contracting agencies. This section identifies costs for serving undocumented persons through county-administered departments.

As should be expected, services and eligibility requirements are locally determined and vary from one county to the next. Most of the counties surveyed provided emergency financial assistance in the form of cash grants for rent, food, and utility payments. Others also offered transportation and general social service counseling. With the exception of the Travis County Emergency Assistance Office, these emergency aid offices categorically deny eligibility to undocumented aliens on the basis of nonresidence. Therefore, funds for emergency aid for undocumented persons are calculated on the basis of a proportion of the "fraud rate" for each agency or on estimates given by providers. In Table 5.7 the Travis County cost is high as the use rate is based on a population proportion of the total caseload. This, of course, assumes that the proportion of undocumented aliens in the city of Austin is similarly represented in the county's caseload.

Locally Contracted Social Services. City and county governments also assist in the provision of social services through contracting arrangements with private, nonprofit organizations. These organizations generally have funding from a variety of sources and typically sponsor specialized programs or services within the community. In the six surveyed areas, local governments extended their social service activities through contracting arrangements with organizations such as Rape Crisis Centers, Family Violence Centers, Big Brothers/Big Sisters, day care centers, and others. These services are often provided on the basis of need and, therefore, stringent eligibility standards are not generally applied. Thus, undocumented persons may be able to use these services with fewer barriers, although the specialization of the programs, and information from the surveyed providers, indicate that this is not the case. Table 5.8 lists the local costs of serving undocumented persons for selected contracted social service programs in the surveyed areas. In most areas, city and county funds could not be disaggregated. Contracted service costs were not extended on a statewide basis, because the specialization of the programs suggests that less populated areas in Texas may not be able to support these services. The estimated total for contracted services in these areas was $403,633 - $573,201. This total is greatly affected by the programs in San Antonio supported by local government. One project alone received one-half of the estimate for all six regions.

ESTIMATING THE COST OF EDUCATING UNDOCUMENTED ALIEN CHILDREN

According to the responses by school district officials to the Texas Education Agency (TEA) questionnaire, there were 19,846 undocumented aliens in Texas public schools in the 1982-1983 school year.

These estimates should be viewed with caution for several reasons. First, schools are not required to ask children for documentation of their status in the country and, therefore, school records are not reliable indicators of the number of undocumented children in school. Second, not every school district replied to the TEA questionnaire, and some of these nonresponding school districts may have significant numbers of undocumented children.

If the number of children counted in the TEA survey is doubled, there would be 39,692 undocumented alien children in Texas public schools. Because the figures derived from our survey of undocumented households were significantly higher than even this doubled figure, even after adjusting for sampling bias (discussed below), the doubled figure will be used in the calculations based on TEA information. At the state average of $2,176

Table 5.7

County Costs for Direct Social Services for the Undocumented

County	Totals Estimate Low	Totals Estimate High	General-Emergency Assistance (1) Estimate Low	General-Emergency Assistance (1) Estimate High	Child Welfare-Foster Care (2) Estimate Low	Child Welfare-Foster Care (2) Estimate High	Misc. (3) Estimate Low	Misc. (3) Estimate High
Travis	9,164	14,995	9,164[1]	14,995[1]	-[5]	-[5]	-[5]	-[5]
Dallas	5,400	6,520	0	223[2]	5,400	5,400	0	897[3]
El Paso	21,014	21,336	483[2]	805[2]	20,531[3]	20,531	-[5]	-[5]
Harris	42,017	42,105	177[2]	265[2]	41,840[3]	41,840	-[5]	-[5]
Hidalgo	18,288	32,868	-[5]	-[5]	18,288	32,868[3,4,6]	-[5]	-[5]
Bexar	-[5]	-[5]	-[5]	-[5]	-[5]	-[5]	-[5]	-[5]
Totals	$95,883	$117,824	$9,824	$16,288	$86,059	$100,639	0	$897

Source: Provider interviews and calculations.

Bean and King population estimates by city (percentage): Austin (3.3-5.4); Dallas (2.3-3.8); El Paso (11.8-19.04); Houston (2.79-4.5); and San Antonio (8.56-13.82).

[1] Calculation based on average cost per case X Bean & King proportion.
[2] Calculation based on fraud rate given by provider X Bean & King proportion X average cost per case.
[3] Calculation based on estimate given by provider on undocumented clients' use X average cost per case.
[4] This high estimate includes medical costs per case.
[5] No additional costs attributed to serving undocumented clients, or program not funded by the county.
[6] Estimate includes medical costs.

Table 5.8

Estimated Costs of Contracted Social Services to Local Governments
(for Undocumented Population)

City/County	Totals	Rape Crisis	Big Brothers/Big Sisters	Day Care	Family Violence Centers	Misc.	Child Guidance
Austin/Travis	20,095 - 20,697	110[6] - 110	0 - 602[2,6]	15,994[3,6] - 15,994	-[5]	3,991[2,6] - 3,991	-[5]
Dallas		No estimates available					761-1,205[7]
El Paso/El Paso	11,991 - 12,007	273 -[2,6] 289[2,6]		11,718 - 11,718	-[5]	-[5]	-[5]
Houston/Harris	77,053 - 83,789		865[2,6] - 865	44,622[6] - 44,622	704 - 3,872[1]	30,862 - 34,430	-[5]
McAllen/Hidalgo		No estimates available					-[5]
San Antonio (City only)	294,494 - 456,708		2,043 -[3,4] 3,193[3,4]		634 - 2,960[3,4]	291,817 - 450,555	-[5]
Totals	$404,394 - $574,406	$383 - $399	$2,908 - $4,660	$72,334 - $72,334	$1,338 - $6,832	$326,670 - $488,976	$761 - $1,205

Source: Provider estimates.

[1] These are high estimates since most funds are used for educational purposes rather than direct costs.

[2] City/County mix.

[3] City only.

[4] Calculation based on estimate given by provider on undocumented clients' use X average cost per case.

[5] This high estimate includes medical costs per case.

[6] No additional costs attributed to serving undocumented clients, or program not funded by the county.

[7] Calculation based on average cost per case X Bean & King proportions.

operating cost per student, the total cost of educating these students in 1982-1983 was $86,369,792. Using the 1979-1980 school year proportions for sources of funding, 48.8 percent of the above figure, or $42,148,458, was provided by the state. Local tax support contributed 40.9 percent of the funding, or $35,325,245. The balance of the cost was covered by federal funds; the estimated federal contribution was $8,896,089. Tables 5.9a and 5.9b show the respective costs to the local districts and to the state based on the TEA survey.

In our survey of undocumented aliens, 202 of 358 children (or 56.4 percent of those under 18 years) were enrolled in school. Of these, 130 were undocumented children attending public schools in the six surveyed areas.* These children represent 22.2 percent of the total undocumented population surveyed. If we use this proportion with the Bean and King state population estimates, there would be 126,296 to 203,885 undocumented children in Texas schools. (One-half of that figure would be 63,148 children to 101,942 children. Twice that figure would be 252,592 to 407,770 children.)

These estimates should also be viewed with caution, since our sample probably included a large number of households with children compared to the undocumented children at large. Using our survey data, a reasonable estimate to use as a basis for cost estimates would be one-half of the estimated number of children, or 63,148 to 101,942. Table 5.10 shows the estimated number of children in public schools (statewide and in our sample regions) based on the 22.2 percent of undocumented aliens in our sample that are children in school, and then applying this percentage to one-half the estimated distribution of aliens in the sample cities (one-half of the Bean and King estimate). For each Standard Metropolitan Statistical Area (SMSA), the cost to the state and the cost to the local school district are estimated using average costs per child for the major district in the area, as presented in Appendix G. This projects a somewhat high cost, since some SMSAs have several school districts, and the major district will have higher expenditures per child in most cases than smaller districts. This is especially true for San Antonio and Houston, which have many districts.

As mentioned in the Appendix, it should be remembered that removal of these children from the schools would not represent a dollar-for-dollar cost savings, since the state bases its funding formula on the average daily attendance in the school.

ESTIMATING THE COSTS OF POLICE SERVICES AND IMPRISONMENT FOR THE UNDOCUMENTED POPULATION IN TEXAS

The justice system in Texas serves the undocumented population in many

---

*Of the 202 total, 59 students were U.S. born or legal residents, while 13 of the undocumented children attended private schools.

Table 5.9a

Cost to District of Undocumented Children
in School

School District	X/2	X	2X
Austin	$ 237,277	$ 474,553	$ 949,106
Dallas	1,110,593	2,221,187	4,442,373
El Paso	189,144	378,288	756,576
Houston	4,893,574	9,787,147	19,574,294
McAllen	375,766	751,531	1,503,062
San Antonio	459,724	919,447	1,838,894
Statewide Totals	$ 7,266,607	$14,532,152	$29,064,302

Source: TEA Survey, 1982, for Dallas and El Paso; Texas Undocumented Survey for others.

X = Cost to district for undocumented children.

Table 5.9b

Cost to State of Undocumented Children
in School

School District	X/2	X	2X
Austin	$ 101,920	$ 203,840	$ 407,680
Dallas	596,153	1,192,305	2,384,610
El Paso	315,695	631,389	1,262,778
Houston	1,862,316	3,724,632	7,449,264
McAllen	585,200	1,170,400	2,340,800
San Antonio	454,518	909,036	1,818,072
Statewide Totals	$21,074,229	$42,148,458	$84,296,916

Source: TEA Survey, 1982, for Dallas and El Paso; Texas
Undocumented Survey for others.

X = Cost to district for undocumented children.

Table 5.10

Estimated Costs for Undocumented Children in School

School District	X/2		Cost to State		Cost to District	
	Low	High	Low	High	Low	High
Austin	1,996	3,221	1,660,672	2,679,872	3,866,152	6,238,916
Dallas[1]	2,349	3,792	1,848,663	2,984,304	3,443,939	5,559,565
El Paso	6,283	10,144	6,326,981	10,215,008	3,790,722	6,120,180
Houston	8,986	14,506	6,433,976	10,386,296	16,906,440	27,291,879
McAllen	4,869	7,860	5,180,616	8,363,040	3,326,550	5,370,031
San Antonio	10,186	16,443	10,450,836	16,870,518	10,570,522	17,063,723
Subtotals of Six Surveyed Areas	$34,669	$55,966	$25,467,768	$51,499,038	$41,904,325	$67,644,294

Source: Texas Undocumented Survey.

Calculations on the estimated number of children in school are based on the Texas Undocumented Survey, where the school population is 22.2% of the sample. This percentage is applied to the Bean and King estimate for each city. Costs to the state and district are average costs for the major school district in each city.

[1] City only.

ways, including general police protection provided for anyone dwelling within the state, responses by police departments to victims of crimes, and general legal services, involving the undocumented, on both the state and local levels. However, when determining the costs to the state and local governments that involve undocumented aliens residing in the state, one must measure only those costs which can be attributed specifically to undocumented aliens. Those costs which would accrue to the government whether or not these persons resided in the state cannot be attributed to the undocumented population. Since the undocumented segment is small in proportion to the total population, the level of police services would not change significantly if there were no undocumented persons in the state. Therefore, this study is limited to estimating the specific costs of incarceration when an undocumented alien is suspected or convicted of a crime; the study does not attempt to estimate the court costs of trials of undocumented aliens.

Costs to the State of Texas of Incarceration
of Undocumented Aliens

The costs to the state of incarceration of undocumented aliens in Texas Department of Corrections (TDC) facilities are estimated as follows: We assume that the number of non-U.S. citizens in TDC facilities on any day is a representative figure of the undocumented population that is being incarcerated. In 1982 there were 34,393 prisoners in TDC facilities. Of this number 501 were found to be non-U.S. citizens on a one day count.* Assuming that all of these persons were undocumented,** and that this day was representative in terms of inmate numbers, the cost to the state, at the rate of $12.11 per prisoner per day, was about $6,067 per day, totaling $2,214,495 for 1982.

Costs to Local Governments of Incarceration of Undocumented Aliens

If each city in the study sample arrests the same percentage of its

---

*Telephone interview by Martha Van Haitsma with J. Byrd, Public Affairs Office, TDC, Huntsville, Texas, June 24, 1983.

**This assumption is made to assure a conservatively high cost estimate. A lower figure might be obtained by taking a ratio of the estimated undocumented population to the total estimated undocumented population plus legal resident alien population. This would give us an estimate of the portion of non-citizens who are undocumented aliens. This percentage could then be multiplied by 501 to get an estimate of the number of undocumented persons who are in state prisons on any given day.

undocumented residents as does San Antonio,* then average costs per city can be computed as shown in Appendix H. These computations use city-specific figures for average length of stay and average cost per day; and, the undocumented jail population range is estimated by taking .40 percent and .65 percent respectively of the average undocumented population for each city. These percentages are the low and high estimates of the percentage of undocumented persons arrested in San Antonio. Taking an average of the high and low cost estimates, the estimated total cost to the six cities for the incarceration of undocumented aliens comes to $61,407.**

Similar computations were performed to estimate the costs of incarceration to county governments, as shown in Appendix H. The estimated cost to county governments is $677,997 (again, an average of the high and low figures).

Table 5.11

Estimated Costs of Incarceration of Undocumented Aliens
for Local and State Governments

	Costs
Local Governments (Cities and Counties in Sample)	$ 739,404
State Government (TDC)	2,214,495

Source: Provider questionnaires and surveys.

SUMMARY

Table 5.12 sums up estimated state and local costs of the various service areas used by undocumented aliens in Texas.

---

*Because San Antonio has a large undocumented population, this is thought be an overestimation.

**Ranges derived were so broad as to be meaningless. Therefore, a point estimate has been made. Other, similar figures were computed using a number of approaches, thus giving us greater confidence in the average figure.

Chapter Six brings together all these cost figures and compares them with revenue data.

Table 5.12

Summary Table

Estimated Costs of Public Services for the
Undocumented (Surveyed Areas and TDC)

Service Area	Totals		Local		State	
	Low	High	Low	High	Low	High
Education [1]	$32,694,375	$80,563,334	$ 7,226,607	$29,064,302	$46,389,377	$93,805,169
Corrections [2]	2,953,899	2,953,899	739,404	739,404	2,214,495	2,214,495
Social Services	1,331,933	1,949,789	500,277	692,230	815,206	1,249,454
Health	4,481,443	5,115,165	4,364,432	4,938,460	117,011	176,705
Totals			$12,830,720	$35,434,396	$49,536,089	$97,445,823

Source: Summary of estimates provided by agency personnel. See Appendices A, E-H.

[1] Cost to local districts was based on Table 5.9a. Cost to state was based on Texas Undocumented
Survey, Bean and King, and TEA cost estimates.
Cost to state of six surveyed areas (i.e. 54.9%) = $25,469,768 (low)
                                                = $51,499,034 (high)

Total cost to state = $25,469,768/54.9% = $46,389,377 (low)
                    = $51,499,038/54.9% = $93,805,169 (high)

[2] State costs are projected for the entire state.

CHAPTER 6

COSTS AND REVENUES SUMMARIZED AND COMPARED

This chapter summarizes the estimated revenues received from undocumented persons residing in the state of Texas and the costs of providing services to them. The revenues and costs are then compared both at the state and local/regional levels.

REVENUES RECEIVED

Income Tax

Although income tax is paid to the federal government, a portion of this money is returned to the state. In fiscal year 1982, an estimated 17 percent or $2.44 billion of the total state budget was comprised of federal funds.* Out of every dollar of income tax paid by Texas residents, 68 cents is returned to the state in the form of grants. These funds are often earmarked for certain purposes; however, the distribution channels are unclear, especially in the areas of health and social services. In 1982, 43.6 percent of the returned federal funds went to the broad category of "welfare", 22.4 percent went to education, and 16.3 percent went to highways. This does not distinguish between grants awarded directly to local governments or agencies and grants to the state, which may or may not be passed along to locally administered programs.

Of the total 1982 state budget, 3.3 percent or $394,744,558 was granted to political subdivisions. It is unclear, however, how much of this redistributed money originated as federal funds.**

---

*Comptroller of Public Accounts, State of Texas, Annual Financial Report, fiscal year ending August 31, 1982 (Austin, Texas: Office of the Comptroller, November 1, 1982).

**We could estimate this to show an order of magnitude. Assuming that federal money received by the state is evenly distributed among the state's expenditures, 17 percent of the money passed down to political subdivisions would have originated as federal funds. Using the formula 3.3 percent X 17 percent to arrive at the portion of state funds received from income tax which

Using the estimated ranges of income taxes paid in by undocumented persons residing in Texas as calculated in Chapter 4, and the 68-cents-to-the-dollar formula for tax money returned to the state, we can calculate the estimated undocumented contribution to the state (see Table 6.1).

Table 6.1

Federal Income Taxes Paid by Undocumented Aliens
Returned to the State of Texas

	Low	High
Income Taxes Paid by Undocumented Aliens	$174,731,356	$282,076,828
Portion Returned to Texas	X .68	X .68
State Revenues (X)	118,817,322	191,812,243
X/2	59,408,611	95,906,122
2X	237,634,694	383,624,486

Source: Chapter 4, Table 4.9.

Excise Taxes

The state levies and collects a number of excise taxes. Most of these taxes go to the state treasury. However, in the case of vehicle registration and certificate of title fees, a portion of the revenues remains with the county of registration. For fiscal year 1982, the fee for a vehicle certificate of title was $3.00 per vehicle and that amount was evenly split between the county and the state. Vehicle registration fees vary with the

---

** Contin.

is passed on to political subdivisions, we estimate the following distribution:

	Low	High
Revenues to the State	$118,817,322	$191,812,243
Revenues to County and Local Units	666,907	1,076,067

Source: Table 6.1 and annual reports of the Comptroller of Public Accounts.

weight of the car, normally ranging from $10 to 20 per vehicle.* Each county retains an allowance of this revenue based on the road mileage in that county. Revenues received above the road allowance figure are split evenly between the county and the state until a county reaches its maximum of $350,000, and all money collected thereafter goes to the state. Because all counties in our sample normally reach the $350,000 maximum, because of their size, the presence or absence of undocumented persons should have no effect on county funds. Therefore, we will assume that registration fees from undocumented persons represents additional funds to the state. All driver's license fees go to the state. The number of certificate of title fees paid which were reported by undocumented persons in our sample was too small on which to base an estimate.** The total excise taxes paid by undocumented persons as estimated in Chapter 4 are as shown in Table 6.2. These revenues are considered to be entirely state revenues.

Table 6.2

Excise Taxes Paid by Undocumented Aliens in Texas

	Low	High
Excise Taxes Paid (X)	$14,034,763	$22,656,928
X/2	7,017,382	11,328,464
2X	28,069,526	45,313,856

Source: Chapter 4, Table 4.14.

Sales Tax

Sales tax is, according to the State Comptroller, the largest source of state revenues (40 percent of all tax revenue). In metropolitan areas, such as those included in this study, sales tax is 5 percent of the purchase price of taxable goods. The state receives 80 percent of this revenue (4 percent of the purchase price) and the metropolitan area retains 20 percent of the

---

*Telephone interview with Travis County Tax Collector's Office, May 23, 1983.

**This question was not asked directly, but a number of persons volunteered the information when asked about paying for driver's licenses and vehicle registration.

revenue (1 percent of the purchase price).* From estimated sales tax payments by undocumented persons (calculated in Chapter 4) the distribution of sales tax revenues may be calculated as shown in Table 6.3.

Table 6.3

Sales Taxes Paid by Undocumented Aliens in Texas

	Low	High
Total Sales Taxes Paid by Undocumented Persons in Texas	$48,242,720	$77,880,320
Amount to the State	38,594,176	62,304,256
Amount to Local Governments	9,648,544	15,576,064

Source: Chapter 4, Table 4.12.

Property Tax

The undocumented persons interviewed were renters, and we can assume that the vast majority of all undocumented persons are renters rather than homeowners. While tenants do pay property taxes indirectly through rent, there is no accepted formula for calculating the amount. We lack estimates of the average property values of the areas in which the undocumented persons interviewed live,** knowledge of current rental rates, size of property holdings of landlords, and other factors which influence the percentage of property tax passed along to the tenant by the landlord. Without suitable information to estimate from, we will make the conservative assumption that undocumented persons pay no property tax.

Social Security Tax

Social security taxes are paid by the majority of employed undocumented persons in this sample. However, this money is federal revenue, and is

---

*Houston and San Antonio charge a slightly higher tax, and the extra revenue goes to pay for public transportation.

**Unless the interview was conducted in the respondent's home, we had no information about where the respondent lived, and to protect subjects, this information, like names, was neither asked for nor recorded if volunteered.

distributed directly to eligible individuals by the federal government.*
Thus, social security taxes do not represent revenues to the state.

Miscellaneous

There are many other local fees which provide some revenue to the state
or to local governments, e.g. park and pool fees, parking meter fees, various
licenses and permits, and others. Most of these fees go to offset the cost of
the service being provided, as in the case of bus fare. While undocumented
persons undoubtedly contribute something through fees such as those listed
above, the amount is unlikely to be significant relative to the total intake,
since the services such fees help to support have low or nonexistent marginal
costs. The addition or subtraction of a small percentage of users should have
no effect on the number of buses running, the upkeep of parks, the number of
lifeguards hired for a pool, and so forth. We will make the conservative
assumption that undocumented persons pay no miscellaneous fees.

SUMMARY OF REVENUES

The total contribution of undocumented persons to the public coffers is
(conservatively) estimated in Table 6.4.

Table 6.4

Revenues Collected from Undocumented Aliens

	State	Local
Income Tax	$118,317,322-191,812,243	$ -
Social Security	-	-
Sales Tax	38,594,176-62,304,256	5,297,050-8,551,259[1]
Excise Tax	14,034,763-22,656,928	-
Property Tax	-	-
Total(X)	157,425,532-276,773,427	5,297,050-8,551,259
X/2	78,714,766-188,386,714	2,648,525-4,275,630
2X	314,851,064-553,546,854	10,594,110-17,102,518

Source: Table 6.3.

[1]Since the six regions used account for 54.9 percent of the
amount of sales tax to all local government, $9,648,544 X
54.9 percent is the low estimate and $15,576,064 X 54.9 percent
is the high estimate.

---

*Some benefits, such as those derived under Titles 19 and 20, are
administered by the state, but the costs of administration are covered by the
federal government out of the social security fund.

COSTS INCURRED

Undocumented persons utilize a number of services which are supported by government funds. Tables 6.5 and 6.6 present summaries of the estimated costs of providing such services to the resident undocumented population. The costs are broken down by government level wherever possible. It should be noted that just as the revenues received from undocumented persons have been systematically underestimated for conservative reasons whenever a choice had to be made, so, too, the costs of providing the services used by undocumented persons will be systematically overestimated whenever a choice must be made. The sources of bias for both costs and revenues will be reviewed prior to a comparison of the two. The estimate of revenues received from undocumented persons is more reliable at the state than at the local level. On the other hand, the estimates of service costs are more reliable at the local level. Our best service cost estimates are for the six cities targeted by this study. The reason for this discrepancy is that while the taxes included here are fairly constant throughout the state, the provision of services is not. Many services available in one city are not available in comparable form, or not at all, in other cities in the state. Many more services are available, and likely to be used by the undocumented, in large metropolitan areas than are available, or likely to be used, in rural areas. Generalizing from urban to rural areas tends to overstate costs.

Table 6.5

Local and Regional Costs of Services Provided
to Undocumented Aliens for Six Cities[1]

	Low	High
Education[2]	$7,226,607	$29,064,302
Corrections	739,404	739,404
Social Services	500,277	692,230
Health	4,364,432	4,938,460
Totals	12,830,720	35,434,396

Source: Chapter 5.

[1]See Table 6.6.

[2]Estimates for Austin, Houston, McAllen, and San Antonio
are based on the Texas Undocumented Survey. Estimates for
Dallas and El Paso are based on TEA data.

Table 6.6

State Costs of Services to Undocumented Persons

	Low	High
Education[1]	$46,389,377	$93,805,169
Corrections[2]	2,214,495	2,214,495
Social Services	815,206	1,249,454
Health[3]	117,011	176,705
Totals	49,536,089	97,445,823

Source: Chapter 5.

[1]Costs are estimated by school district.

[2]This figure is a statewide estimate rather than an estimate for the six cities only.

[3]This includes regional services contracted out by the state.

COMPARING COSTS AND REVENUES

In order to compare the costs of providing services to undocumented persons in the six cities in our survey with the revenues paid in by those same persons, it is necessary to compute estimates of revenues for the six cities only. We are assuming that the undocumented population is distributed across Texas in roughly the same manner as the total Hispanic population. Therefore, since 54.9 percent of "persons of Spanish origin"* reside in the six cities targeted by this study, we are assuming that the same proportion of the total undocumented population of Texas resides in these cities as well. Since revenues were computed on a per capita basis, we can simply take 54.9 percent of the total revenues to arrive at a figure for the six cities. We believe that this biases revenue downward because of the more sophisticated tax collections systems in urban than in rural areas. We will show a separate estimate of costs and revenues for the state as a whole. Then, total costs and revenues will be compared in the six cities.

Before comparing costs with revenues, a listing of the sources of bias for overestimation of cost and underestimation of revenues is given in order to clarify the results.

---

*Census definition.

Sources of Downward Bias in Revenue Estimations

Income taxes. Income taxes represent the largest single source of revenue to the state from undocumented persons. Assuming that there is a constant percentage of undocumented workers whose employers do not deduct taxes, the amount of income taxes paid in is dependent on the percentage of the undocumented population that is working. In our sample, we assume that only 52 percent of the undocumented population is working. Not only does this exclude working minors in our own sample, but it also assumes an age/sex distribution similar to ours in the entire undocumented population—an extremely unlikely assumption. Because we sampled through agencies, we were more likely to find women, children, and entire families. These in turn are more likely to be long-term settlers. Young single migrants, who appear to comprise the bulk of the undocumented population, will have a much higher proportion of workers than settled families that include dependent children.* Calculating that only 65.3 percent of the working undocumented population pays income taxes, as we do here, and that only 52 percent of the population is working, we are assuming that only 34 percent of the entire undocumented population pays income taxes. This figure is considerably lower than percentages found in other studies (North and Houston, 1975: 73.2 percent; Cardenas, 1975: 59.5 percent; Cornelius, 1976: 64 percent; Villalpando, 1976: 81 percent; Orange County Task Force, 1977-1978: 70 percent).**

Property Taxes. Property taxes, because they could not be calculated, were simply dropped from the analysis. However, we know that undocumented residents are paying property taxes, some directly, and many more indirectly in their rental payments. These taxes support schools and hospitals, both of which are figured in as major costs despite the fact that no revenues are calculated.

Excise Taxes. Only those excise taxes with significant response levels were added in to the revenue sums. Other taxes which did not appear on the questionnaire, because they were unlikely to be significant, may still represent some revenue to the state.

Fees. Many services carry a fee, which, even if nominal, somewhat offsets the cost of the service. A number of the hospitals studied financed

---

*We can surmise that this is correct from the labor force participation rate of the detainees in our sample. As many as 54 percent of the household members reported by detained respondents—including the respondents themselves—were working at the time of apprehension. Only 39 percent of the respondents were working because many of them had been apprehended while crossing the border, and so had not yet had the opportunity to find work. However, 90 percent of the detainee respondents reported economic reasons as their motivation for coming to the U.S., so we can assume that had they not been apprehended, many more of the detainees would have found jobs.

**See Annotated Bibliography, Appendix I.

their bad debt with high patient fees for those who did pay their bills. Since most undocumented patients did pay their bills at these hospitals, they too were subsidizing those who did not pay. However, this was not calculated as part of the revenues.

Sources of Upward Bias in Cost Estimations

Cost Calculation. Most service costs were based on average rather than marginal cost. This means that the entire cost of the service, including overhead, is divided by the total number of users to determine the average cost per person. Such figures overstate the actual cost, because the cost of an additional person is not as large as the average total cost. It takes very large differences in user numbers to affect certain overhead costs. It would take a very large number of undocumented persons, indeed, to affect the number of school buildings provided for children, the number of wardens hired by state prisons, or the amount of equipment owned by a hospital. The plant and equipment a facility has must be maintained regardless of the number of users. Social service agencies often provide whatever level of service their budgets allow since demand always exceeds supply. In such cases undocumented users might represent a "cost" to citizens in terms of access, but the marginal monetary cost would be zero.

Estimate Choice. Because service providers were interviewed as well as undocumented persons directly, we had two bases from which to calculate service usage. Service providers gave estimates of the numbers of undocumented aliens they felt were using their facility, and undocumented persons reported the number and kinds of services they or someone in their household had used. Service provider estimates were routinely higher than estimates derived from the undocumented sample, and in each case we based our calculations on the higher estimates.

Sampling Method. Because we located undocumented persons for interviews largely through social service agencies, our population was by definition a service-using group. In addition, the large percentages of women and children in our sample create a further upward bias in that these two groups are more likely to use services than are adult males.

Overall Bias in Comparison Method

Cities as Target Areas. Targeting cities for cost and revenue estimation has the effect of biasing costs upward and revenues downward. The reason for this imbalance is that while revenues may be paid in fairly uniformly by all undocumented persons residing in the state, services and their costs are concentrated in urban centers. Persons from outside the metropolitan area use facilities located within the city, particularly hospitals. Thus, while the cost of providing services to such people is included, the contributions those people make through taxes are not included. In addition, funding goes where services are offered. A disproportionate amount of the total money for social and health services will go to agencies in cities. Thus, a disproportionate amount of the tax dollars from undocumented persons all over the state will be funneled into urban areas. Again, the revenues of those not residing in the urban centers are not included in the calculations, even though they may in fact be subsidizing those services.

COMPARISON OF TOTAL COSTS AND TOTAL REVENUE

As shown in Table 6.7, revenue to the state exceeds cost to the state. The high cost estimate is still considerably smaller than the low revenue estimate. Undocumented aliens in Texas contribute more revenue to the state than the cost to the state to provide them with public services.

Table 6.7

Costs and Revenues to State

	Low	High
Cost	$ 49,536,089	$ 97,445,823
Revenue[1]	157,425,532	276,773,427

Source: Previous tables, Chapters 4 and 5 of this report.

[1]Based upon X in Table 6.4.

Table 6.8

Costs and Revenues to Six Cities Surveyed

	Low	High
Cost	$12,830,720	$35,434,396
Revenue[1]	5,297,050	8,552,259

Source: Previous tables, Chapters 4 and 5 of this report.

[1]Based upon X in Table 6.4.

Table 6.8 illustrates that costs to provide services exceed revenue for the six cities considered by the study. The low cost estimate is larger than the high revenue estimate. Undocumented aliens place a burden on the local governments, since revenue contributed by these persons is smaller than the cost to provide them with services.

The consistent downward biasing of revenues and upward biasing of costs is done in an effort to make the relationship of the final totals more reliable. That is, since total revenues exceed total costs despite the systematic bias, we can be quite certain that such is in fact the case. The numbers which appear in this report are all estimates and should be treated as such. The broad ranges which are calculated for every cost are an indication of the necessary roughness of the figures. Because undocumented persons are not countable in any exact way, because no official statistics are kept of numbers of undocumented clientele using most public services, because we had no way to draw a representative sample of undocumented persons to interview, and because sources of funding of public services are often difficult to trace, there are numerous points in our calculations where rough estimates had to be used. Given so many possible sources of error, the deliberate exaggeration of costs and minimization of contributions is a method of ensuring that even if individual estimates are not accurate, the general relationship between costs and revenues would be reliable.

There is, however, a discrepancy between the level at which revenues are collected and the level at which the services used are funded. Those services funded at the local level are those most heavily utilized by undocumented aliens, but the revenues contributed by these persons go primarily to the state and federal government. Thus, while the state realizes a bonus from taxes attributable to undocumented residents, local governments and agencies often experience a deficit.

We conclude that it is almost certain that undocumented persons contribute more to the revenue of the State of Texas than it costs the state to provide services. The opposite is true for county and local governments. At this level of government, the estimated costs exceed the estimated revenues.

It should be noted that, taken together, state and local contributed revenues exceed the combined estimated cost of services. This is true despite the consistent biasing used to obtain these estimates. It must also be remembered that social security taxes are not treated here because such revenue is federal rather than state. To the extent that undocumented aliens pay social security but do not receive benefits, this represents a contribution by the undocumented to the social security fund. Insofar as Texas residents receive social security benefits, there is an indirect contribution made to Texas by undocumented aliens.

CHAPTER 7

CONCLUSIONS AND RECOMMENDATIONS

The purpose of this study was to estimate the costs to the State of Texas and specified localities of providing services to undocumented aliens and to compare these costs with the revenues received from undocumented persons in the state and the specified localities. Metropolitan localities were targeted for the survey sample because research indicates a continuing shift of the undocumented population to urban destinations and because services, being more numerous and more accessible in cities, are more likely to be used there. The cost and revenue estimates generated by this study have been disaggregated where possible by state and regional/local levels.

In the course of our research, we learned much about the habits of undocumented persons. This knowledge leads us to question many stereotypes that are accepted about the characteristics and behavior of the undocumented.

We would like to stress seven points.

1. Undocumented persons do, indeed, use public services and they also pay taxes. The total revenues received exceed the total costs of providing services. This is particularly true at the state level. Faced with a number of estimation procedures, we consistently chose the lowest reasonable revenue estimate and the highest reasonable cost estimate. This was done in the interest of conservatism. Thus we have confidence that, despite the range within which the true figures can be expected to fall, the overall relationship--revenues exceed costs--is correct.

2. Education is the most costly service at both the state and local level. Health services are one of the most frequently used public services, but most undocumented clients pay for such services. Our findings show that there is little use by undocumented aliens of social services, such as food stamps and AFDC, from which undocumented persons are explicitly not excluded. When costs and revenues are disaggregated by state and local levels, our conclusion is that local governments bear the brunt of the cost burden and the state receives the bulk of the revenues.

3. Because illegal immigration is an emotionally and politically charged issue, unsupported, exaggerated figures are frequently used. If we have any central recommendation to policy makers, it is that they should be cautious about making any exaggerated public statements on this point.

4. A second recommendation is that policy makers should look at the methodology of studies before drawing conclusions. We found significant differences in service usage and demographic characteristics between samples of detained and undetained undocumented persons. The two should be treated almost like separate universes for policy purposes. Neither is likely to represent an accurate reflection of the total undocumented population. Young,

single males are overstated in the detained population, and settled families with women and children are overstated in the undetained population.

5. A large percentage of households in which undocumented persons reside include both legal and illegal residents. Undocumented adults frequenty live with legal resident aliens and/or have citizen children. Attempts to deny services to undocumented persons are likely to exclude numerous legal residents as well. The problem of undocumented immigration is very complex. The legal-illegal distinction may be valid at the level of the individual, but becomes tenuous at the household level. Oversimplification can thus lead to injustice.

6. Many public services, such as health care and education, are social goods from which the society benefits when universally available. Since children of undocumented residents are likely to remain in this country, it would be "pound foolish" to deny education to them and to transform them from a future tax benefit to a tax burden. Also, the failure to inoculate even one undocumented child can lead to a costy epidemic.

7. It is precisely those services from which the entire society benefits whose costs are borne disproportionately at the local level. Just as Texas has complained that the federal government should bear more of the cost burden to educate undocumented children, so the local communities have a valid complaint that the state is not bearing its fair share of these costs. We conclude that the state should make more funds available to local governments for providing health and education services.

APPENDIX A

METHODOLOGY

The information contained in this report was obtained from a variety of
sources. There were two primary data-collecting groups: those collecting
information from service providers and those collecting information directly
from undocumented aliens. The group collecting provider information was
further subdivided into groups targeting health services, social services,
educational services and police-protection/correctional services. Each group
relied to varying degrees on one or more of the following: face-to-face
interviews, mail surveys, telephone interviews and library research. The
methods of each group are specified in more detail below.

UNDOCUMENTED ALIEN INTERVIEW TECHNIQUES

Those gathering information from undocumented persons relied on face-to-
face interviews. First, it was determined that information would be gathered
at the household level. Demographic and service utilization information was
to be gathered for all persons sharing a household. A household was
determined on the basis of shared expenses. Those who lived together, but who
paid their expenses separately, were treated as separate households; such
persons were interviewed separately. A second preliminary decision was made
to target only Spanish-speaking undocumented persons, since it was felt that
these would account for the bulk of all undocumented aliens in Texas.

The questionnaire used for the survey was therefore composed and
administered in Spanish. After determining the kind of information sought, a
pretest questionnaire was devised. The interviewers (all bilingual) were
given formal training and interviewing practice. In addition, each
interviewer helped administer at least one pretest questionnaire. Several of
the interviewers had contacts in the undocumented community and solicited the
help of these persons for the pretest. Ten pretest surveys were administered
in teams of two, with one person asking the questions and marking the
responses, and the other person observing any weaknesses in the questionnaire
or its administration. After the interview, comments and suggestions from the
interviewees were actively solicited. We asked that they make comments about
the wording of the questions, that they suggest other questions which might be
useful to add, and that they indicate any questions which should be omitted.
These suggestions and those of the interviewers were considered in the
revision of the pretest questionnaire. A copy of the final survey instrument
is contained in Appendix D; the English translation of the questions is given
in Appendix C.

To protect the respondents, a cover letter included at the front of the
survey was read prior to each potential interview. The respondents were
advised of the confidential, voluntary and anonymous character of the survey,

as well as their right to omit a response to any question or to terminate the interview at any time. The letter also briefly explained the nature of the survey. Questionnaires took between 5 and 140 minutes to administer, with an average time of 40 minutes and a most common time of 30 minutes. The wide variation in the time it took to administer the questionnaires was primarily due to interviewee eligibility and to the variation in settings (those conducted in the home of the respondent were more conversational and took longer than those conducted at agencies or holding centers) and to the variation in the number of household members for which information had to be collected.

The sample for the interview was generated in a variety of ways. The primary sources of interviews were agencies, such as those providing immigration legal services, that have occasion to deal with undocumented clients on a regular basis. A number of respondents were obtained by "snowball sampling," that is, by interviewers who knew undocumented persons asking these persons for help in contacting others who might be willing to be interviewed. Several interviews were conducted at worksites, others in the respondents' homes, but most were held at the agency or office through which the contact had been made. A small sample of persons detained at Immigration and Naturalization (INS) holding facilities were also interviewed to provide a comparison sample group. Interviewers traveled to each of the six targeted cities (El Paso, McAllen, Houston, Austin, Dallas, and San Antonio) to interview respondents. Additional interviewers were located and trained in each of the cities except Austin. Table A.1 is a breakdown of the setting in which interviews were given:

Table A.1

Setting of Interviews

Place of Interview	Number	Percent
Agency (church, atty.'s office, social service agency, etc.)	109	43.1
Home of Respondent	61	24.1
Worksite	6	2.4
Detention Center	39	15.4
Other	38	15.0
Totals	253	100.0

Source: Texas Undocumented Survey.

It should be made clear that this method of sampling tends to greatly overestimate the number of service users, since 43.1 percent of the total sample and 51 percent of the undetained population were contacted through agencies by virtue of their being service users. By definition, these people were using at least one service. Those interviewed at home may also have been contacted through a respondent obtained by an agency. This adds a considerable upward bias to our estimates of service usage.

SERVICE PROVIDER DATA COLLECTION TECHNIQUES

Education

Criteria for Selecting Agencies. For the six targeted cities, all school districts were originally considered for a mail survey. The plan was to contact each school principal. However, initial research indicated that given time and budget constraints this would be impractical. Therefore, questionnaires were mailed only to school district superintendents of the central school district of each of the six cities. The already existing Texas Education Agency (TEA) survey of school principals, asking for estimates of undocumented students enrolled, was then used as supplementary information.

Data Collection. Initial contact was made with TEA for referrals and overall school budgets. Additionally, the TEA made data available from its 1982 internal survey of school principals, which asked for estimates of the number of undocumented children enrolled in the school. These data were later compared to those obtained from the survey of school superintendents. The TEA survey counted as undocumented any children of Spanish surname whose legal status was not known from documents presented at registration. It is assumed that the superintendents used the same criteria. A questionnaire (included in Appendix G) was mailed to superintendents of seven school districts for each of the targeted cities and Brownsville. Information requested included the marginal cost of educating enrolled undocumented children. Of particular interest were costs associated with special programs such as bilingual education. All questionnaires mailed were returned; however, the El Paso Independent School District supplied no estimates of the number of undocumented children enrolled.

Health

Criteria for Selecting Agencies. Preliminary research was done to determine the organizational structure of health institutions, the sources of funding for these institutions, and budgetary information. Supervisors were identified from organizational charts and then contacted. After discussing the project with a number of supervisors, it was decided that facilities with high Spanish-speaker usage would be targeted. This targeting was based on the assumption that undocumented persons generally do not use facilities not used by the general Spanish-speaking population. An upward bias of estimated service usage by undocumented persons is likely to have resulted from this choice of health facilities.

   Data Collection. The Texas Department of Health was contacted along with public regional clinics, hospitals, and other health facilities in each of the six cities. Supervisors of public health areas, administrators and billing personnel in hospitals, and supervisors and Spanish-speaking nurses in health clinics were questioned. Face-to-face interviews were conducted with hospital personnel in all cities, except McAllen where appropriate persons were interviewed by telephone. Information from clinics was obtained by telephone interview for Dallas, Houston, and McAllen (including some surrounding areas). Attempts to contact clinic personnel in El Paso and San Antonio were not successful;* thus, no information is available for clinics in these cities. Because the project's location in Austin facilitated follow-up visits, all health personnel in Austin were interviewed in person. Public health personnel were also interviewed in person in El Paso, Houston, and San Antonio, whereas those in McAllen and Dallas were interviewed by telephone. Each health organization contacted was asked about budgetary allocations and funding sources, including revenues from fees. Information was sought both about average as well as marginal cost of service provision. Also requested was information about organizational structure, eligibility requirements for receipt of services, total number of clients served, and the proportion of clients believed to be undocumented. Personnel were asked to report any seasonality they noticed in the use of the facility by undocumented persons, and to describe the criteria used to determine who was undocumented. Hospital and public health administrators and staff were very helpful and cooperative. The overall response from health clinics was more guarded. In many cases personnel from health agencies were either unwilling or unable to assist the project; thus information about many clinics in the target cities must be inferred from the minority which did respond. Because immigration status was not recorded by clinics, no public health agency was able to provide an official estimate of usage by undocumented persons; hospitals, which do maintain such records, were able to do so. Hospital patients, however, are classified as undocumented by staff at any stage, usually at the time of admission, and official documents are not generally used in this determination.

Protection and Correctional Services

   Criteria for Selecting Agencies. All city police departments were targeted for study as were city and county jails. The state prisons were also included. It was decided to focus on police protection and incarceration facilities, rather than the court system, for a number of reasons, such as the difficulty of calculating marginal costs in the court system, the intricacy of the system, and the difficulty of tracing persons through it. Information

---

*In these cities, clinics were especially wary and protective of their clients. This made it particularly difficult to make estimates of the number of undocumented clients attended to by these clinics.

about the use of the courts was gathered from the undocumented persons surveyed, but was not gathered from the service provider side.

Data Collection. Information was obtained from police officers of the Austin and San Antonio city police departments. A questionnaire was constructed and revised according to the suggestions of planners in the Research and Planning division of the Austin Police Department. All city police departments were contacted and asked to participate in the survey, but time and manpower limitations prevented all but Austin and San Antonio from being able to take part. In Austin, 325 questionnaires were distributed by the Police Department to the mailboxes of sworn officers. A cover letter was attached by the Department to explain the purpose of the survey and to solicit the officers' cooperation. A total of 112 questionnaires were completed and returned. In San Antonio, 400 questionnaires were distributed to the mailboxes of police officers. Those who patroled areas of high concentrations of Spanish-speaking persons were given more complete coverage than those who patroled other areas of the city. Of the 400 distributed, 175 questionnaires were completed and returned. A copy of the questionnaire form can be found in Appendix H. Information about overall departmental budgets and policy regarding undocumented aliens was obtained from the research and planning divisions of each city police department. The questionnaire used to obtain information from police departments was administered in person in Austin and San Antonio, and by telephone in the other four cities. A copy of the questions asked of each police department research and planning division is found in Appendix H. Information about city and county jails was obtained by telephone from each office. Information about the state prisons was obtained by telephone from the Texas Department of Corrections (TDC) central office in Huntsville. Additional information about incarcerated undocumented persons was supplied by the Immigration and Naturalization Service (INS). While TDC officials were quite helpful in supplying us with any pertinent information they had available, they keep no statistics about undocumented inmates brought in under charges other than that of illegal entry into the country. There is a figure for non-citizens; however, this number includes legal resident aliens. Because no official statistics about undocumented offenders are kept by either the state prisons or the city police departments, all numbers from these agencies reflect estimates based on known populations, such as all non-citizens or all Spanish-speaking groups.

Social Services

Criteria for Selecting Agencies. The area of social services is one with many diverse programs, many of which are often funded by a mix of private and public funds. All state agencies providing social services which are entirely publicly funded were targeted for study. It was determined, however, that programs with a mix of private and public funding were too numerous to cover completely. Based on preliminary research in Austin, it was decided that agencies with high average and marginal costs with public funding of at least $50,000 per year be the focus for study. Also, similar agencies were studied in each city in order to get comparable information. Programs for the elderly were not covered, because the population of undocumented persons has been characterized by all previous research as a young population. Using these criteria, city and county budgets were reviewed to determine programs meriting inclusion in the study. Emergency assistance programs became an area of special emphasis.

Data Collection. Questionnaires (see Appendix F for copies) were sent to the regional offices of the Texas Employment Commission (TEC) and Texas Rehabilitation Commission (TRC). All of the eight survey forms sent to regional TEC offices were completed and returned; five of the seven forms sent to the TRC offices were completed and returned. Face-to-face interviews were conducted with five people at the Texas Department of Community Affairs, including the migrant workers' advocate and the director of the local government services division. Information was obtained by telephone from the state offices of the Texas State Commission for the Blind and the Texas State Commission for the Deaf. Information about Aid to Families with Dependent Children (AFDC), food stamps, day care, child welfare (protective services), and family violence was obtained by telephone from the following persons and offices: In the Texas Department of Human Resources (TDHR), persons contacted include the executive director, eligibility specialist, program specialists and planners for TDHR day care, child protective service workers, fraud control personnel for food stamps and income assistance, the budget director, and the assistant commissioner for family self-support services. The regional heads of child protective services were contacted in all six cities in addition to the supervisors of the county offices, child welfare workers and intake workers. Also contacted in each of the six regional offices of TDHR were statistics personnel, state food stamp and AFDC statistics personnel, regional directors and supervisors of family self-support units (these handle day care contracts), and regional directors of the income assistance program. Additional regional level data were obtained from the assistant director for child protective services and the director for family planning, both in Austin (region 6), and the regional directors for income assistance in Houston and McAllen (regions 11 and 9). State level information about funding, eligibility, and family planning programs was obtained from the TDHR state office. Information on the local level was obtained from at least two day care centers in each of the six cities. The largest centers were targeted and their directors, intake workers and budget officers interviewed. In Houston and Austin, child welfare case workers and food stamp and AFDC intake workers were contacted. In Austin, only the Planned Parenthood Clinic supervisor was contacted, and in McAllen, food stamp and AFDC intake workers were contacted. For those services contracted out to smaller agencies or provided by subsidized private agencies, the selective criteria discussed earlier were used to narrow the study to a manageable size. These latter agencies were contacted primarily by telephone, as they are located in many places all around each city, making face-to-face interviews difficult. Some intake workers were contacted, but supervisors supplied the primary information. It should be noted, however, that many of the programs were small enough or had been cut back to the point that their directors were in direct contact with clients. Among such agencies contacted in all six cities were Big Brother/Big Sister (in El Paso this is the Boy's Club, a United Way Agency), neighborhood centers (with the exception of McAllen, which has no such centers), and county youth assistance programs. Neighborhood centers are "umbrellas" for many kinds of social and medical services. A number of social service agencies exist in each city which have no counterparts in other cities. Also, each city contracts some social services out to private agencies. A listing of those contacted includes the following:

In El Paso: the social services funding worker for United Way; the Women's Resource Center; the vice president of the Private Industry Council (formerly the City Department of Human Development); the Community Development Division (information about the following programs funded by this agency were obtained: the Youth Assistance Program, Aliviane, the El Paso Guidance Center, two YWCA child care programs, and Trinity Coalition Day Care); recreation center superintendents; and the El Paso County Transitional Living Center and Child Guidance Center.

In Dallas: the City Department of Human Services; the Community Development Program; Martin Luther King Jr. Community Center; Dallas Parent-Child Center; the County Department of Human Resources and Employment Services; CETA; the Community Action Committee; the Family Outreach Program; the Human Resources Aid Program; the Dallas Child Guidance Program; the Community Council of Dallas; and the Dallas Service Program.

In Austin: the head of planning for social services programs, Human Services Department; Rural Centers; the former director of the Family Self-Support Program (now defunct); the Caritas Clinic; the Urban League; the Capital Area Food Bank; the Center for Battered Women; Child and Family Services; the South Austin Neighborhood Council of Youth Bureaus, Youth Employment Services; the Teenage Parent Council; and the Youth Advocacy Program.

In San Antonio: the Ella Austin Youth Advocacy Guidance Program, Ella Austin Community Center; the vice president for human resources of the Mexican American Unity Council; and the program director of the Centro del Barrio.

In Houston: the community development division of the City of Houston Human Resources Department (this department funds ten private day care centers, seven programs for the aging, eight programs for youth, and one social service program for AFDC recipients); and Private Sector Initiatives, a group that spearheads and coordinates corporate involvement in job training and social services.

APPENDIX B

TEXAS DEMOGRAPHICS RELEVANT TO THE USE OF PUBLIC
SERVICES BY UNDOCUMENTED ALIENS IN TEXAS

According to the United States Census, the population of Texas in 1980 was 14,229,191; of these, 50.8 percent were female. The urban population was 11,114,017, or 78.9 percent, while the population of the six cities involved in this study was 6,833,513 (excluding Fort Worth) or 48 percent of the Texas population. The population of persons of Spanish origin (Census Bureau classification) living in Texas was 2,985,824, or 20.9 percent, while the number of persons (over age 5) speaking Spanish in the home was 2,485,324*, or 17.5 percent. Another pertinent figure, the number of foreign-born persons, was 856,327 or 6 percent of the population of Texas.

Figure B.1 shows the concentration of persons of Spanish origin by percent of population for the state of Texas. Figure B.2 represents the relationship between the overall population of Texas and the population being studied here. The sector under study includes Houston, Dallas, San Antonio, Austin, El Paso, and McAllen/Rio Grande Valley. Figure B.3 breaks down the population and Hispanic concentration data by Standard Metropolitan Statistical Area (SMSA). Table B.1 gives numbers and percentages of Hispanics for all locations surveyed, broken down by city, by county and by SMSA. The demographic profiles of the six cities in question are detailed below.

HOUSTON

In 1980, the metropolitan population of Houston (SMSA) was 2,905,353, of which 424,903 persons, or 14.6 percent, were of Spanish origin. The greatest concentration of persons of Spanish origin within Houston was in the center of the city; the least was in the suburbs. The most predominantly Spanish-origin region was the southeast side, followed by the northwest area of downtown. However, there were several areas outside of downtown that had Spanish-origin concentrations of from 10 to 20 percent. The only discernible pattern in those areas was a decrease in concentration of persons of Spanish origin as one moved further from the center of the city. Data were collected from the Houston Chamber of Commerce, which derived the concentration figures from the 1980 U.S. census tracts.

---

*U.S. Bureau of the Census, Census of Population and Housing: 1980, Supplementary Report Series PHC 80-S2-45, Table P-2. Washington, D.C., Government Printing Office.

Figure B.1

Persons of Spanish Origin in Texas

1980 Census (Total Pop.= 14,229,191)

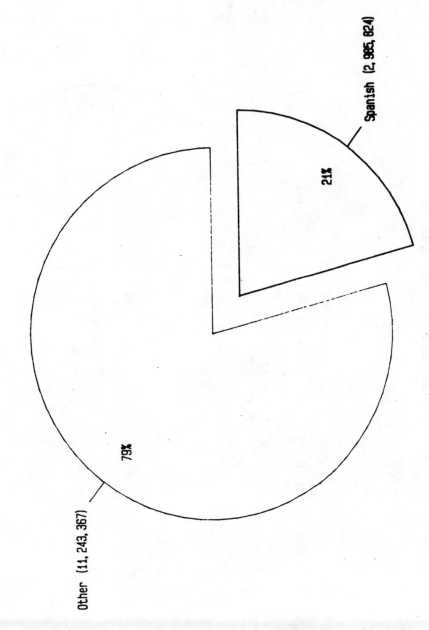

Other (11,243,367)

79%

21%

Spanish (2,985,824)

Source: U.S. Bureau of the Census, Census of Population and Housing: 1980, General Population Characteristics, Texas, PC80-1-B45 (Washington, D.C.: U.S. Government Printing Office).

Figure B.2

Persons of Spanish Origin in Six Cities

1980 Census (Total Pop. = 6, 833, 513)

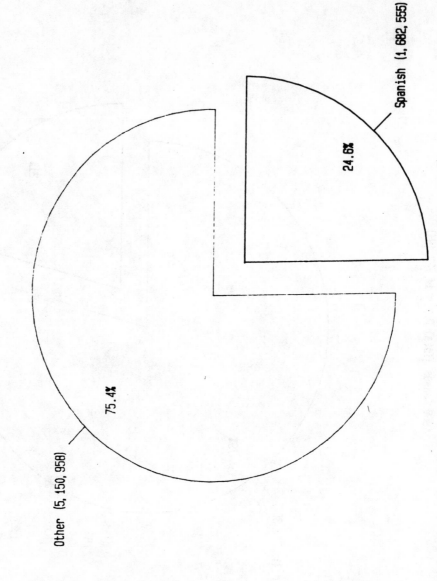

Spanish (1, 682, 555)

24.6%

Other (5, 150, 958)

75.4%

Source: U.S. Bureau of the Census, Census of Population and Housing: 1980, General Population Characteristics, Texas, PC80-1-B45 (Washington, D.C.: U.S. Government Printing Office).

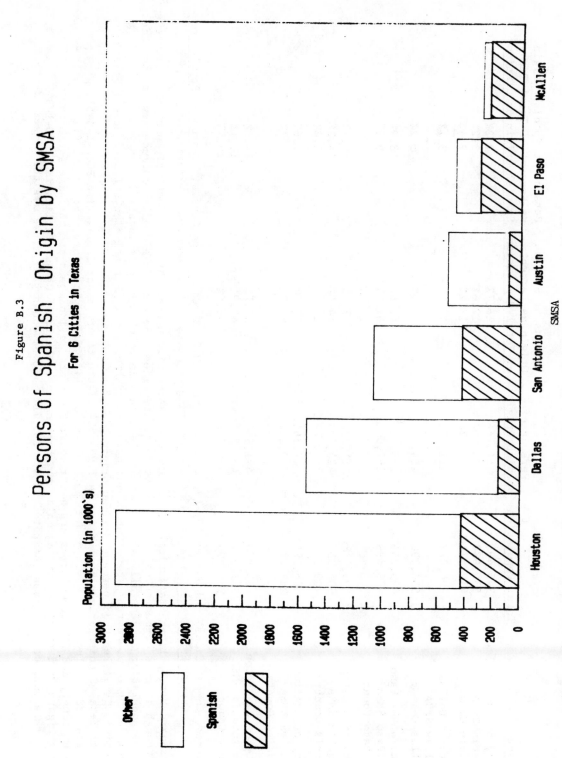

Figure B.3

Persons of Spanish Origin by SMSA

For 6 Cities in Texas

Source: U.S. Bureau of the Census, Census of Population and Housing: 1980, General Population Characteristics, Texas, PC80-1-B45 (Washington, D.C.: U.S. Government Printing Office).

Table B.1

Persons of Spanish Origin for Relevant Cities, Counties and SMSA's[1]

Place	Total Population	Persons of Spanish Origin[2]	Persons of Spanish Origin as Percent of Total Population	Persons of Spanish Origin as Percent of Total Texas Spanish Origin Population[3]
City of Austin	345,496	64,766	18.7%	2.2%
Austin SMSA	536,688	94,367	17.6%	3.2%
Travis County	419,573	72,228	17.2%	2.4%
City of Dallas	904,078	111,083	12.3%	3.7%
Dallas SMSA[4]	-	-	-	-
Dallas County	1,556,390	154,561	9.9%	5.2%
City of El Paso	425,259	265,819[6]	62.5%	8.9%
El Paso SMSA[5]	479,899	297,001	61.9%	9.9%
El Paso County				
City of Houston	1,595,138	281,331	17.6%	9.4%
Houston SMSA	2,905,353	424,903	14.6%	14.2%
Harris County	2,409,547	369,077	15.3%	12.4%
City of McAllen	66,281	47,361	71.5%	1.6%
McAllen SMSA[5]	283,229	230,212	81.3%	7.7%
Hidalgo County				
City of San Antonio	785,880	421,954	53.7%	14.1%
San Antonio SMSA	1,071,954	481,511	44.9%	16.1%
Bexar County	988,800	460,911	46.6%	15.4%

Source: Computations, and Tables 16, 19, 25 and 31 from U.S. Bureau of the Census, Census of Population Characteristics, Texas, PC80-1-B45 (Washington, D.C.: U.S. Government Printing Office).

[1]Standard Metropolitan Statistical Area. Includes metropolitan area that is effectively part of a city even though it goes beyond actual city limits to county lines. Because SMSA's often include several counties, the population is generally above that of the county in which a city is located.

[2]Includes Mexican, Puerto Rican, Cuban, and other Spanish origins. For all places listed above, Spanish origin is at least 88 percent Mexican origin.

[3]Total Texas Spanish origin population is 2,985,824 (Table 16 of Census Publication PC80-1-B45).

[4]Dallas SMSA includes Ft. Worth, which was not part of this study. Therefore, the county figures will be used.

[5]Here, county and SMSA boundaries are contiguous; therefore, all numbers are the same for both.

[6]This figure is derived by summing males and females in Table 25 of Census Publication PC80-1-B45. Table 31 of this publication gives the total figure 265,762. To be conservative, we use the higher figure.

Figure B.4

Concentration of Persons of Spanish Origin

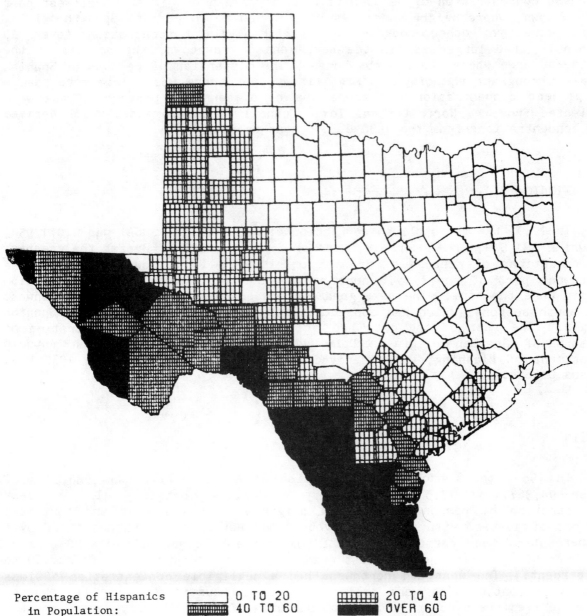

Percentage of Hispanics
in Population: ☐ 0 TO 20   ▦ 20 TO 40
                 ▨ 40 TO 60   ■ OVER 60

Source: Data prepared by Jerome A. Olson, Bureau of Business Research, The University
          of Texas at Austin, 1983.

DALLAS

In 1980, the metropolitan population of Dallas (Dallas County) was 1,556,390, of which 154,561, or 9.9 percent, were of Spanish origin. The greatest concentration of persons of Spanish origin was in the southwest part of downtown, where neighborhoods varied from 20 to 60 percent Spanish origin. There were two other pockets of Spanish-origin concentration (over 20 percent): the larger was in the north end of downtown, the smaller in the southeast area where the suburbs began. The dispersion of persons of Spanish origin throughout the city was significant, yet there was seldom more than a 10 percent concentration and there was no discernible pattern. Data were collected from the North Central Texas Council of Governments, which derived the concentrations from the 1980 U.S. census tracts.

SAN ANTONIO

In 1980, the metropolitan population of San Antonio (SMSA) was 1,071,954, of which 481,511, or 45 percent, were of Spanish origin. By far the greatest concentrations of persons of Spanish origin were found downtown and in the southwest part of the city, where neighborhoods of over 80 percent Spanish origin were the norm. The next greatest concentrations were in the northwest and south sectors, which had concentrations of from 40 to 60 percent Spanish origin. The rest of the city had a less than 40 percent concentration of persons of Spanish origin. Data were collected from the San Antonio Department of Planning, which derived the concentrations from the 1980 U.S. census tracts.

AUSTIN

In 1980, the metropolitan population of Austin (SMSA) was 536,688, of which 94,367, or 17.5 percent, were of Spanish origin. The greatest concentration of persons of Spanish origin was in the east and southeast sectors of Austin, with several neighborhoods having a concentration of over 50 percent of such persons. Most of the southeast quadrant had a 20 percent concentration, while the northeast quadrant had a concentration of from 10 to 20 percent. The west and northwest had a negligible concentration of less than 5 percent. Data were collected from the Austin Planning Department, which derived the concentrations from the data of the 1980 U.S. census tracts.

EL PASO

In 1980, the metropolitan population of El Paso (SMSA) was 479,899, of which 297,001, or 61.8 percent, were of Spanish origin. El Paso is situated along the Rio Grande River and adjoins the city of Juarez, Mexico, which has a population of over one million people. Not surprisingly, the overwhelming majority of residents of Spanish origin in 1980 lived along the border; every border sector was made up of at least 60 percent persons of Spanish origin. There was also a heavy concentration (from 40 to 60 percent) in the downtown area, while concentration declined to below 20 percent in the most northern parts of the city. Data were collected from the Department of Planning, Research and Development, City of El Paso, which derived the concentrations from the 1980 U.S. census tracts.

MCALLEN/RIO GRANDE VALLEY

In 1980, the population of Hidalgo County (which includes the sister cities of Pharr, Edinburg and McAllen, and is the same as the McAllen SMSA) was 283,229, of which 230,212, or 81 percent, were of Spanish origin. This area thus has the greatest such concentration in Texas. The concentration for McAllen in particular was very high, with portions of downtown having a concentration of 98 percent, and the western and southern parts of the city ranging from 80 to 92 percent. The less populated eastern and northeastern sectors of McAllen ranged from a 40 to 65 percent concentration of persons of Spanish origin. Data were collected from the McAllen Planning Department, which derived the concentrations from the 1980 U.S. census tracts.

To obtain further details, the Bureau of Business Research or the Population Research Center, The University of Texas at Austin, can be contacted.

ENGLISH TRANSLATION OF THE TEXAS
UNDOCUMENTED QUESTIONNAIRE

(The actual Spanish version used is given in Appendix D.)

First I am going to read you a letter from our professors at The University of
Texas:

Dear Participant:

As part of The University of Texas at Austin, we are conducting a study
regarding the situation of undocumented people in the State of Texas.

Our study specifically deals with the use of public services by undocumented persons and the taxes paid by the same people.

We would like to interview you for this study. If you decide to participate, we will not ask your name or address and you may choose to not answer
any question; also, you may terminate the interview at any point. The
information which you give us is confidential and your personal data will
not be revealed. There are no risks in your participating in this study.
We thank you for your participation in this study, for you will give us
information which will help us to understand the situation of undocumented
persons in the State of Texas.

Sincerely,

Gilberto Cardenas
Assistant Professor of Sociology
    and LBJ School of Public Affairs

Sidney Weintraub
Dean Rusk Professor of the LBJ
    School of Public Affairs

Academic Year 1982-1983

Section I: Demographic Characteristics

First I want to ask you some questions about yourself.

1.   Sex (check)

_____F   _____M

2.   How old are you? _____

3.   Where were you born? _____

4.   Are you married?

_____ no   _____ yes

5.   Is this the first time you have come to the United States?

_____ no   _____ yes

6.   When you came to the U.S. --this time-- did you have papers to enter?

_____ no

_____ yes

Which documents did you have? _____

Are they still valid?   _____ no

_____ yes

Do you work?   _____ no

_____ yes

7.   What was the reason you came to the U.S.?

_____

_____

8.   Prior to coming to the U.S. where did you live?

In what state? _____

In what country? _____

9.   [SEE THE FOLLOWING PAGE]

108

9. Please answer the following questions for each person who lives in your house. Let's begin with you and then with each one of the people who live with you, from the oldest to the youngest. (RECORD BELOW)

Instructions

1. Fill in columns 1 through 3 simultaneously.
2. Fill in adults across.
3. Fill in children down by question.
   (i.e., ask for all children)
4. Fill in column 10 after the others are complete.

Person's relation to you?	Sex	What is this person's age?	Person's place of birth	When did he/she come to U.S.?	How many yrs. of school has he/she fin-ished?	Is this person enrolled in school now?	Does this person go to private or public school?	Employed?	How many of the people in your house are un-docu-mented?
(1)	(2)	(3)	(4)	(5)	(6)	(7)	(8)	(9)	(10)
1. respondent									
2.									
3.									
4.									
5.									
6.									
7.									
8.									
9.									
10.									

Section II: Wages, Taxes and Expenses

In this section I am going to ask you about your earnings, taxes and expenses.

10.   What kind of place are you employed at? _____

What do you do at this place? _____

11.   How much are you paid per hour? (piece)

$_____ per _____

12.   How many hours do you work? _____ per week

13.   How much are you paid per week, bi-weekly, monthly?

between _____ per _____ and _____ per _____

14.   How are you paid? (check, cash, etc.)

_____ _____ _____

15.   Do you receive any other compensation for your job? (e.g., tips, food, room)

_____

16.   Is medical insurance deducted from your pay?

_____ no

_____ yes   [IF YES] Does it cover your family?

_____ don't know   _____ no

_____ no response   _____ yes

_____ don't know

_____ no response

17.   Is social security deducted from your pay?

_____ yes   [IF YES] How much?_____

_____ no

_____ don't know

_____ no response

18.   Are taxes deducted from your pay?

_____ yes   [IF YES] How much? _____

_____ no

_____ don't know

_____ no response

JOB S-INTERVIEW RESPONSE

19. Are there any other deductions from your pay? (e.g., uniform, tools, food, room)

_____ no

_____ yes   How much? $ _____ per _____

20. Do you have another job?

_____ no   [IF NO, GO TO QUESTION 31]

_____ yes

21. What kind of place are you employed at? _____

What do you do at this place? _____

22. How much are you paid per hour? (piece)

$ _____ per _____

23. How many hours do you work per week? _____

24. How much are you paid per week, bi-weekly, monthly?

between $_____ per _____ and $_____ per _____

25. How are you paid? (check, cash....)

_____

26. Do you receive any other compensation for your job? (e.g., tips, food, room)

_____

27. Is medical insurance deducted from your pay?

_____ no

_____ yes   [IF YES] Does it cover your family?

_____ don't know   _____ no

_____ no response   _____ yes

                            _____ don't know

                            _____ no response

28. Is social security deducted from your pay?

_____ yes   [IF YES] How much? _____

_____ no

_____ don't know

_____ no response

29. Are taxes deducted from your pay?

_____ yes   [IF YES] How much? _____

_____ no

_____ don't know

_____ no response

30. Are there any other deductions from your pay? (e.g., uniform, tools, food, room)

_____ no

_____ yes   How much? $ _____ per _____

31. Did you report and pay income tax this past year?

_____ no

_____ yes and paid   [PROCEED TO A]

_____ yes and got a refund   [PROCEED TO B]

_____ no response

A. How much did you pay? _____

B. How much were you refunded? _____

32. Does your spouse work?

_____ no [IF NO, THEN ASK --WHO SUPPORTS THE HOUSE? _____]

_____ yes   (Relationship to respondent)

33. What kind of place is spouse employed at? _____

What does spouse do at this place? _____

34. How much is spouse paid per hour? (piece)

$_____ per _____

35. How many hours does spouse work per week? _____

36. How much is spouse paid per week, bi-weekly, monthly?

between $ _____ per _____ and $ _____ per _____

37. How is spouse paid? (check, cash...)

_____

38. Does spouse receive other compensation for job? (e.g., tips, food, room)

_____

39. Is medical insurance deducted from spouse's pay?

_____ no

_____ yes   [IF YES] Does it cover family?

_____ don't know   _____ no   How much? _____

_____ no response   _____ yes

                              _____ don't know

                              _____ no response

40. Is social security deducted from spouse's pay?

_____ yes   [IF YES] How much? _____

_____ no

_____ don't know

_____ no response

41. Are taxes deducted from spouse's pay?

_____ yes   [IF YES] How much? _____

_____ no

_____ don't know

_____ no response

42. Are there any other deductions from spouse's pay? (e.g., uniform, tools, food, room)

_____ no

_____ yes   How much? $_____ per _____

43. Is there anyone else living with you who works and contributes to the household expenses?

_____ no   [PROCEED TO Q. 45]

_____ yes

_____ no response

44. How much does this person contribute to the household expenses?

$_____ per _____

45. The following question is about your expenses. There is a special section where I will ask about things which have special taxes because these provide income to the state.

[IF NO EXPENSE RECORD ZERO (∅)
IF DON'T KNOW RECORD NA]

Amount

X	X	X
week	month	year

a. How much do you pay for rent?   _____   _____   _____

b. How much do you spend on clothes?

c. Do you send any money to your country? If so, how much?

d. How much do you spend on food?

e. Do you pay any money for child care? If so, how much?

f. Do you save any money? If so, how much?

46. The following expenses have special taxes.

    a. public services:

        gas

        electricity and water

        telephone

        telegraph

    b. cigarettes

    c. alcoholic beverages

    mixed drinks

    liquor

    wine

    beer

47. Do you have other expenses which you are paying on credit?

    _____ no   [PROCEED TO Q. 48]

    _____ yes

    _____ no response

47. (continued)

	Amount		
	X week	X month	X year
a. furniture	_____	_____	_____
b. electric appliances	_____	_____	_____
c. car	_____	_____	_____
d. clothing	_____	_____	_____
e. travel	_____	_____	_____
f. smuggler (to enter U.S.)	_____	_____	_____
g. hospital	_____	_____	_____

48. Do you have a car(s)?

_____ no   [PROCEED TO QUESTION 50]

_____ yes   How many? _____

49. Which expenses do you have for your car?

	X week	X month	X year
a. gas	_____	_____	_____
b. repairs	_____	_____	_____
c. insurance	_____	_____	_____
d. vehicle registration	_____	_____	_____
e. vehicle inspection	_____	_____	_____
f. vehicle license (sticker)	_____	_____	_____

50. Do you have other expenses which I have not mentioned?

_____ no

_____ yes   What are they?

	X week	X month	X year
_____	_____	_____	_____
_____	_____	_____	_____
_____	_____	_____	_____

Section III: Public Services

[--IF A PUBLIC SERVICE OR FACILITY IS USED, NOTE THE NAME OF THE AGENCY/FACILITY.

--INFORMATION IS NOT NEEDED FOR SERVICES RECEIVED FROM PRIVATE (PROFIT-MAKING)
    AGENCIES OR PRACTITIONERS].

Now I am going to ask you for information regarding the public services which
you may have received in the state of Texas.

A. Health Services

Let's begin with the different types of medical services which are provided
by the state of Texas. Specifically I'm interested in the type of medical assistance which you, or someone who lives with you, use for sickness or accidents.

(Note: The following are the questions pertaining to each section, health section
        first. See page 11 of Spanish questionnaire for format used in actual
        survey.)

51. Have you or anyone who lives with you been treated in an emergency room during
     the past year?

     _____ no

     _____ yes   [NAME OF FACILITY]   [PERSON TREATED]

52. During the past year, did you or anyone who lives with you get treated at a
     public hospital?

     _____ no

     _____ yes

53. Have you or anyone who lives in your home been treated at a public clinic?

     _____ no

     _____ yes

54. Have you or anyone who lives in your home been treated at a public dental clinic?

     _____ no

     _____ yes

55. Have you or anyone who lives in your home used services from a mental health clinic?

     _____ no

     _____ yes

56. Have you or anyone who lives with you used ambulance services in the past year?

_____ no

_____ yes

57. Have you or anyone who lives with you received medical attention which I have not mentioned?

_____ no

_____ yes

(Note: Along with questions 51-57 we asked for the following information:)

What type of service/treatment did you receive?

How many times?

How much did they charge?

How much did you pay?

How much do you still owe?

Method of payment? (cash, insurance, etc.)

58. (no question)

59. Were there any other medical services that you or anyone who lives with you requested but did not receive?

A. What kind of service did you request?

    a. medical _____
    b. dental _____
    c. other (specify)

    _____ _____

    _____ _____

B. Were services denied to you?

    _____ no

    _____ yes   Why? _____ because of undocumented status
                          _____ because of inability to pay
                          _____ other (specify)

    _____

60. Were there any medical services which you or anyone who lives in your house needed but did not request?

_____ no

_____ yes   Why?   _____ because of undocumented status
                             _____ believed you did not meet the requirements
                             _____ did not know services existed
                             _____ do not speak English
                             _____ they do not speak Spanish
                             _____ for lack of money
                             _____ other (specify)

_____

B. Educational Services

This section is about education.

[IF NO CHILDREN IN HOUSEHOLD, GO TO Q. 63]

61. Of the children living with you, how many went to school in the U.S. in the last year? _____

62. Of these, how many participated in any of these programs?

Programs   # of Children

school breakfast
school lunch
bilingual programs
special education
bus
driver's training

63. Have you or anyone who lives in your home participated in adult education programs?

_____ no
_____ yes   Which programs?   # of people?

            GED
            English
            Vocational Training
            Other (specify)

64. Were there any educational services that you or anyone who lives in your house needed but did not receive?

_____ no

_____ yes   What service did you need?

               Why did you not receive the services?

         A.   _____ denied services
             Why?   _____ because of undocumented status
                      _____ other (specify)

         B.   _____ didn't request the services
             Why?   _____ because of undocumented status
                      _____ unfamiliar with services
                      _____ services did not exist
                      _____ other (specify)

         C.   _____ other   Explain _____

C. Social Services

The following questions are about social services.

65. In the last year, have you or anyone who lives in your house received any of these services?

Type of Aid	how much time	week	amount month	year
a. AFDC				
b. Help to pay water, electric, or gas bill				
c. Help to pay the rent				
d. Food stamps				
e. WIC				
f. Unemployment compensation				
g. Workman's compensation (for an accident)				

If they cut off any of these services: Can you tell me why?

66. In the last year when you, or anyone who lives in your house, needed help:

     A.   To find work
         Where did you go? _____
         What help did you receive? _____
         Did it cost you?
         _____ no
         _____ yes   How much?_____

     B.   To buy or get food
         Where did you go? _____
         What help did you receive? _____
         Did it cost you?
         _____ no
         _____ yes   How much? _____

C. To translate something (e.g., an ad, a letter, to fill out a form)
Where did you go? _____
What help did you receive? _____
Did it cost you?
____ no
____ yes   How much? _____

67. D. Transportation (e.g., tickets for the bus, rides to services)
Where did you go?_____
What help did you receive?_____
Did it cost you?
____ no

____ yes   How much? _____

E. With information on some service you needed?
Where did you go? _____
What help did you receive?_____
Did it cost you?
____ no
____ yes   How much? _____

68. Did someone who lived in your house in the last year receive aid for the elderly? (like Meals on Wheels)
____ no
____ yes   Which ones?_____

Did it cost you? ____ no
____ yes   How much?_____

69. There are professional counseling services that various agencies offer. For example, Planned Parenthood, help with alcoholism or drug abuse, and help with family budgeting. In the last year have you or anyone who lives in your house received any of these types of counseling?
____ no
____ yes   Which ones? _____

Did it cost you? ____ no
____ yes   How much? _____

70. In the last year, was there any service which I have mentioned (e.g., food, transportation, translation, employment) which you or someone who lives in your house requested but did not receive?
____ no
____ yes   Which one?_____

Why did they deny you the service?
____ for being undocumented
____ for not being able to pay
____ other (specify) _____

71. In the last year, was there a service that you or anyone who lives in your house needed but did not request?
_____ no
_____ yes   Which one? _____

Why did you not request it?
_____ for being undocumented
_____ believed you did not meet the requirements
_____ did not know the services existed
_____ did not speak English
_____ they did not speak Spanish
_____ for lack of money
_____ other (specify)

Legal Services

The following questions are about the legal system in Texas.

72. Have you or anyone else who lives in your house used any legal service in the last year?

What type of service?	Who provided the service? (notary, lawyer)	What type of agency did you go to? (private, church, public)	Cost?
_____	_____	_____	_____
_____	_____	_____	_____

73. Did you or anyone who lives in your house get a traffic ticket in the last year?
_____ no
_____ yes   Did you pay a fine? _____ no
                                 _____ yes   How much? _____

74. The following questions refer to the police, and not to immigration officials. Have you or anyone who lives in your house been arrested in the last year?
_____ no
_____ yes   Who arrested you?   _____ Local police
                                    _____ State police
                                    _____ Sheriff
                                    _____ Don't know
                                    _____ Other (specify)_____

75. Have you or anyone in your house been in jail in the last year?
_____ no
_____ yes   How many days? _____
             Which jail were you in? _____

76. During the last year, did you or someone who lives in your house appear before a judge? (PROCEED TO Q. 77)
   _____ no
   _____ yes

   a. Did the court appoint you a lawyer? _____ no
                                          _____ yes
   b. Did the court appoint you an interpreter? _____ no
                                                _____ yes
   c. Did you pay a court fee?
      _____ no
      _____ yes   How much? _____
   d. Did you pay a fine?
      _____ no
      _____ yes   How much? _____

77. In the last year, did they appoint a probation officer for you or someone who lives in your house?
   _____ no
   _____ yes   For how long? _____

78. In the last year, have you or someone who lives in your house filed a suit in any court?
   _____ no
   _____ yes

   a. Did you pay something? _____ no
                            _____ yes   How much? _____
   b. Did you use a private lawyer or a public agency?
      _____ private   Cost? _____
      _____ public   Cost? _____
   c. Did you have to pay the other party?
      _____ no
      _____ yes   How much?
   d. Was there any other cost or fine that you paid?
      _____ no
      _____ yes   How much?

Other Services

79. Do you or anyone in your family use the public transportation system?
   _____ no
   _____ yes   How many times? _____ every _____

80. Do you or anyone in your family use recreation facilities?
   _____ no
   _____ yes   Which ones?   _____ pool
                                     _____ park
                                     _____ recreation center
                                     _____ other (specify)

81. Has the fire department gone to your house in the last year?
    _____ no
    _____ yes   Why? _____

82. Do you live in housing subsidized by the government?
    _____ no
    _____ yes

Primero le voy a leer una carta escrita a Ud. por los profesores
de la Universidad de Texas:

Estimado Participante:

Por medio de la Universidad de Texas en Austin estamos condu-
ciendo un estudio sobre la situación de las personas indocumentadas
en el estado de Texas.

Nuestro estudio específicamente trata del uso de los servicios
públicos por personas indocumentadas y los impuestos pagados por
esta misma gente.

Nos gustaría entrevistarle para este estudio. Si Ud. decide
participar, no le vamos a preguntar su nombre ni su domicilio y puede
no contestar las preguntas que quiera, y también puede terminar la
entrevista en cualquier momento. La información que Ud. nos dé es
confidencial y sus datos personales no serán revelados. No existen
riesgos con su participación en el estudio. Le agredeceríamos su
participación en este estudio, pues nos dará más información para
entender la situación de las personas indocumentadas en el Estado
de Texas.

Sinceramente,

Gilberto Cárdenas
Assistant Professor of Sociology
and LBJ School of Public Affairs

Sidney Weintraub
Dean Rusk Professor of the LBJ
School of Public Affairs

Academic Year 1982-1983

APPENDIX D

TEXAS UNDOCUMENTED QUESTIONNAIRE

(Spanish version used)

Interview Number_____

1982 - 1983

Study of Use of Public Services by Undocumented Persons

in the State of Texas

Date_____

City_____

Interviewer _____

Source of Contact_____

Time Begun:_____

Time Ended:_____

SECCION I: CARACTERISTICAS DEMOGRAFICAS

Primero le voy a preguntar unos datos personales.

1.   Sexo   [CHECK]

   ___F   ___M

2.   ¿Cuántos años tiene? _____

3.   ¿Dónde nació? _____

4.   ¿Está Ud. casado(a)?

   ___no ___sí

5.   ¿Es ésta la primera vez que viene a los EEUU?

   ___no ___sí

6.   ¿Cuando vino a los EEUU -- esta vez -- tenía papeles para entrar?

   ___no   [PROCEED TO QUESTION 7]

   ___sí

        ¿Cuáles? _____
                [FILL IN]

        IF GREEN CARD, TERMINATE INTERVIEW.
        ANY OTHER CATEGORY

        ¿Válidos? ___no   [PROCEED TO QUESTION 7]

               ___sí

               ¿Trabaja?   ___no [TERMINATE]

                          ___sí [PROCEED]

7. ¿Cuál fue la razón por la que vino a los EEUU?

    _____

    _____

8. ¿Antes de venir a los EEUU, dónde vivía?

    _____

    ¿En qué estado? _____

    ¿En qué país? _____

9. [SEE THE FOLLOWING PAGE]

SECCION II: INGRESOS, IMPUESTOS Y GASTOS

En esta sección le voy a preguntar sobre sus ingresos, impuestos y
gastos.

10. ¿En qué trabaja? _____

    ¿Qué hace en este trabajo? _____

    _____

11. ¿Cuánto le pagan por hora? (pieza)

    $_____ por _____

12. ¿Cuántas horas trabaja? _____ por semana.

13. ¿Cuánto le pagan por semana, quincena, o mes?

    entre $_____ por _____ y $_____ por _____

14. ¿Cómo le pagan? (con cheque, en efectivo...)

    _____

127

9. Para cada una de las personas que viven en su casa, me puede contestar las siguientes preguntas. Empecemos con sus datos y después de cada una de las personas que viven en su casa del mayor al menor. [RECORD BELOW]

<u>INSTRUCTIONS</u>

1. Fill in columns 1 through 3 simultaneously.
2. Fill in adults across.
3. Fill in children down by question.
   [i.e., ask for <u>all</u> children]
4. Fill in column 10 after <u>all</u> the others are complete.

	¿Cuál es su rela-cion?	Sexo	¿Cuantos años tiene?	¿En qué país nacio?	¿Cuándo vino a los EEUU?	¿Cuántos años de escuela ha terminado?	¿Está en la escuela?	¿Va a escuela pública o privada?	¿Trabaja?	En su casa, cuantos son indo-cumentados?
	(1)	(2)	(3)	(4)	(5)	(6)	(7)	(8)	(9)	(10)
1. respondent										
2.										
3.										
4.										
5.										
6.										
7.										
8.										
9.										
10.										

RESPONDENT'S JOB

15. ¿Hay algo más que recibe por su trabajo? (por ejemplo: propinas, comida, cuarto, etc.) ____________________

____

16. ¿Le descuentan seguro médico de su salario?

___no

___sí [IF YES] ¿Cubre a toda su familia?

___no sabe

___no contestó

___no

___sí

___no sabe

___no contestó

17. ¿Le descuentan seguro social de su salario?

___sí [IF YES] ¿Cuánto? ________________

___no

___no sabe

___no contestó

18. ¿Le descuentan impuestos sobre sus ingresos?

___sí [IF YES] ¿Cuánto? ________________

___no

___no sabe

___no contestó

19. **¿Le descuentan algo más de su salario? (Por ejemplo: para uniforme, herramientas, comida o habitación).**

___**no**

___**sí** ¿Cuánto? $ __________ **por** __________

20. ¿Tiene otro empleo?

   ___no   [IF NO, GO TO QUESTION 31]

   ___sí

21. ¿En qué trabaja? _____

   ¿Qué hace en este trabajo? _____

   _____

22. ¿Cuánto le pagan por hora ? (pieza)

   $_____ por _____

23. ¿Cuántas horas trabaja? _____ por semana.

24. ¿Cuánto le pagan por semana, quincena, o mes?

   entre $_____ por _____ y $_____ por _____

25. ¿Cómo le pagan? (con cheque, en efectivo...)

   _____

26. ¿Hay algo más que recibe por su trabajo? (por ejemplo:

   propinas, comida, cuarto, etc.) _____

   _____

27. ¿Le descuentan seguro médico de su salario?

   ___no

   ___sí   [IF YES] ¿Cubre a toda su familia?

   ___no sabe   ___no

   ___no contestó   ___sí

                       ___no sabe

                       ___no contestó

RESPONDENT SECONDJOB

28. ¿Le descuentan seguro social de su salario?

___ sí   [IF YES]   ¿Cuánto? _____

___ no

___ no sabe

___ no contestó

29. ¿Le descuentan impuestos sobre sus ingresos?

___ sí   [IF YES]   ¿Cuánto? _____

___ no

___ no sabe

___ no contestó

30.. ¿Le descuentan algo más de su salario? (Por ejemplo: para uniforme, herramientas, comida o habitación).

___ no

___ sí   ¿Cuánto? $ _____ por _____

31. ¿En este último año reportó y pagó impuestos sobre sus ingresos?

___ no

___ sí y pagó   [PROCEED TO A]

___ sí y le devolvieron dinero   [PROCEED TO B]

___ no contestó

A. ¿Cuánto pagó? _____

B. ¿Cuánto le devolvieron? _____

32. ¿Trabaja su esposa/esposo?

   ___no [IF NO, THEN ASK-- ¿Quién mantiene la casa _____]

   ___sí   [RELATIONSHIP TO RESPONDENT]

33. ¿En qué trabaja? _____

   ¿Qué hace en este trabajo? _____

   _____

34. ¿Cuánto le pagan por hora? (pieza)

   ¿ _____ por _____

35. ¿Cuántas horas trabaja? _____ por semana.

36. ¿Cuánto le pagan por semana, quincena, o mes?

   entre $_____ por _____ y $_____ por _____

37. ¿Cómo le pagan? (con cheque, en efectivo...)

   _____

38. ¿Hay algo más que recibe por su trabajo? (por ejemplo:

   propinas, comida, cuarto, etc.) _____

   _____

39. ¿Le descuentan seguro médico de su salario?

   ___no

   ___sí   [IF YES]   ¿Cubre a toda su familia?

   ___no sabe   ___no

   ___no contestó   ___sí

                           ___no sabe

                                  ¿Cuánto? _____

                          ___no contestó

132

40. ¿Le descuentan seguro social de su salario?

___sí   [IF YES] ¿Cuánto? _____

___no

___no sabe

___no contestó

41. ¿Le descuentan impuestos sobre sus ingresos?

___sí   [IF YES] ¿Cuánto? _____

___no

___no sabe

___no contestó

42. ¿Le descuentan also más de su salario? (Por ejemplo: para uniforme, herramientas, comida o habitación).

___no

___sí   ¿Cuánto? $ _____ por _____

43. ¿Hay otra persona en su casa que trabaja y contribuye a los

gastos de la familia?

___no [PROCEED TO Q. 45]

___sí

___no contestó

44. ¿Cuánto contribuye esta persona a los gastos de la familia?

$_____ por _____

45. La siguiente pregunta es sobre sus gastos. Hay una sección
especial donde le voy a preguntar sobre cosas que tienen
impuestos especiales porque estos le dan ingresos al estado.

[IF NO EXPENSE, RECORD ZERO (∅);
IF DON'T KNOW, RECORD NA]

	Cantidad		
	X semana	X mes	X año
a. cuánto paga de renta	_____	_____	_____
b. cuánto gasta en ropa	_____	_____	_____
c. cuánto dinero manda a su país	_____	_____	_____
d. cuánto gasta en comida	_____	_____	_____
e. cuánto gasta por el cuidado de sus niños	_____	_____	_____
f. cuánto ahorra	_____	_____	_____

46. Los siguientes gastos tienen impuestos especiales.

	X semana	X mes	X año
a. servicios públicos:			
gas	_____	_____	_____
luz y agua	_____	_____	_____
teléfono	_____	_____	_____
telégrafo	_____	_____	_____
b. cigarros	_____	_____	_____
c. bebidas alcohólicas			
bebidas mixtas	_____	_____	_____
liquor	_____	_____	_____
vino	_____	_____	_____
cerveza	_____	_____	_____

47. ¿Tiene otros gastos que esté pagando a crédito?

___no   [PROCEED TO QUESTION 48]

___sí

___no contestó

		X semana	X mes	X año
a.	muebles	____	____	____
b.	aparatos eléctricos	____	____	____
c.	carro	____	____	____
d.	ropa	____	____	____
e.	viajes	____	____	____
f.	coyote	____	____	____
g.	hospital	____	____	____

48. ¿Tiene coche(s)?

___no   [PROCEED TO QUESTION 50]

___sí   ¿Cuántos? _____

49. ¿Cuáles son los gastos que tiene para su carro (coche)?

		X semana	X mes	X año
a.	gasolina	____	____	____
b.	composturas	____	____	____
c.	aseguranza	____	____	____
d.	registro de vehículos	____	____	____
e.	inspección de vehículos	____	____	____
f.	licencia de vehículos	____	____	____

50. ¿Hay otros gastos que tenga que no he mencionado?

                                                      Cantidad

___no

___sí   ¿Cuáles?

	X semana	X mes	X año
_____	_____	_____	_____
_____	_____	_____	_____
_____	_____	_____	_____

SECCION III: SERVICIOS PUBLICOS

[--IF A PUBLIC SERVICE OR FACILITY IS USED, NOTE THE NAME OF THE

   AGENCY/FACILITY.

 --INFORMATION IS NOT NEEDED FOR SERVICES RECEIVED FROM PRIVATE

   (PROFIT-MAKING) AGENCIES OR PRACTITIONERS.]

Ahora le voy a pedir información sobre los servicios públicos que

ha recibido en Texas.

A. SERVICIOS DE SALUD

Vamos a empezar con los diferentes tipos de servicios médicos del

gobierno en Texas. Específicamente sobre el tipo de atención médica

utilizada para enfermedades o accidentes por Ud. o alguién que vive

en su casa.

136

¿Qué tipo de servicio o tratamiento recibió?	¿Cuántas veces?	¿Cuánto le cobraron?	¿Cuánto Pagó?	¿Cuánto debe?	¿Cómo pagó?

51. ¿Ha sido atendido Ud. o alguien que vive con Ud. en una sala de emergencia durante el último año?

____ no [PROCEED TO Q. 52]

____ sí

[NAME OF FACILITY]   [PERSON]

52. ¿Durante el año pasado, Ud. o alguien que vive con Ud. ha estado internado o fue atendido en un hospital público?

____ no [PROCEED TO Q. 53]

____ sí

[NAME OF FACILITY]   [PERSON]

¿Qué tipo de servicio o tratamiento recibió?	¿Cuántas veces?	¿Cuánto le cobraron?	¿Cuánto Pagó?	¿Cuánto debe?	¿Como pagó?

53. ¿Ha sido atendido en una clínica pública?

_____ no [PROCEED TO Q. 54]

_____ sí

[NAME OF FACILITY]   [PERSON]

54. ¿Ha recibido servicios de una clínica dental?

_____ no [PROCEED TO Q. 55]

_____ sí

[NAME OF FACILITY]   [PERSON]

¿Qué tipo de servicio o tratamiento recibió?	¿Cuántas veces?	¿Cuánto le cobraron?	¿Cuánto Pagó?	¿Cuánto debe?	¿Como pagó?

55. ¿Ha utilizado Ud. o alguien que vive en su casa servicios de una clínica de salud mental (MHMR)?

   ___ no   [PROCEED TO Q. 56]

   ___ sí

[NAME OF FACILITY]   [PERSON]

56. ¿Ha usado Ud. o alguien que vive en su casa servicios de ambulancia?

   ___ no   [PROCEED TO Q. 57]

   ___ sí

[NAME OF FACILITY]   [PERSON]

¿Qué tipo de servicio o tratamiento recibió?	¿Cuántas veces?	¿Cuánto le cobraron?	¿Cuánto Pagó?	¿Cuánto debe?	¿Como pagó?

57. ¿Ha recibido Ud. o alguien que vive con Ud. atención médica de alguien que no he mencionado?

___ no   [PROCEED TO Q. 58]

___ sí

[NAME OF FACILITY]   [PERSON]

58. No hay pregunta.

59. ¿Hubieron otros servicios médicos que Ud. o alguien que vive en su casa solicitó pero no recibió?

___ no

___ sí   A.   ¿Qué clase de servicio solicito?

             a.   _____   médico

             b.   _____   dental

             c.   _____   otro (especifique)

_____

_____

          B.   ¿Le negaron los servicios?

            ___ no

            ___ sí   ¿Porqué?   _____   por ser indocumentado

                                     _____   por que no podía pagar

                                     _____   otro (especifique)

_____

_____

60. ¿Hubieron otros servicios médicos que Ud. o alguien que vive en su casa necesito˜ pero no los pidio?

___ no

___ sí   ¿Porqué?   _____   por ser indocumentado

                         _____   pensó que no llenaba los requisitos

                         _____   no sabia que existían estos servicios

                         _____   no habla inglés

                         _____   ellos no hablan español

                         _____   por falta de dinero

                         _____   otra razón (especifique)_____

_____

B. SERVICIOS EDUCACIONALES

Esta sección es sobre educación.

[IF NO CHILDREN IN HOUSEHOLD, GO TO Q. 63]

61. De los niños que viven con usted: ¿Cuántos fueron a la escuela el año pasado en Los Estados Unidos? _____

62. De estos, cuántos han participado en alguno de los siguientes programas?

Programas	# de niños
desayuno en la escuela	_____
comida en la escuela	_____
programa bilingüe	_____
educación especial	_____
camión ("Bos")	_____
lecciones de manejar	_____

63. ¿Ha participado usted o alguien que vive en su casa en programas de educación pública para adultos?

____ no

____ sí

¿Cuáles programas?	# de personas
GED	_____
inglés	_____
entrenamiento vocacional	_____
otro	_____

64. ¿Hubieron algunos servicios educacionales que usted o alguien que
vive en su casa necesitó pero no recibió? (por ejemplo: "bos",
programa bilingüe, educación especial, comida en la escuela).

___no   [IF NO, PROCEED TO QUESTION #65]

___sí

       ¿Cuáles servicios necesitó?

       _____

       _____

       _____

       ¿Porqué no recibió los servicios?

       A. _____ Le negaron los servicios

            ¿porqué?   _____ por ser indocumentado

                     _____ otro (especifique) _____

       _____

       _____

       B. _____ No solicitó los servicios

            ¿porqué?   _____ por ser indocumentado

                     _____ desconocía los servicios

                     _____ no existe

                     _____ otro (especifique) _____

       _____

       _____

       C. _____ Otro   Explique: _____

       _____

       _____

C. SERVICIOS SOCIALES

Las siguientes preguntas son sobre servicios sociales.

65. ¿En el último año, ha recibido usted o alguien que vive en su casa alguno de estos servicios?

Tipo de asistencia	Por cuento tiempo	Cantidad		
		X semana	X mes	X año
a. AFDC (ayuda para familias con niños dependientes)	_____	____	____	____
b. ayuda para pagar el agua, luz o gas	_____	____	____	____
c. ayuda para pagar la renta	_____	____	____	____
d. estampillas para la comida (cupones)	_____	____	____	____
e. WIC (ayuda para madres y niños para comprar leche y huevos)	_____	____	____	____
f. beneficios de desempleo	_____	____	____	____
g. seguro de incapacitación para trabajadores (por algún accidente en el trabajo)	_____	____	____	____

Sí le discontinuaron alguno de estos servicios (a-g listed above), ¿me puede decir porqué?

_____

_____

_____

_____

_____

_____

66. En el último año cuándo Ud. o alguien que vive en su casa necesitó
    ayuda: [READ ENTIRE PHRASE PREVIOUS TO EACH AREA]

    A.   A encontrar trabajo

        ¿Adónde fue (o quién le ayudó)? _____

        _____

        _____

        ¿Que ayuda recibió? _____

        _____

        _____

        ¿Le costó algo?

        ___no

        ___sí   [IF YES]   ¿Cuánto? _____

    B.   Para comprar o conseguir comida

        ¿Adónde fue (o quién le ayudó)? _____

        _____

        _____

        ¿Que ayuda recibió? _____

        _____

        _____

        ¿Le costó algo?

        ___no

        ___sí   [IF YES]   ¿Cuánto? _____

67. C. A traducir algo (e.g. como un anuncio, una carta, para llenar
una forma)

¿Adónde fue (o quién le ayudó)? _____

¿Que ayuda recibió? _____

_____

_____

¿Le costó algo?

___no

___sí   [IF YES]   ¿Cuánto? _____

D. Transportación (por ejemplo, con boletos para el "bos",
"aventones" a recibir servicios, etc.) [PROBE]

¿Adónde fue (o quién le ayudó)? _____

¿Que ayuda recibió? _____

_____

_____

¿Le costó algo?

___no

___sí   [IF YES]   ¿Cuánto? _____

E. Con información sobre algun servicio que necesitaba?

¿Adonde fue (o quién le ayudó)? _____

¿Que ayuda recibió? _____

_____

_____

¿Le costó algo?

___no

___sí   [IF YES]   ¿Cuánto? _____

68. ¿Alguien que vivió en su casa durante el último año recibió
    servicios para ancianos? [como comida sobre ruedas (Meals-on-
    Wheels)]

    ___no

    ___sí   ¿cuáles? _____

                                       _____

                                       _____

           ¿Le costó algo? ___no

                           ___sí   ¿cuánto? _____

69. Hay servicios de consejo profesional que dan varias agencias.
    Por ejemplo, consejos sobre planificación familiar, consejos sobre
    el alcoholismo o uso de drogas, y consejos para hacer un
    presupuesto familiar. ¿En el último año, Ud. o alguien que vive
    en su casa recibió algun tipo de consejo profesional?

    ___no

    ___sí   ¿cuáles? _____

                                       _____

                                       _____

           ¿Le costó algo? ___no

                           ___sí   ¿cuánto? _____

70. En el último año, ¿había algún servicio como los que acabamos de nombrar (e.g. comida, transporte, traducción, encontrar trabajo) que Ud. o alguién que vive en su casa solicitó y no recibió?

___ no

___ sí   ¿cuáles? _____

                                        _____

                                        _____

¿porqué se los negaron?

_____ por ser indocumentado

_____ por no poder pagar

_____ otro (especifique) _____

                                        _____

71. ¿En el último año, hubo algún servicio que Ud. o alguien que vive en su casa necesitó y no lo pidió?

___ no

___ sí   ¿cuál(es)? _____

                                        _____

                                        _____

¿porqué no lo pidió?

_____ por ser indocumentado

_____ pensó que no llenaba los requisitos

_____ no sabía que existían estos servicios

_____ no habla inglés

_____ ellos no hablan español

_____ por falta de dinero

_____ otra razón _____

_____

D. SERVICIOS LEGALES

Las siguientes preguntas son sobre el sistema legal de Texas.

72. ¿Ud. o alguien que vive en su casa utilizó algún servicio legal en el año pasado? [READ ENTIRE "por ejemplo" UNDER COLUMNS 2 and 3].

¿Qué tipo de servicio recivió?	¿Quién le dío el servicio? (por ejemplo, notario, abogado).	¿A que tipo de agencia fue? (por ejemplo, agencia particular, agencia de la iglesia, agencia pública, o agencia de la ciudad).	Costo

73. ¿Recibió Ud. o alguien que vive en su casa infracciones de tránsito en el último año?

___no

___sí   ¿Pagó una multa?

                     ___no

                     ___sí   ¿cuánto?_____

74. Las siguientes preguntas se refieren a la policía, y no a los
oficiales de migración. ¿Arrestaron a Ud. o alguien que vive en
su casa en el último año?

___no

___sí   ¿Quién lo arrestó?

           _____ policía municipal

           _____ policía estatal

           _____ sheriff

           _____ no sabe

           _____ otro

           _____

           _____

75. ¿Ha estado Ud. o alguien que vive en su casa en la cárcel en el
último año?

___no

___sí   ¿cuántos días? _____

           ¿en cúal cárcel estuvo? _____

76. ¿Durante el año pasado, Ud. o alguien que **vive en su casa** tuvo una audiencia ante un juez?

___no   [PROCEED TO Q. 77]

___sí

   a. ¿Le designó un abogado la corte?   ___no

                                              ___**sí**

   b. ¿Le designó un intérprete la corte?   ___no

                                              ___**sí**

   c. ¿Pagó algún costo a la corte?

     ___no

     ___sí   ¿cuánto? $_____

   d. ¿Pagó alguna multa?

     ___no

     ___sí   ¿cuánto? $_____

77. ¿A Ud. o alguien que vive con Ud. se le **designó un oficial de** "probation" en el último año?

___no

___sí   ¿Por cuánto tiempo?

78. En el último año: ¿Ud. o alguien que vive con Ud. ha iniciado una demanda en alguna corte? (Por ejemplo, para iniciar un divorcio, o una demanda).

___no   [PROCEED TO Q. 79]

___sí

      a. ¿Pagó algo?   ___no

                       ___sí   ¿cuánto? $_____

      b. ¿Usó un abogado particular (privado) o de una agencia pública?

                                                    COSTO

          _____ privado/particular $_____

          _____ público $_____

      c. ¿Tuvo que pagar algo al otro partido del pleito?

         ___no

         ___sí   ¿cuánto? $_____

      d. ¿Hubo algún otro costo o multa que Ud. pagó?

         ___no

         ___sí   ¿cuánto? $_____

E. OTROS SERVICIOS

79. ¿Usa usted o alguien de su familia el sistema público de tranportación?

___no

___sí   ¿cuántas veces?   _____ por _____

80. ¿Usa usted o alguien de su familia servicios recreativos?

_____no

_____sí   ¿cuáles?

_____ alberca/picina

_____ parque

_____ centros recreativos

_____ otro (especifique)

_____

_____

_____

81. ¿Han tenido que ir los bomberos a su casa en el último año?

___no

___sí   ¿porqué? _____

_____

_____

82. ¿Vive usted en viviendas subsidiadas por el Gobierno?

___no   ___sí

REMEMBER TO FILL IN TIME ENDED ON THE COVER SHEET

APPENDIX E

THE USE OF STATE- AND LOCALLY FUNDED PUBLIC HEALTH
SERVICES BY UNDOCUMENTED ALIENS IN TEXAS

By law, each city and county in Texas is responsible for providing comprehensive health care services to those residents who cannot afford, or do not choose, private sources of health care. This appendix examines the use of state- and locally funded public health services by one segment of the population of Texas: namely, undocumented aliens. The opening section provides background information on the organization, funding, service provision and eligibility requirements of the state and local health departments in general. The following section then provides a more detailed examination of the ways in which health services are provided through state and local agencies in Austin, Dallas, El Paso, Houston, McAllen/Rio Grande Valley, and San Antonio, and specifically focuses on the use of these services by undocumented persons. Finally, some general conclusions are made about the use of health services by illegal aliens and the financial impact of this usage on the State of Texas and the localities mentioned above.

It should be emphasized at the outset that much of the information contained in this report is based on the "best estimates" of health care workers. Little concrete information regarding the use of public health services by undocumented persons exists, and this portion of the report depends heavily on estimates made by health care personnel who serve clients and patients who may be undocumented.

BACKGROUND

State and Local Public Health Departments

Public health services in Texas are provided through the combined efforts of the Texas Department of Health and local (city and/or county) health departments. Approximately 75 percent of the population of Texas is served by local health departments. The remaining 25 percent had no access to comprehensive public health services until 1975, when the Department of Health Regional Health Program was created to fill the existing service gap. Today, the state health department supplements the services provided by the local health departments where those local departments exist, contributing funds, training programs and other resources, in addition to providing public health services directly to the 25 percent of the population which is not served by local departments.

The Texas Department of Health has divided the state into twelve Public Health Regions, each of which has its own headquarters. Each of the regions contains some cities and counties that have their own health departments. Since each of the areas covered in this study is served by a city and/or a county health department, we shall consider the Texas Department of Health's input into illegal alien health care only insofar as it contributes to the operations of these specific local health departments, or operates health service organizations independent of the local departments.

The state health department receives approximately 45 percent of its funding from the federal government in the form of block grants, entitlements, and other funds. Some of this money is earmarked for specific purposes such as family planning, and some is not. The health department then parcels out its funds to its regional offices and clinics and to the local health departments. The local departments combine the state funds they have received with the funds they have raised locally through taxes, bonds and service fees. Although the proportion of state funds (this includes federal money that has been funneled through the Texas Department of Health) and local funds used by local departments can be determined, in most cases the specific services provided by each local health department cannot be separated on the basis of their funding sources. In other words, local health departments mix their funds together, regardless of source, and services provided are financed from this general fund. This fact is significant to this study, because often estimates of the use of services by illegal aliens will be made by service, and the cost can then not be traced back to a specific local, state or federal funding source. As a general rule, however, state and federal contributions to local health departments are used directly for programs (immunizations, family planning, etc.) and not for administration, capital improvements or other operating expenses.

Table E.1 shows the breakdown of state and local funding for the local health departments covered in this study.

Services Provided

Public health department services can be divided into two main categories: environmental control (animal control, food, air and water quality, etc.); and personal health services. In this study, the environmental responsibilities of the health departments will not be considered, since the marginal cost of providing these services to the undocumented segment of the population is negligible. However, information regarding the use of personal public health services by illegal aliens is germane to this study.

Personal health services are provided through two basic kinds of health care organizations: (1) hospitals, which provide primary care; and (2) clinics or health centers, which provide preventive and, to a lesser extent, primary care. Since hospital funding, administration, service and eligibility differ from one place to the next, we shall examine the public hospital care provided in each specific city in the following section. Local health department clinics, however, provide similar services throughout the state, and some general statements can be made about the provision of these services by local clinics. Following is a list of the various clinics, programs, and services which are state and/or locally funded and offered by all local health department clinics.

Table E.1

State and Local Funding for Local Health Departments

City/Area	Health Dept.	Total $	State $	Local $	% State	% Local
Austin	Austin/Travis County	18,229,741	359,000	17,870,741	2	98
Dallas	Dallas City	9,276,184	268,750	9,007,434	2.9	97.1
	Dallas County	4,715,907	220,395	4,495,512	4.7	95.3
El Paso	El Paso City/County	4,041,357	166,985	3,874,372	4.1	95.9
Houston	Houston City	23,801,389	1,945,170	21,856,219	8.2	91.8
	Harris County	4,540,086	388,798	4,201,288	8.6	91.4
Valley	Hidalgo County	1,198,060	221,130	976,930	18.4	81.6
San Antonio	San Antonio Metropolitan	11,747,769	516,340	11,231,429	4.4	95.6

Source: Texas Department of Health, State Participating Local Health Department Budgets With Bureau of Community Health Services, October 1, 1982-September 30, 1983.

1. <u>Child</u> <u>Health</u> <u>Services</u> <u>Program</u> offers preventive health care and maintenance for children. Includes physical examinations, developmental assessment, nutritional counseling. Staffed by nurses and doctors. Service is provided free of charge. Eligibility: residency within the local health department's district (either city or county, whichever applies).

2. <u>Family</u> <u>Planning</u> provides physical examinations, family planning and counseling for both men and women, pregnancy testing and birth control supplies. Sliding fee scale (client pays 0, 10, 20, 30, or 100 percent of his or her bill). Eligibility: residency within the local health department's district.

3. <u>Maternal</u> <u>Health</u> provides prenatal care, examinations, lab work, health counseling, and home visits for pregnant women. Service is provided free of charge (this service does not include delivery; women are usually referred to the appropriate public hospital for delivery, which must be paid for). Eligibility: residency within the local health department's district.

4. <u>Immunization</u> <u>Program</u> provides immunizations for polio, pertussis, mumps, measles, rubella, diphtheria, tetanus, as well as phenylketonuria and tuberculosis screening. Service provided free of charge. Eligibility: residency within local health department's district.

5. <u>General</u> <u>Communicable</u> <u>Disease</u> <u>Program</u> provides surveillance and epidemiology for diseases such as hepatitis, rubella and salmonella. Service provided free of charge. Eligibility: residency within the local health department's district.

6. <u>Tuberculosis</u> <u>Control</u> <u>Program</u> provides diagnosis, treatment, and follow-up for residents of the local health department district. No charge is made for the service.

7. <u>Venereal</u> <u>Disease</u> <u>Program</u> provides diagnosis, treatment, follow-up, education and counseling. Service provided free of charge. Eligibility: residency within local health department's district.

8. <u>Dental</u> <u>Clinic</u> provides comprehensive dental care service to adults and children. Service may be provided free of charge or for a fee. Eligibility: residency within the local health department district is required; U.S. citizenship may also be required.

Most of these services are designed to encourage health maintenance and to prevent disease, malnutrition and unwanted pregnancies. Generally, they are provided free, and proof of residency within the applicable local health department district--not proof of U.S. citizenship--and a demonstration of need are the only eligibility requirements for receipt of service. Generally, any needy undocumented person residing within the domain of a local health department is officially eligible to receive these services. The reasoning underlying this policy is that the primary goal of preventive medicine is to protect as many people as possible, which means nobody is excluded. In the eyes of public health administrators, it is worth the price the local department might have to absorb in providing health care for undocumented aliens to prevent community-wide health hazards, unwanted pregnancies, and so on. Hence, public health administrators, doctors and nurses in local health departments throughout the state say that they do not want to know whether a client applying for service might be undocumented, as long as U.S. citizenship is not required for service. For this reason, all of the following information regarding service usage by illegal aliens is based solely upon estimates made by public health officials administering programs for which undocumented persons may be eligible.

According to public health nurses, doctors, and staff members, illegal aliens generally do not apply for services which have citizenship eligibility requirements.* They do not apply for two reasons: first, the requirements are strictly enforced and those who do not meet the criteria are not served; and secondly, they fear that their undocumented status will be detected when they cannot produce the proper documents required for service (birth certificate, passport, etc.).

Public Hospitals

Public hospitals are run by the cities or counties in which they are located. In general, there are two primary types of public hospitals which are of interest to this report. The first, commonly called a "welfare hospital," is funded directly by local property taxes, and provides health care for all residents of its district regardless of their ability to pay. These hospitals typically receive little or no payment for their services, and usually only 10 to 15 percent of their operating expenses are covered by patient fees. The second type of public hospital is the general hospital, which attempts to cover its operating expenses with the fees it collects from patients. Although a general hospital operates under the jurisdiction of a local health department, tax money is only used to contribute to operating expenses if the hospital runs in the red at the end of the year. Neither welfare nor general hospitals may turn away a patient in an emergency situation, but general hospitals make every effort to collect their bills, whereas welfare hospitals may write off their bad debt. Of the cities considered in this study, only Houston and Dallas are served by welfare hospitals; the other localities are served by general hospitals.

In general, the hospitals in each city seemed to provide more precise and accurate information than did clinics on the cost of providing services to undocumented aliens. This was due to the fact that hospitals have more sophisticated billing systems than do clinics, and their operations are conducted under one roof, rather than being spread out over a large number of facilities. Furthermore, it is possible that because undocumented aliens go

---

*For example, the Austin-Travis County Medical Assistance Program provides payments for complete medical services. Legal residence is an eligibility requirement.

to hospitals only when they have a serious medical problem, they may be more honest in providing information (such as, true name, immigration status, and so on) than they are when they are well. Clinics generally do not treat people in life-threatening situations, and we do not have the same confidence in their estimates of undocumented usage.

To what extent do undocumented aliens take advantage of those services for which they are eligible? The following section examines how public hospital and clinic services are provided in Austin, Dallas, El Paso, Houston, the Rio Grande Valley, and San Antonio, and assesses the extent to which these services may be used by undocumented persons.

THE USE OF HEALTH SERVICES BY UNDOCUMENTED ALIENS

Austin

Hospital Care. Brackenridge Hospital is a public hospital for the residents of Travis County, but, since it is the only hospital within a ten-county area with an emergency/trauma center, it has in effect become the center for the indigents of nine counties surrounding Travis County. This presents the hospital, the City of Austin and Travis County with a logistical and financial burden.

Brackenridge has 397 beds. Its annual operating budget, based upon 85 percent occupancy, was $66.5 million for fiscal year 1982. The hospital's net revenue for fiscal year 1981 was $62 million. Direct funding for the hospital from the Austin/Travis County Health Department covers only capital improvements; operating expenses must be covered by revenues. In order to make the budget balance, when the budget is prepared each year, the bad debt for the coming year is estimated and fees are adjusted to compensate for the predicted bad debt. In effect, those patients who pay their bills are actually paying a higher rate than they would if all patients paid their bills; they are subsidizing those who do not pay.

For the past few years, the bad debt has run at approximately 17 percent of the operating costs. This percentage translated into a figure of approximately $12 million in 1982--an extremely large amount compared with other area hospitals. Austin's private hospitals, for example, have an average bad debt of only 2 percent. The hospital's bad debt is largely due to the fact that the hospital must by law admit anyone in need of hospitalization, regardless of the ability to pay. As noted, uncollectible bills are absorbed into operating expenses and are not normally covered by taxpayers. However, if initial estimates of uncollectibles are too low, the City of Austin must cover the difference at the end of the fiscal year. The City controls the hospital's books and its funds.

According to an estimate that is generally accepted among Brackenridge's administrative and billing staffs, approximately 4 to 5 percent of the hospital's bad debt can be attributed to undocumented persons. In 1981, this translated into around $500,000.

In admitting a patient, the hospital is concerned with whether he can pay his bills, not whether he is an American citizen. No proof of ability to pay is required in an emergency situation, but, in non-emergency situations, a person may be asked to return with proof of ability to pay his bills. According to Brackenridge's billing supervisor, most undocumented persons do pay their bills. The most common method of payment is through a contract which can be arranged with the hospital; under such a contract a $500 down payment (negotiable) is required, and the balance must be paid off over a period of months or even years. Many undocumented persons seem to fear that the INS will be notified if they do not pay their bills. However, some bills are so large that they cannot be paid. Outstanding examples of this problem include the well-publicized case of an undocumented teenage boy who was frostbitten in 1982, and whose medical bills have already reached $75,000; and an undocumented woman whose complications in giving birth to twins have cost $66,000 so far. The hospital reportedly has ten to twelve such high-cost undocumented patients each year. The expenses for these cases can rarely (if ever) be covered by the patient; this, in large part, explains the $500,000 estimate of undocumented persons' debt to Brackenridge last year.

One factor which makes payment difficult for undocumented persons in these high-cost cases is a lack of third-party coverage (insurance). In some cases, a person may be insured but carrying the policy under a different name, or he may simply be afraid of using the insurance for fear of being caught by the INS.

Brackenridge employees provided some general characteristics of undocumented persons seeking health care at the hospital. In general, most wait until they have an emergency or serious problem before seeking hospital care. This leads to a higher than average per-person expense. Most have substandard health care and personal hygiene. More undocumented males than females are treated at the hospital; often they are the victims of accidents or fights. Most undocumented women seen at the hospital are admitted to deliver children.

For the past year and a half, approximately three out of the twelve babies delivered each day have been born to undocumented mothers. Most of these women are in the hospital for two days and incur bills of $1,500 to $2,000. It should be noted, however, that women who can afford care at other hospitals generally do not use Brackenridge, as the hospital's staff doctors, rather than obstetricians, deliver the babies there. An average of three undocumented males are admitted each weekday, and an average of six each weekend day; their bills run between $3,000 and $4,000 for a three-to-four-day stay. Most of these "routine" patients pay their bills on a contract basis.

In sum, while most undocumented patients do pay their bills, a small group of very high-cost treatment patients cannot; approximately $500,000 of Brackenridge's bad debt last year was due to undocumented persons who could not pay their bills. None of the hospital's other expenses can be attributed solely to illegal aliens; for example, no Spanish-speaking employees had to be added to staff to serve undocumented patients, since the hospital also serves large numbers of legally-resident Spanish-speaking patients.

Clinics and Health Centers. The Austin/Travis County Health Department operates a number of health centers in various parts of the city and county. Six of these centers offer most of the services outlined in the background section of this report (immunizations, family planning, etc.) for which undocumented persons are eligible. Funding for the services provided by these centers comes primarily from the City of Austin's general fund (tax-supported), although contributions are also made by the state health department. The cost of providing each of the health services city-wide (in all six health centers combined) can be broken down; however, there is no available information which shows what the cost is to provide each service within each of the six separate centers.

Of the six health centers, three--East Austin, South Austin, and Montopolis--reportedly serve significant numbers of undocumented persons, while the other three serve few, if any, illegal aliens. At each of the centers which serve undocumented clients, estimates of the undocumented proportion of clients served ranged from 1 percent (low) to 5 percent (most common) to 17 percent (high). Table E.2 presents budget information for each of the health center services that can be used by undocumented persons, and provides high, low and most common estimates of service usage and cost to the Austin/Travis County Health Department. It should be noted that the information given for "3 clinic total cost" and "3 clinic total usage" refers to the usage and cost for the three clinics thought to be serving undocumented clients. This calculation is an estimate, and is based on the assumption that each of the six clinics serves roughly the same number of people for the same average cost per service; hence, the cost of providing services to all comers in three centers used by undocumented persons is estimated to be 50 percent of the total cost for all centers. In short, the resulting cost figures for undocumented persons' use of health centers are rough.

To sum up: it is likely that the cost of providing health services to undocumented aliens in Austin through local health departments ranged between $504,500 ($500,000 for Brackenridge and $4,500 for clinics) and $576,814 ($500,000 for Brackenridge and $76,814 for clinics) in fiscal year 1982.

Dallas

Hospital Care. Parkland Hospital is a public hospital operated by the Dallas County Hospital District. It has 932 beds, provides comprehensive medical care, and serves as a regional emergency/trauma center. Parkland's mandate is to provide health care for the indigent population of Dallas County; hence, residency within the county, rather than ability to pay, is the primary eligibility requirement for service. The majority (80 percent) of its patients are admitted through the Emergency Room (compared with an average of 20 percent for private hospitals in the area), and one out of three patients is admitted for obstetrical care. Parkland's annual operating budget is $112.7 million, 57 percent of which is funded through local ad valorem taxes. Parkland is known as a "welfare" hospital, and 67 percent of its budget is spent on treatment for indigents who cannot pay their bills.

Table E.2

Budget Information for Health Center Services Used by Undocumented Persons

Service	Austin Total # Served[1]	Total Budget[2] ($)	Source(s)	3 Clinic Total Usage[1]	3 Clinic Total Cost ($)	Low=1% of 3 Clinics Usage[1]	Cost ($)	5% of 3 Clinics Usage[1]	Cost ($)	17% of 3 Clinics Usage[1]	Cost ($)
Child Health	4,491	106,510	106,510 Local (100%)	2,245	53,255	22	532	110	2,260	382	9,052
Family Planning	6,241	395,820	9,860 Fees (2.5%) 101,866 Fed via TDH (Title X) (25.7%) 134,920 Fed via TDH (Title XX) (34%) 149,154 Local (37.7%)	3,120	197,910	31	1,979[3]	156	10,350[3]	530	33,643[3]
Immunizations	46,802	142,747	340,000 State (80.5%)	23,401	71,373	234	714	1,170	3,570	3,978	12,138
VD	25,284	138,561	82,471 Local (19.5%)	12,642	69,280	126	693	630	3,465	2,142	11,781
TB		141,163	N/A--Cost of Treatment Too Variable to be Applied Here								
Maternal Health	8,654	120,035	120,035 Local (100%)	4,327	60,017	43	600	216	3,000	736	10,200
Total		1,044,836	458,170 Local (43.9%) 340,000 State (32.5%) 236,786 Fed via State (22.7%) 9,860 Fees (.9%)				4,518		23,000		76,814

Source: Total number served and budget figures from Austin-Travis County Health Department. Usage estimates made by method explained in text.

[1]Encounters.
[2]Budget for programs only--excludes administrative, personnel, capital, and other "overhead" expenses.
[3]Based on assumption that patient pays 0% on the sliding scale.

In 1982, Parkland conducted a study to determine the extent to which the hospital was being used by persons who did not reside in Dallas County. This issue was of great interest to taxpayers, who were in effect subsidizing the hospital's treatment of indigents. The results of the study showed that 12 percent of the hospital's patients were non-residents. Of these non-residents, 23.4 percent were undocumented aliens. Such persons are not considered residents of the county even if they live there; therefore, this figure should include all undocumented aliens. This percentage translated into approximately 3 percent of all Parkland's admissions. The portion of the hospital's bad debt attributed to these undocumented patients was $1,630,980 ($1,004,328 inpatient, and $626,652 outpatient/Emergency Room) in fiscal year 1982.

Three out of four undocumented patients admitted to the hospital in fiscal year 1982 entered to give birth. Many of these patients did, in fact, pay their bills, at least in part. Of those who paid, 90 percent used a self-pay method (cash or contract); 7.5 percent had commercial insurance; and 2.5 percent had "other" means of payment. None used Medicaid, Medicare, Blue Cross, or Workers' Compensation to pay their bills. The bulk of the bad debt attributable to undocumented aliens at Parkland is generally incurred when an illegal alien who does not have insurance has an accident or complicated illness, and runs up a large bill which cannot be paid. Thus, as in Austin, a few patients with unusually high-cost treatment account for most of the unpaid bills.

Clinics and Health Centers. Clinic health care in Dallas is provided by the Dallas City Health Department in conjunction with the Dallas County Hospital District. These organizations act as a single unit, operating six health centers throughout Dallas which offer dental health care, immunization clinics, maternal health care, child health care, prenatal care, and tuberculosis and venereal disease clinics. The only eligibility requirement for any of these services is residency in the City of Dallas, not U.S. citizenship. No fees are charged for any of the services.

Out of the six health centers, two--West Dallas and Swiss Avenue (also known as North Dallas)--serve significant numbers of undocumented persons, according to staff members. Of the range of services offered, it is believed that immunization and child health clinics are used most often by undocumented aliens. Family planning and maternal health services, which are under a combined program, are also used, though to a much lesser extent. The average cost of an immunization in fiscal year 1982 was $1.05, while the average cost of a child health visit was at least $4 and the cost of the typical family planning/maternal health visit was also approximately $4. Table E.3 shows the cost of providing these services to undocumented aliens at the West and North Dallas clinics (based on estimates of service usage and average cost).

In addition, a significant number of undocumented aliens are believed to be using VD clinics in Dallas. Because of their anonymity, V.D. clinics serve a wide cross-section of the city's population, rather than only the poor or disadvantaged. Because only one clinic staff member would venture a guess

Table E.3

Cost of Providing Services to Undocumented Aliens
at West and North Dallas Clinics

Service	Av. Cost	Tot.# Undoc.	Tot. Cost Undoc.	West Dallas			North Dallas		
				Tot.# Served	% Undoc.	# Undoc.	Tot.# Served	% Undoc.	# Undoc.
Immunization	$1.05	3,296	$ 3,461	2,467	52%	1,283	6,709	30%	2,013
Child Health	$4.00	3,651	$14,604	5,643	40%	2,257	5,577	25%	1,394
Maternal Health/ Family Planning	$4.00	508	$ 2,032	5,083	10%	508	1,128	"few"	--
Total			$20,097						

Sources: Average cost and total number served provided by Dallas City Health Department. Estimates of service usage by undocumented aliens made by staff persons at each clinic.

as to the proportion of undocumented patients--and this was "something less than 30 percent"--we will assume that the proportion of patients who are undocumented persons is the same as the proportion of residents of the city who are undocumented persons. If 3.8 percent, or 5,130 patients (the high estimate), were undocumented at an average cost of $3.14 a visit, the total cost for treating undocumented patients was $16,108 in fiscal year 1982.

In sum, the city and county of Dallas spent around $1,667,185 in fiscal year 1982 for the health care of the city's undocumented population (based on estimates of $1,630,980 on hospital care, $20,097 in health clinics, and as much as $16,108 on veneral disease treatment).

El Paso

Hospital Care. R. E. Thomason is the public hospital serving El Paso and the surrounding area. It is located just six blocks from the Mexican border. In fiscal year 1982 the hospital's operating budget was approximately $28 million, of which 60 percent was covered by patients' fees, and 40 percent by local taxes. The hospital provided $13 million in "charity" care (46 percent of the operating budget). Of that amount, $10 million was covered by tax dollars so that the hospital could maintain its low patient fee structure. If it did not do this, more patients could not pay their bills, and the bad debt would increase even more. The hospital is in financial straits, and is currently trying to decide whether to request a tax increase and/or increase its patient fees to help offset its bad debt.

The hospital's policy toward undocumented persons is to treat them as it does any other patient who is not a resident of El Paso County. Although any person who arrives at the hospital in an emergency situation must be treated regardless of nationality or ability to pay, in theory, non-residents must pay their bills in full and are not eligible for any discount. In practice, of course, non-residents often cannot pay their bills, and their expenses must be absorbed into the hospital's bad debt.

A large proportion of the undocumented persons admitted to R.E. Thomason are women in labor. In 1982, out of a total 2,751 babies born at the hospital, an estimated one in ten (around 275) had undocumented mothers. In general, undocumented women experience more complications than the average woman during delivery, due to inferior prenatal care. The hospital personnel believe that there has been an increase recently in the number of undocumented women who try to give birth in the United States so that their babies will be American citizens. While many use the services of lay midwives in El Paso so that they will not have to run the risk of being turned away from the hospital, others wait until they are in advanced stages of labor before presenting themselves at the hospital emergency room. In such an emergency situation they must, by law, be treated.

Most of the other illegal aliens treated at R.E. Thomason are also admitted through the emergency room. Most are male victims of stabbings or shootings, or accident victims, and they account for approximately 20 percent of the hospital's emergency room activity. At any given time, an estimated 5 percent of all the hospital's patients are undocumented. The amount of the hospital's bad debt that can be attributed to these patients totaled at least $750,000 in fiscal year 1982. A major portion of this figure can be attributed to patients with severe injuries or complicated illnesses or deliveries (so-called "big ticket" patients) who had no insurance to cover their bills. One accident victim, for example, ran up a $100,000 hospital bill that could not be paid. The rest of the undocumented patients' bad debt is attributable to patients with more "standard" ailments who simply would not or could not pay their bills. Since El Paso is so close to the Mexican border, the undocumented do not fear deportation because crossing back and forth is quite easy; hence, they are not afraid that the INS may be notified if their bills are not paid. In general, however, most undocumented persons pay their bills on a self-pay basis, usually with cash. Contracts between the hospital and undocumented patients are not as common at R.E. Thomason as in other public hospitals in the state; with so much of the undocumented population shifting back and forth between El Paso and Juarez, address verification and billing are difficult at best.

Clinics and Health Centers. Because of the large, dense population of El Paso (approximately 500,000) and Juarez (approximately one million), the El Paso City and County Health Department is most concerned with preventing epidemics of infectious diseases. All of the city's public health clinics provide preventive services to any person on demand, regardless of nationality. Because of the large proportion of people of Mexican origin living in El Paso, it is impossible to single out clinics that might be used by more undocumented persons than others; rather, it is believed that all of the clinics are used equally by illegal aliens.

The El Paso City and County Health Department's operating budget for fiscal year 1982 was $4,675,000. Of this, $2,038,000 was devoted to Emergency Medical Services (EMS); a substantial portion provided general public goods, such as air pollution control and animal regulation; and the remainder supported general personal health, services and clinics. Public health officials and administrators were unable to guess what percent of EMS use was devoted to undocumented persons, but asserted that, of all the services provided, only immunization clinics and tuberculosis control centers were used by illegal aliens. Table E.4 shows the budgets for the health services that are known to be used by undocumented persons; indicates the proportion of clients using each service that are believed to be undocumented; and presents a derived estimated cost to the El Paso City and County Health Department of providing each service to these clients in fiscal year 1982.

In sum, last year in El Paso, the minimum cost to the city and county of providing public health care to undocumented persons ranged between $849,000 and $915,000 for hospital and clinic care (the higher figure includes TB victims living in El Paso on temporary border crossing cards). It should also be noted that American public health officials in El Paso and Mexican officials in Juarez cooperate with one another to a great extent, so that many

Table E.4

Budgets for Health Services

Service	Budget($)	Source	% Undoc.	$ for Undoc.
Immunizations	116,118	State	20%	23,223
TB Control	600,000	State	11.0-12.6%	66,000-75,600[1]

Source: Budget information obtained from Texas Department of Health. Estimated usage by undocumented aliens made by Dr. Earl Gorby, Region 3 Deputy Director and Director of Tuberculosis Control. Dollar cost for undocumented derived from budget and usage estimates.

[1] Ranges are derived by including or excluding those using temporary border crossing cards.

undocumented aliens in El Paso reportedly cross back to Mexico for the treatment of many of their health problems.

Houston

Hospital Care. There are two public "welfare" hospitals in Houston, both operated by the Harris County Hospital District, which provide care for the city's indigent population. The first, Jefferson Davis Hospital, provides a variety of services but it is primarily an obstetrical hospital. It has only 278 beds, but in fiscal year 1982 approximately 16,000 babies were delivered there. The second, Ben Taub Hospital, provides comprehensive medical care and serves as a regional emergency/trauma center. It is substantially larger than Jeff Davis, with 475 beds.

Both hospitals are funded, as is the Harris County Hospital District as a whole, through a combination of patient fees (15 percent) and a local property tax of 19 cents per million dollars of property value (85 percent). Essentially, the taxpayers of Harris County subsidize the health care of the county's indigent. Jeff Davis Hospital's operating budget for fiscal year 1982 was $28,668,729, while Ben Taub's operating expenses over the same period were $58,450,464. Each hospital's bad debt runs between 80 and 85 percent annually.

At Jeff Davis 43 percent of the patients and at Ben Taub 27.8 percent of the patients are Hispanic. Of these, 10 to 15 percent are thought to be undocumented (based on estimates by intake personnel). Table E.5 summarizes estimates which can be made about the use and cost of providing hospital services to undocumented persons at the two hospitals in fiscal year 1982. It assumes that all costs attributed to the undocumented become bad debt. This

Table E.5

Summary of Estimated Costs of Providing Hospital
Services to Undocumented Persons in Houston

Facility	Budget($)	Bad Debt($)[1]	% Undoc.[2]	Amt. Bad Debt Attrib. Undoc.($)[3]
Jeff Davis	28,668,729	24,368,419	5.4	1,315,895
Ben Taub	58,450,464	49,682,894	3.5	1,738,901
Total				3,054,796

Source: Budget figures from Harris County Hospital District Budget.
Estimates of Undocumented alien and Hispanic usage made by
Curtis Baker, Assistant Fiscal Administrator, Harris County
Hospital District.

[1]Estimate derived from total budget X .85.

[2]Estimate derived from percent Hispanic X .125.

[3]Inferred from estimates of bad debt and percent undocumented patients.

is therefore a known overestimation, because we know that many undocumented patients do pay their bills.

Ben Taub and Jeff Davis Hospitals are extremely overcrowded. At Jeff Davis, women admitted in labor are often discharged the same day, because there simply is not enough bed space in the hospital for all of the patients who need care. Neither hospital has a computerized billing system or any means of verifying patients' addresses, and these factors make the difficult billing situation even more burdensome. Those patients who pay their bills are the exception, rather than the rule.

Most undocumented aliens admitted at both hospitals come through the facilities' emergency rooms where, by law, they cannot be turned away. In non-emergency situations, they must only present proof of residency within Harris County (a paid electric bill, for example) in order to receive treatment. According to the hospital administrators, undocumented patients are neither worse nor better off than most other patients. Most of the hospital's clients are desperately poor and suffer from substandard health, and they seek health care only when it is absolutely needed.

Clinics and Health Centers. Public health centers in Houston are operated by both the Harris County Hospital District and the City of Houston Department of Health. Those clinics which provide services available to undocumented persons receive funds from both the city and the county departments, and in most cases share common facilities.

Three facilities in Houston that are believed to serve large numbers of undocumented aliens are run jointly by the two health departments; these are the West End and Casa de Amigos Health Centers, and Ripley House. Each provides a full range of preventive health services, including family planning, maternal health care, prenatal counselling, child health care, immunizations, TB and VD treatment, and so on. Unfortunately, although budget information is available for each health center as a whole, there is no available information on the breakdown of services offered within each clinic, their cost, or their usage. The best estimates that can be made of health center usage by undocumented aliens must be applied to the centers as units, not to specific programs offered by the centers. Table E.6 provides a summary of the budgetary information, estimated undocumented use and associated (inferred) cost to the health departments in fiscal year 1982.

In sum, according to best estimates, the cost to the city of Houston and the Harris County Hospital District of providing health care to undocumented aliens in fiscal year 1982 was approximately $3,162,319 (this includes $3,054,796 for hospital care and 107,523 for clinic care).

McAllen/Rio Grande Valley

Hospital Care. There are three public hospitals in Hidalgo County in and around the town of McAllen. All three are funded by the cities in which they

Table E.6

Budgetary Information, Estimated Undocumented Use and Associated Cost
to Harris County Hospital District and City of Houston Department of Health

Facility	Budget ($)[1]	Source($)	% Hisp.[2]	% Undoc.[3]	Undoc. ($)[4]
West End	896,789	238,038 County 658,751 City	32	4	35,872
Ripley House	261,627	County	50	6.25	16,352
Casa de Amigos	460,833	268,774 County 192,059	90	12	55,300
Total					107,523

Source: Budgets for Harris County Hospital District and City of Houston. Estimates of % Hispanic and % undocumented made by Curtis Baker, Assistant Fiscal Administrator, Harris County Hospital District.

[1] Budget for services and supplies only. Personnel, administrative, capital costs, etc., were not included since use of facilities by undocumented proportion of clients would have a minimal marginal effect on these costs.

[2] Percentage estimated by health center administrators.

[3] Derived by taking percentage Hispanic clients multiplied by .125 (estimated percentage of Hispanics that are undocumented).

[4] Only a derived estimated cost based upon budget for facility's programs and rough estimate of percentage undocumented clients.

are located: McAllen, Mission, and Edinburg. Of these, the McAllen General Hospital is the largest, with 270 beds, followed by Edinburg General Hospital with 106, and Mission Municipal Hospital with 58. All three serve substantial numbers of undocumented persons. As in other cities, patients admitted in non-emergency situations must prove that they are residents of the city in which the hospital is located; however, any person arriving at the hospital in an emergency situation must be admitted. All of the hospitals are funded through patient fees and local taxes. In the past year, each of the hospitals has experienced an increase in the number of patients who are unable to pay their bills; this may in large part be due to the fact that unemployment in the Valley has skyrocketed.

Even though many undocumented women in the Valley use midwives to deliver their children, a substantial percentage of the illegal patients admitted to the hospitals are women ready to give birth. In general, these women have had inadequate prenatal care, and therefore have higher risk of complications in childbirth. Because of the proximity to the border, women may readily obtain 72-hour border passes, cross into the United States and have their children in one of the public hospitals in the Valley. Most of the other undocumented patients admitted to Valley area hospitals are males, often the victims of accidents, fights or work-related injuries.

The Rio Grande Valley is located at the Mexican-American border, and many undocumented Mexican nationals live in the Valley on the American side. Because a substantial portion of the Valley's population shifts back and forth between the U.S. and Mexico, it is extremely difficult to tell who is an undocumented alien and who is an American citizen. For this reason, hospital administrators in McAllen, Mission, and Edinburg did not feel confident in estimating the proportion of their patients who might be undocumented. Therefore, no service usage or cost estimations could be made for the hospital care of undocumented aliens in the Rio Grande Valley.

In addition, the Harlingen State Chest Hospital, which provides care for TB victims from all over the state, is located in the Valley. The hospital has 125 beds. It is unknown how many undocumented aliens are served by the hospital. When illegal aliens are found or known to have contracted TB, public health officials are presented with a difficult problem. Private hospitals will not accept them because they may be a financial burden. The State Chest Hospital is now required by law to report any patients who are known to be undocumented to the INS for deportation. However, if an undocumented person is deported, there is a good chance that he will spread the disease during deportation, back in Mexico, and in the U.S. if he attempts another entry into Texas. In order to control a potential TB epidemic, the Harlingen Chest Hospital has adopted a "don't see" attitude. The hospital does treat undocumented persons, although it does not know (officially, at any rate) how many are treated. No estimates of undocumented patient usage were available for this report, although it is known that the incidence of TB among illegal aliens in the U.S. is higher than the average for the United States.

Clinics and Health Centers. The Hidalgo County Health Department provides public health services throughout the Rio Grande Valley. It operates family planning, maternal health, immunization and child health clinics, as well as counseling on nutrition and other health-related matters in the towns of Donna, Edinburg, Elsa, Hidalgo, McAllen, Mercedes, Mission, Pharr, and Weslaco. The department does not break down its budget for each clinic, so estimates of usage by undocumented persons must be based upon total costs for clinic services and average estimates of usage across all nine clinics.

In fiscal year 1982, the Hidalgo County Health Department's budget was $1,653,371. Of this, $518,259 (31 percent) was devoted to the programs offered by the department's health centers and clinics. Estimates of the proportion of clients served that were undocumented ranged from 15 percent to 25 percent at each of the health centers except Hidalgo, for which information was unavailable. None of the administrators or staff members at that clinic would venture a guess as to how many of its patients were undocumented aliens; this is unfortunate, because Hidalgo is located right next to the border and its health center is reputed to have the largest proportion of undocumented aliens of all the clinics in Hidalgo County. Based on an estimate of 20 percent undocumented use at each clinic, it is likely that about $104,000 (20 percent of $518,259) was spent by the Hidalgo County Health Department in serving undocumented aliens in fiscal year 1982.

According to staff members at the various clinics, child health, immunization, and maternal health clinics are the services in the greatest demand by undocumented aliens. Immunization clinics are popular, because the estimated 3,000 children of undocumented parents living in the Valley must be immunized before they can start school. Maternal health clinics are in great demand, and this demand has been increasing, perhaps in part due to the fact that even though many undocumented women go to midwives to deliver their babies, many of those midwives are now demanding that their clients attend prenatal clinics and have blood testing done for syphilis, along with other prenatal tests.

To sum up, in Hidalgo County an unknown amount was spent by the cities of McAllen, Mission and Edinburg for hospital care of undocumented persons, while an estimated $104,000 (at least) was spent by the Hidalgo County Health Department on preventive health care services for undocumented aliens in fiscal year 1982.

San Antonio

Hospital Care. Bexar County Hospital, the only public hospital in the San Antonio metropolitan area, is operated by the Bexar County Hospital District. The hospital has 564 beds, and in fiscal year 1982 it had an operating budget of $76 million, $26 million of which was covered by county taxes, and $50 million by patient fees. The hospital receives no federal or state support.

Many undocumented aliens treated at the Bexar County Hospital are admitted through the emergency room, because, as in other cities, state law requires that no one be denied emergency care. Proof of residency and U.S.

citizenship are required for "normal" admittance, which entitles a patient to a discount on his hospital bill. To prove eligibility, the patient may be asked to produce a paid utility bill to prove residency within Bexar County, and AR Form 3A, INS Form 94, or a certifying letter issued by the INS to prove U.S. citizenship. Since undocumented persons cannot meet the citizenship requirements, they must, at least in theory, pay their bills in full.

Approximately 3 percent (9,960 of a total 332,000) of all outpatients at the hospital in 1982 were undocumented, as were 7 percent (1,911 out of 27,300) of all inpatients. Of the illegals admitted, 40 percent were obstetrical cases, 30 percent were the victims of shootings or stabbings, and 30 percent were accident victims or had other ailments. Approximately 90 percent were unable to pay their bills in full.

In fiscal year 1982, the hospital's bad debt amounted to approximately $38 million (approximately 50 percent of the operating budget), of which $1 million (2.6 percent) was attributed to undocumented patients. This bad debt was absorbed by patients who did pay their bills (and had to pay a higher fee to subsidize those who did not), and by Bexar County tax dollars. The hospital's administrators have characterized two types of undocumented patients using the hospital's facilities. The first type of individual is poor, uneducated and unskilled, living in fear of being picked up by the INS and subsisting in a hand-to-mouth fashion. The second type is the transient who is injured in San Antonio on his way to or from Mexico. Such individuals present a special problem to the hospital, because often they need care after they are discharged, and may have to be transported back to Mexico to rejoin family.

The Bexar County Hospital is confident about the accuracy of its statistics regarding the use of its services by undocumented aliens. Hospital intake workers conduct intensive interviews, and the institution enjoys a sophisticated, computerized patient classification and billing system. It maintains careful records of the use of its services by undocumented patients, in part so that it can justify its ever-increasing budget requests to the county taxpayers.

Clinics and Health Centers. The San Antonio Metropolitan Health District provides public health clinic care to residents of San Antonio. The District's budget in fiscal year 1982 was approximately $8.9 million, 75 percent of which was financed through the City of San Antonio's general fund.

Staff members at city-funded health centers in San Antonio refused to make even rough estimates of the extent of clinic use by undocumented persons in San Antonio; they even refrained from guessing which clinics might serve more undocumented patients than others. This was apparently due to the fact that San Antonio has such a large Hispanic population; estimating the proportion of that population which might be undocumented was thought to be risky and unreliable. Although workers in federally funded clinics, such as the Barrio Comprehensive Clinic, were able to estimate the percentage of their clientele that were undocumented (up to 40 percent), local health department employees refused to venture guesses.

It is difficult to obtain estimates of the number of potential health clinic clients that might be undocumented. Information from different sources is conflicting. For example, one study conducted for the Bexar County Hospital District indicated that 16 percent of the potential population need for public health clinical services could be generated by undocumented persons. However, the same study then qualified this statement by admitting that while the typical undocumented alien in San Antonio was a single male in his twenties, the typical public health patient is either a child, a woman, or elderly. A second study, done for the San Antonio Express News (a city newspaper), found that some 4 percent of all Bexar County residents were undocumented; however, it did not volunteer what proportion of those, if any, were potential public health service recipients.

In short, no reliable estimates exist for the proportion of San Antonio public health clients that might be undocumented. Table E.7 presents the various programs offered by the city's clinics, budgets for each, and funding source information. However, no estimates can be made about the amount of money that might be attributable to service usage by undocumented persons in San Antonio.

According to the San Antonio Task Force on Immigration, the "grapevine" operating among undocumented persons in the city discourages the use of public services that are offered at no charge (as are all of the city health centers' services), with the exception of family planning. There are two reasons for this. First, if an undocumented person wants to legalize his status, he must declare to the INS all of the public services he has used. If he has used many free services, he may be viewed as a potential burden to society, and therefore unfit for citizenship. Second, in applying for services, an undocumented person risks being detected, reported to the INS and deported. Whether or not these fears are valid, they may have an impact on the undocumented community in San Antonio. If many undocumented persons in the city have been warned not to use public services, it may be that few of them use the health centers provided by the city.

CONCLUSION

Undocumented persons in Austin, Dallas, El Paso, Houston, the Rio Grande Valley, and San Antonio were found to be using state- and locally-funded public health services. Although the extent of their use of these services varied from place to place, some general observations can be made about the use of public health services by undocumented aliens, and about the financial impact of this usage on the specific localities studied in this report, and, indirectly, on the State of Texas.

In all of the places studied, public hospitals absorbed much more of the cost of providing health care to illegal aliens than did health clinics. Each of the hospitals studied noted that a large proportion of its undocumented patients were women admitted to deliver children, while the others were primarily men suffering from injuries sustained in accidents or fights. Very few of the undocumented patients were covered by medical insurance, and the

Table E.7

Programs and Budgets for San Antonio Health Clinics

Service/Facility	Budget($)	Source(s)
Eastside General Clinic	175,978	City Health Dept.
Southwest Gen. Clinic	225,932	City Health Dept.
Nursing Services in Clinics	2,530,084	2,262,400 - City Health Dept. 267,684 - State Health Dept.
Family Planning	200,000	Federal Govt.
VD/Communicable Diseases	576,885	310,468 - City Health Dept. 229,694 - State Health Dept. 36,723 - Federal Govt.
Tuberculosis Control	512,476	420,480 - City Health Dept. 91,996 - Federal Govt.
Immunizations	611,410	369,038 - City Health Dept. 39,114 - State Health Dept. 203,258 - Federal Govt.
Dental Clinics	497,336	City
TOTAL	5,330,101	

Source: City and state health departments.

vast majority of them were admitted through emergency rooms. There are two reasons which explain why they are generally admitted in this fashion. First, most wait until they actually do have a medical emergency before seeking health care. Second, although they might be barred from normal admittance due to a lack of citizenship, state law requires that no one be denied treatment in an emergency.

All of the hospitals studied operated on funds gathered through both local taxes and patient fees. In some places, such as Austin, where patient fees theoretically cover 100 percent of the hospital's operating expenses, care for undocumented persons who cannot pay their bills is directly subsidized by those patients who can pay. In other places such as Houston, where property taxes cover 85 percent of operating expenses, the burden falls on the taxpayer, rather than on other patients. At any rate, since the hospitals receive no state or federal funds, the financial burden of providing hospital care for undocumented aliens who cannot pay their bills falls on the local governmental unit—either the city or county.

Health clinic services are also used by undocumented persons. In general, this report showed that undocumented aliens use most of the services for which they are eligible to some extent. However, they tended to use services which were necessary more readily than services which were nonessential. For example, immunization clinics were heavily used, since children must be immunized before they can enter school, and tuberculosis can be fatal if it is not treated. However, nutrition counseling, preventive dental care, and other such "nonessential" services were not sought nearly as much as the more essential services. As in hospital care, the financial burden of providing these services falls on the local health departments, and, to a lesser degree, on the state, which does contribute funds to every local department.

In general, the hospitals studied were able to provide more specific information than could the clinics on the use of their services by undocumented aliens. Information gathered from clinics was based largely on estimates and inferences, while the hospital data seemed to be more exact and reliable. In addition, hospital administrators were open to discussing the issue of health care for the undocumented, while clinic staff persons were often very reluctant to engage in such discussions. Although the cost of providing health care to undocumented aliens in each of the cities studied was significant, it is still likely that such persons do not use public health services to the degree that they might.

In sum, while it is known that many undocumented aliens do, in fact, take advantage of state and local public health programs in Texas, the exact extent to which they use services is not known. The burden of providing care does, however, appear to fall upon local units of government, rather than upon the state.

APPENDIX F

THE USE OF SOCIAL SERVICES BY THE
UNDOCUMENTED POPULATION IN TEXAS

INTRODUCTION

To determine the cost to the State of Texas and its local governments of social services used by undocumented aliens, one must look at two factors: first, the patterns of use of social services by the undocumented; and second, the average and marginal cost per unit of these services, broken down by source of funding. This appendix will first provide some background and methodological information regarding social services and undocumented persons in Texas. Then it will describe the patterns of funding for the major social services supported by public funds. Next, it will trace the costs to the funding sources for specific services in the six geographic areas covered by our research. Finally, it will estimate the level of use of the services by undocumented aliens.

OVERVIEW

Governmental entities are involved in social services in Texas both as direct providers of services and as sources of funding. The federal and state governments serve primarily as funding sources; they award grants to city and county governments and private nonprofit agencies for the delivery of services. City and county governments provide direct services as well as award grants to local nonprofit agencies. Other taxing authorities, such as school districts, also play a small role in funding and providing social services.

Eligibility

Eligibility standards for social services vary considerably. Many publicly funded services require foreign-born recipients to have legal immigration status within the U.S.; however, the methods for determining the client's legal status vary. Federally funded programs, such as Aid to Families with Dependent Children (AFDC) and Food Stamps, require official proof of status, while for other programs the client's personal testimony of legal status may be sufficient. Even when there are statewide or citywide standards, the methods of checking on eligibility will vary from social worker to social worker.

Other programs, particularly city and private programs, may require only proof of residency. In some cases, eligibility may be based solely on need, as in the case of battered women's shelters and Child Protective Services.

The variations in eligibility standards and their enforcement make it difficult to count the numbers of undocumented aliens using social services in Texas. Undocumented aliens are eligible for many programs by virtue of low-income status or other needs; where such persons are eligible, program administrators do not keep records of their clients' immigration status. In other programs, where undocumented aliens are ineligible for services, some undocumented persons may receive services through fraud, or because of varying enforcement of eligibility standards. In this report, numbers given for undocumented persons using social services are based on estimates from administrators, social workers, and demographers.

Regional Variations

The use of social services by undocumented aliens varies from region to region of the state. One of the reasons for this variation is that the percentage of the undocumented in the population varies regionally, affecting the level of need within a particular area. Other reasons for the variations in use stem from differences in availability of the services from city to city as well as from variations in eligibility requirements and the enforcement of these requirements. (Whether regions, counties, or cities were investigated depended on the particular service being studied. The survey used the major city in the area as a focal point; for example, if foster care in Harris County was being studied, Houston was the focus of concentration for collecting data.)

Under the Constitution of the State of Texas, the county is obligated to provide assistance to its indigent legal residents. Therefore, the county generally funds emergency financial assistance programs for the indigent within the county. However, county budgets vary in their commitment to emergency financial help. Cities vary widely in the amount and types of services provided directly by city agencies, and in the amount of money budgeted for the nonprofit agencies that are city-supported.

The local economy and industrial base affect the number of individuals in need of funded social services. Also, the location of the city and the types of jobs that are available affect the number of undocumented aliens migrating to the city and subsequently needing assistance.

Data Collection

Two approaches were used to identify the costs to the various governmental bodies of social services for undocumented aliens: document research and face-to-face or telephone interviews. State, city, and county budgets and program descriptions were examined for information about programs and their costs. Public administrators, administrators of nonprofit agencies receiving public funds, and social workers in both public and private agencies were interviewed for further cost and background information, to determine eligibility standards, and for estimates of the number of undocumented workers using the services.

SOURCES OF PUBLIC FUNDING FOR SOCIAL SERVICES IN TEXAS

Social services in Texas are funded by state agencies, city, county, and other local taxing authorities. The largest source of funding for social services, by far, is the Texas Department of Human Resources. However, five other smaller state agencies which were examined, the Commissions for the Blind, Deaf, Employment, and Rehabilitation, and the Texas Department of Community Affairs, are also important sources of assistance for social services in the state. This section will describe the major funding sources, their programs, the amounts devoted to various programs, and the eligibility requirements that might affect the use of the services by undocumented aliens.

State Funding for Social Service Programs

Texas Department of Human Resources (TDHR). Five TDHR-administered or supported services were examined to determine their use by undocumented aliens during the course of this study: the Food Stamp Program, Aid to Families with Dependent Children (AFDC), Child Protective Services (Child Welfare), Day Care, and the Family Violence Program.

These programs were selected and included in the study because they were funded with a significant proportion of state money and/or they have eligibility requirements which allow non-citizens to receive the service. The Food Stamp Program was included because of its prominence as a social program, even though the State of Texas is only an administrative agent for the program and not a contributor of funds (except for 50 percent of the administrative costs).

1. Aid to Families with Dependent Children (AFDC). AFDC receives significant funding from the State of Texas. For FY'82, Texas paid 45.87 percent of the total AFDC bill of $140.9 million, with the federal government absorbing the rest.

Being eligible for AFDC allows a family to receive several other state-sponsored social services, such as food stamps, Medicaid, employment services and day care. By determining the use of AFDC by undocumented aliens, it was thought possible to gain an insight into the proportion of the undocumented using these other programs.

AFDC's goals and objectives are to provide financial support to families who are deprived of support because of the absence or disability of one or both parents. AFDC also funds a foster care program (administered by the Protective Services Branch of TDHR) which protects abused and neglected children who are eligible for AFDC but have been removed from their homes by court order.

To be eligible for the AFDC program requires that children be either citizens of the United States or aliens lawfully admitted for permanent residence. Children must also be residing with a relative with the required degree of relationship, and this relative and the child must be residents of the State of Texas. Citizen children of undocumented aliens are eligible to receive AFDC benefits. Eligibility is determined for every applicant at an interview with a local TDHR intake worker. From information received from the state office of TDHR, the average grant for FY'82 for one person in a family was $34.52, with the average family size generally consisting of one parent and two or three children. This brings the usual payment within an estimated range of between $102.56 and $138.08 per month. Each person in the family is also entitled to two $50-a-year payments to purchase clothing and other essentials.

Although no precise data are kept on undocumented aliens applying for or receiving AFDC, it appears that very few attempt to receive benefits. It is the general feeling of TDHR regional directors that the number of undocumented persons receiving AFDC for their families is not significant. TDHR has an extensive quality control branch which evaluates the AFDC Program (and the Food Stamp Program), and the control reports show a very slight error for questions of citizenship and alien status (see Table F.1).

The figures for Table F.1 are taken directly from the state AFDC quality control reports produced by TDHR for the time periods of October 1981 through September 1982. The category or element of error is listed as number 160 in the reports under the heading of citizenship and alienage error. This category lists the number of cases in error (determined from a statewide sample) due to client failure to meet the citizenship or alienage requirements.

In the period October 1981 through March 1982, the number of cases reported in error within the statewide sample was 1 out of 1,159. In the period from April 1982 through September 1982, the number of cases found to be in error were 2 out of 1,233 cases sampled statewide. These cases made up approximately 0.1 percent of the total sample. It was calculated that these three cases cost the state $209, of which Texas pays only 45.87 percent.

If a range of 0.1 to 1.0 percent is assumed to be the approximate number of undocumented aliens using AFDC, and it is assumed the average AFDC family has three to four members, a figure can be calculated for an approximate statewide estimate of payments to undocumented aliens (see Table F.2). It should be emphasized that these figures are approximations. The range 0.1 to 1.0 is an estimation on the high side based on the quality control reports and telephone interviews with intake workers. Because it is difficult to determine the average length of time families remain on AFDC, costs were estimated for a twelve-month period. This can only be considered a rough guideline for estimating purposes.

TDHR does keep statistics on families having a parent or guardian classified as an ineligible alien of a citizen child receiving AFDC. An ineligible alien is defined generally as a citizen who is not lawfully admitted for residence.

Table F.1

FY'82 AFDC Figures from State Quality Control Reports

STATEWIDE:

# of families on AFDC monthly average	# of recipients monthly average	Total Payments
93,399	287,275	$118,979,340

Total State dollars spent on AFDC for FY'82, $140,905,979; 54.13% federal money, 45.87% state money

Regions	# of cases of error from illegal alienage Oct. 1981 through March 1982		# of cases of error from illegal alienage April 1982 through Sept. 1982	
9 (San Antonio)	0		0	
11 (Houston)	0		1 case	Amount in error $62
6 (Austin)	0		0	
8 (McAllen)	1 case	Amount in error $62	1 case	Amount in error $85
5 (Dallas)	0		0	
03/12 (El Paso)	0		0	
State total for period	1 case	Amount in error $62	2 cases	Amount in error $147

Source: TDHR, quality control reports, October 1981–September 1982.

Amount in error is the cost to the state, but this does not include administrative costs.

Table F.2

Estimated Cost to the State for AFDC Payments to Undocumented Aliens

---

These figures include only payments, and do not include administrative costs, e.g., worker time.

93,399 is the state-estimated, monthly average of the number of families on AFDC (this figure comes from the TDHR FY'82 Annual Report).

Estimated number of cases receiving AFDC payments is 0.1% of the monthly average (this was estimated from the higher rate of error recorded in the quality control reports).

<u>0.1% of 93,399 = 93 families of undocumented aliens estimated receiving AFDC. $34.52 is average payment to 1 person.</u>

With a Family of 3	With a Family of 4
For 3 people payment = $103.56/Mo.	For 4 people payment = $138.08/Mo.
(93) X $103.56 = $9,631.08 per month for state	(93) X $138.08 = $12,841 per month for state
$9,631 X 12 months = $115,573 cost to the state for the year	$12,841 X 12 months - $154,097 cost to the state for the year

The State of Texas, however, pays only 45.87% of these costs, as the federal government pays 54.13% of the payments through Title XX money.

Costs are then estimated for the state at:

$53,013 for the year if all families have 3 recipients $70,684 for the year if all families have 4 recipients

---

Source: Calculated from TDHR provider estimates and quality control reports, October 1981-September 1982.

In this situation, the child is entitled to AFDC payments because of citizenship, but the ineligible parent receives no payment. This of course is different from the regular AFDC situation where the parent receives a monthly payment along with the children. In the time period between January and April of 1982, only 0.5 percent of the total AFDC cases in the state were coded under this heading.

2. Food Stamp Program. Although the Food Stamp Program is totally federally funded, half of the administrative costs of the program are carried by the State of Texas.

TDHR intake workers are required to verify a person's claim to be a U.S. citizen, if it is at all questionable. Alien status also must be verified before a person can be certified as eligible; however, alien status verified for AFDC grants can also be used for food stamps. Citizen children of undocumented aliens are eligible to receive food stamps.

As with AFDC, the Food Stamp Program is administered at local TDHR offices, and eligibility is determined by the intake worker using state and federal guidelines.

It is difficult to determine how many undocumented aliens are receiving food stamps, although TDHR maintains a quality control program, similar to the AFDC program, which samples for citizenship and alienage error.

Table F.3 shows figures taken from the quality control reports for the time period from October 1981 through September 1982.

In the period from October 1981 through March 1982, the number of citizenship or alienage cases reported in error were 3 cases, or 0.2 percent of the total sample of 1,141 cases statewide. In the period from April through September 1981, there were 7 cases of this type of error, or 0.6 percent of the 1,193 cases sampled.

Using the 0.6 percent figure, a rough estimate of the dollar payments of food stamps to undocumented aliens per month can be made (see Table F.4). The 0.6 percent figure was chosen because it was the highest figure on the quality control reports, and because it fit the estimations of most of the intake workers interviewed. The final payment figure in Table F.4 includes costs to the federal government, which pays for the food stamps, as well as 50 percent of the administrative costs for the state. The state's costs are then the administrative costs of processing and serving 7,139 people a month.

TDHR last year carried out a study in conjunction with the U.S. Department of Agriculture (USDA is the federal agency responsible for the Food Stamp Program) to determine the use of food stamps by Mexican nationals. The bulk of the study took place between June 28 and July 9, 1982, and the counties sampled were: Cameron, El Paso, Hidalgo, and Webb, all on the

Table F.3

FY'82 Food Stamp Program Figures

Statewide: # of participants on food stamps, monthly average: 1,189,855

Food stamp value for FY'82: $548,057,320

Regions	# of cases of error from illegal alienage Oct. 1981 through March 1982		# of cases of error from illegal alienage April 1982 through Sept. 1982	
9 (San Antonio)	1 case	Amount in error $52	0	
11 (Houston)	0		2 cases	Amount in error $135
6 (Austin)	0		0	
8 (McAllen)	0		5 cases	Amount in error $240
5 (Dallas)	1 case	Amount in error $44	0	
03/12 (El Paso)	0		0	
State total for the period	3 cases, from the entire state during this period. Amount in error $140[1]		7 cases	Amount in error $375

Source: TDHR, quality control reports, October 1981-September 1982.

Food Stamp payments are funded 100% by the federal government.

Administrative costs are 50% federal and 50% state.

[1]These totals are for the entire state; of these, only 2 cases occurred in the 6 regions surveyed.

Table F.4

Estimated Statewide Food Stamp Payments to
Undocumented Aliens in Texas for FY'82

$42.91 = average food stamp payment per person per month
$142.92 = average family payment per month
$60 million = average total benefits statewide per month
1,189,855 = average monthly participants in the food stamp program
.6% X 1,189,855 = 7,139 undocumented aliens receiving food stamps
per month
7,139 X $42.91 = $306,344 dollars per month to undocumented aliens[1]

State TDHR estimates that: 28% receive benefits 6 months or less
9.5% receive benefits 6 months to 1 year
9.2% receive benefits 1 to 1-1/2 years
8.5% receive benefits 1 to 2 years
13% receive benefits 2 to 3 years
The remainder for longer periods

Source: Calculated from TDHR quality control reports, 1982.

[1]The State of Texas pays 50 percent of the administrative costs for
this program.

Mexico-U.S. border. In home visits to 602 recipient households (2,303 individuals) selected in a random statistical sample, it was found that only 1 Mexican national was improperly certified for participation in the Food Stamp Program. The study concluded that less than 1 percent of ineligible Mexican nationals were certified for participation in the program.

Based on the conclusions from this study, on interviews with intake workers, and on the quality control reports from TDHR, alien participation probably makes up less than 1 percent of the total food stamp population.

3. Protective Services for Children (Child Welfare). The Protective Services for Abused and Neglected Children Program, or to use the more common term, Child Welfare, is designed to protect children from harm by their parents or others responsible for their care. This protection takes the form of ongoing services to children and their families in the child's own home as well as foster care services for children whose home situation is intolerable.

Eligibility for these services is not limited to citizens or those who meet income requirements. All children and their families may receive these services, if the need for protective services is documented. The exception is with the foster care program. Foster care is administered at the county level, with the TDHR worker acting for both the state and the county welfare board. Most foster care clients are able to receive AFDC benefits, with the AFDC program of TDHR reimbursing the county for the cost of foster care.

However, in the case of an undocumented alien child, who is not a citizen and so does not qualify for AFDC, the county must pay the entire foster care cost and this is not reimbursed by the state (see Table F.5). If the family is detained by the Border Patrol, and the child or children are placed in temporary foster care or emergency shelters provided by the county, the cost of the stay and care is reimbursed by the federal government. Families in this situation are not included in Table F.5.

The figures in Table F.5 showing the costs to the various counties are based, in part, on state guidelines. The state sets the rates for the amount of money paid for a child in foster care. The county also follows these guidelines as the state and county are essentially working partners in this area. The reimbursement rate is $7 per day for children up to 9 years old, $8 a day for age 10 to 18, and $12 to $46 a day for exceptional cases. Using $7.50 as the average cost per child, the yearly cost comes to $2,738 per child.

As indicated in Table F.5, El Paso figured an additional 4 percent for medical, clothing, and incidental expenses, raising the average to $2,933 per year. The addition of 4 percent is realistic, given that the state requires a medical and dental examination for a child at some point during the year. The examinations, as well as clothing costs, are absorbed by the county in the case of the undocumented child.

The expenses listed for Hidalgo County were estimated to be $2,604 per child, because these children were under ten years of age and the $7 figure was used. The children in Dallas County received funds for medical costs, bringing that total to an estimated $5,400 for the year.

In the Own-Home Protective Service Programs (see Table F.6), the figures on the number of undocumented aliens estimated are based on the memories of intake workers at the county or regional offices. TDHR does not keep statistics on the average costs of providing these services to families or individual children. This is because the services are individualized for each family and child and costs vary considerably. Average cost figures in this study, therefore, can only be rough estimates. The figures were determined by dividing the number of clients served during FY'82 by the total budget.

Having interviewed TDHR welfare workers in all of the regions covered by the current study, estimates show that only a small percentage of undocumented aliens use Own-Home Services or the Foster Care Program.

4. Day Care. Day Care is one of the variety of social service programs brought together in September 1981 under the umbrella of the Family-Self Support Services Program. Day Care services for eligible families are purchased by the state from public or private agencies, centers, individual day care homes, or group home providers. State day care slots are provided for families, so that parents may train for and maintain employment. Day care centers are also used by the state to prevent abuse and neglect of children; children are frequently referred to these state-contracted day care centers by the Protective Service Branch. State day care is also provided for low-income families not receiving other state or federal benefits.

Table F.5

Estimated Costs for Protective Services-Foster Care for Undocumented Children in 1982

(6 Counties)

Region	County	# of Children in County Foster Care FY'82	Undoc. Children in County Foster Care %	Undoc. Children in County Foster Care #	Average Cost of Child to the County Year	Comments
03/12	El Paso	187	4	7	$2,933	Children in foster care for a year. Figure includes a 4% medical fee for each child.
5	Dallas	510	Less than 1%	1	$5,400 Actual Cost From County Office	Child in care for a year. Had extra medical expenses.
11	Harris	1,500	1	20	$2,790	This does not include medical costs to county.
9	Bexar	--	0	0	0	In last 15 years there has probably not been one. There were 8 undoc. children this year, taken by county, but Border Patrol reimbursed.
6	Travis	--	0	0	0	No undoc. in foster care in FY'82.
8	Hidalgo	80	7.5%	6	$5,478	Undoc. under care for the year. Does not include medical costs. Others, however, paid by Border Patrol.

Source: Provider interviews.

100 percent of the costs of these children are absorbed by the county.
Total costs to the counties, not including medical or administrative costs, are: El Paso, $20,531; Dallas, $5,400; Harris, $55,800 for year, $27,900 for 6 Mos.; Bexar, 0; Travis, 0, Hidalgo, $32,868. (Add 4% to these if medical costs are to be estimated.)

Table F.6

Protective Services: Own—Home or Ongoing Services

County	Approximate # of Cases per County	Cases of Undoc. Families or Children for Year %	#
Dallas	5,490	.3	20
Hidalgo	1,527	8.0	128
Bexar	3,270	0	0
El Paso	1,573		
Harris	8,545	1.0	100[1]
Travis	1,423	0	0

State's Total Budget = $70,386,551 (includes foster care).

Clients served in an average month (August 1982) = 66,418.

Funding sources: 60% federal; 35-40% state; 5% local.

Source: Provider interviews.

[1]Children of illegal parents—children may be citizens.

Income eligible and protective service cases are not asked to provide documentation of citizenship or legal alien status. AFDC recipients using day care have, of course, already established their eligibility along AFDC guidelines.

Funding for the Day Care Program for FY'82 was $30 million, of which about 48 percent came from federal Title XX money, about 44 percent from state revenues, and about 7 percent from local funds.

Estimates given by TDHR workers and local day care centers indicate that only a small percentage of undocumented aliens are using this service. Those that are receiving services fit into the income eligible category. Because strict proof of status is not required, these figures are only estimates (see Table F.7).

In Table F.7 the average cost per child per day was provided by the individual day care centers which were a sample of the funded centers in each city. The average statewide rate provided by TDHR was $8.40 to $8.75 for FY'82, and this range was used to build up the state figure (see Table F.8).

Yearly budget figures were also provided by the individual centers, or, in the case of certain San Antonio centers, by the City of San Antonio Human Resources Department. Each city in the survey has many day care centers or organizations. The survey attempted to sample the organizations or centers in each location with the largest number of day care slots funded by public money. Fiscal years did differ within these various centers, but it was felt that the figures given provide a fairly stable overall average for the number of children and the average expenses. Average length of stay in these centers is undetermined, hence a twelve month range is provided. The average number of TDHR funded children in day care in a month in FY'82 was 13,685.

Because the undocumented aliens who send their children to day care do so because they are income eligible, most pay the center between 2 percent and 4 percent of their gross monthly income per week. This lessens the cost to the state to a small degree, but is not reflected in the table estimates.

5. Family Violence Program. The Family Violence Program is a cooperative effort between TDHR and local community-supported, nonprofit shelters. These centers provide immediate protecton and other services to adult victims of family violence. Children and other household members who are potential victims are also protected at these shelters, and violent family members are helped to establish nonviolent behavior through counseling. These centers are generally equipped with facilities for between 15 and 30 women and their families. Many have counseling, psychological, and legal services for the benefit of the clients.

Any adult who is subjected to physical force or the threat of physical force by another family member, a former spouse, or a person residing in the same household is eligible. There are no legal residency requirements.

Table F.7

TDHR-Funded Day Care

(Sampled Centers in Surveyed Areas)

Region	Estimates of Undoc. Children %	Avg. Cost Per Month	6 Month Costs Cost to DHR	6 Month Costs Local Cost	12 Month Costs Cost to DHR	12 Month Costs Local Cost
Travis County	4	$238	$31,987	$7,997	$63,974	$15,994
Dallas County	5	$299	$19,770	Unknown	$39,540	Unknown
El Paso County	17	$163	$30,553	$5,164	$61,106	$10,328
	0.8	$193	$ 4,574	$695	$9,148	$1,390
Harris County	0.9	$213	$13,036	Unknown	$26,071	Unknown
	39	$185	$52,059	$22,311	$104,118	$44,622
Hidalgo County	6	$216	$ 6,921	Unknown	$15,841	Unknown
Bexar County	2	$153	$ 1,689	Unknown	$3,378	Unknown

Source: Provider interviews.

Table F.8

Cost of Undocumented Aliens in TDHR Day Care

to the State of Texas

3 Months	6 Months	12 Months
$535 X 821[1] = $439,235	$1,071 X 821[1] = $879,291	$2,210 X 821[1] = $1,814,410
$131,770 = approximate cost for 3 mo. period	$263,787 = approximate cost for 6 mo. period	$544,323 = approximate cost for 12 mo. period

TDHR money for day care is 70% federal and 30% state.

Source: Provider interviews.

[1]821 figure is calculated from 6 percent estimate of the undocumented, using day care of the 13,685 monthly average day care population.

For FY'82, with a total state budget of $792,000, a total of $300,000 was funded by the state, and $492,000 by federal Title XX money.

From shelter estimates, it appears that only a very small proportion of undocumented aliens use this service (see Table F.9). The estimates of undocumented persons were provided by the shelter administrators, although several administrators were unable to estimate the number or percentage of undocumented aliens, and only provided statistics regarding their clients' ethnic background. The numbers include residential clients only, and omit telephone or walk-in counseling.

There is no shelter in Hidalgo County or McAllen. The nearest one, in Brownsville, houses only 8 women with their children at any one time, and was not included in the survey.

Texas Commission for the Deaf (TCD). The goal of the Texas Commission for the Deaf is to develop and implement a statewide program to ensure continuity of services to the deaf. In addition to central administration, there are four major program areas: Direct Services Program; Special Services Program; Interpreter Development Program; and Community Assistance and Resource Development Program.

Virtually 100 percent of the costs (estimated at $773,594 for FY'82) are paid for out of the state general revenue fund. The only requirements for using this service are that the recipient be deaf (or hearing-impaired) and residing in Texas. Despite the lack of rigid eligibility requirements, agency personnel maintain that use of this service by illegal aliens is almost zero. This is a result of the rather low profile of the TCD, and the fact that the services provided by the Commission are not of a life-and-death nature.

Texas State Commission for the Blind (TSCB). The Texas State Commission for the Blind is the state agency with primary responsibility for providing "all services to visually handicapped persons except welfare services and services for children provided by regularly established agencies and state authorities" (Texas Administrative Code). The Commission provides services to adults under the Vocational Rehabilitation Program and services to children under the Visually Handicapped Children's Program.

About 75 percent of the costs (estimated at $15,973,140 for FY'82) are paid for out of federal funds. Agency personnel explained that in order to utilize the TSCB service a recipient must prove he is legally residing in Texas. A social security card is the usual means of identification. The use of this service by undocumented persons is believed to be very low. TSCB is a small agency with a low profile. For four years, until FY'82, there was a migrant worker program, administered out of a TSCB office in the Rio Grande Valley area (in Laredo). The total cost of this program, borne entirely by the federal government, was $200,000. Lorenzo Garcia, the person in charge of this program, believes that its use by illegal aliens was almost zero.

Texas Rehabilitation Commission (TRC). The Texas Rehabilitation

Table F.9

Family Violence Program

Location	Number of Families Served	% Undocumented Served	Avg. Cost Per Family	Total Budget	Funding Source (%)		
					State	City	County
Austin	176 families resident (900 people directly counseled)	1-3	$123	$176,376	27	21	19
Dallas	155	No estimates	$2,323	$360,000	19	--	--
El Paso	250 families	Less than 5	$360	$90,000	47	--	1
Houston	210	No estimates	$880	$185,000			
San Antonio	267	2	$881	$235,488	a	24	--

Source: Provider interviews.

aInformation unavailable.

Commission is the principal state agency for matters relating to the rehabilitation of handicapped and disabled individuals (except those with visual disabilities), and provides handicapped citizens with services that will enable them to enter or return to gainful employment. It has two main divisions: the Vocational Rehabilitation Program and the Disability Determination Division.

About 80 percent of the costs (estimated at $84 million for FY'82) are paid for out of federal funds. The bulk of the state's costs for the TRC fall under the Vocational Rehabilitation Program. This program includes the following subprogram areas: academic/vocational training; orthopedic; alcohol; mental health; development of on-the-job training; medical programs; neuromuscular disabilities; arthritis; diabetes; respiratory diseases; hearing-impaired; mental retardation; and worker's compensation.

The use of Vocational Rehabilitation Program services by handicapped and disabled individuals cannot be refused because of lack of state residence. U.S. citizenship (or papers providing legal permission to be in the U.S., such as a work permit) is required. A social security card is the usual means of identification. Agency policy explicitly dictates that "illegal aliens (individuals present in the United States without legal status) are not eligible for VR services."* Thus, the use of TRC services by undocumented persons is presumed to be very low--a judgment confirmed by our survey of TRC offices in most of the six regions covered in this study. Only one regional director went so far as to explain that some illegal aliens had actually asked for services. This information was received from Harlingen; the respondent claimed that from 50 to 75 illegal aliens request TRC services each year, but that the service was not given because these persons were unable to satisfy the identification requirement.

Texas Employment Commission (TEC). The Texas Employment Commission's general responsibilities include:

1. the operation of an employment service program. The major employment service is an automated job placement system;

2. the operation of an unemployment insurance program; and

3. the development of labor market information and related data for the valid assessment of personnel problems and the promotion of overall economic development and stability.

The federal government is responsible for all (100 percent) of TEC's costs, estimated at $117,178,583 for FY'82. Applicants must be here legally.

---

*Texas Rehabilitation Commission, TRC RSM No. 02-4, Revised May 1, 1982, pp. 25-26.

Migrant applicants must show a work permit (e.g., an IB-151). Without such documentation an applicant will be denied service.

Despite the fact that the state bears no cost for TEC's functions, it is worth noting that there may be some illegal aliens utilizing the Migrant and Seasonal Farm Workers Program of the Commission, although program personnel at the state office say that the numbers are believed to be small. Statewide, for regional offices which were surveyed, this same theme (no use of TEC services by illegal aliens) was echoed by regional directors.

Texas Department of Community Affairs (TDCA). The Texas Department of Community Affairs, working out of a single, administrative office in Austin, provides a broad range of services designed to aid communities in the delivery of essential public services. It also coordinates federal and state programs affecting local governments, and informs state officials and the public about the needs of local governments.

The TDCA has seven divisions: Local Government Services; Children and Youth Services; Drug Abuse Prevention; Economic Opportunity; Housing; Employment and Training; and Migrant Services. At least 95 percent of the funds (estimated at $44,068,788 for FY'82) are from federal sources. Only the first three of the divisions mentioned above have enough substantial state support to warrant our concern.

Local Government Services. This division distributes monies for improving the governments of Texas' towns and cities--especially the smaller ones. There is no money from this division directly affecting illegal aliens.

Drug Abuse Prevention. This division currently has $150,000 of state revenue in its budget (for FY'83). Agency personnel stated that no citizenship requirement is attached to any of their dozens of contracts. Based on experience for other services, we estimate that between one and five percent of this money is going toward servicing illegal aliens. In dollar terms, this translates to a total of from $1,500 to $7,500 for the six regions.

Children and Youth Services. This division is the largest state-supported division of TDCA. For FY'82, the state contribution totaled over $900,000. Table F.10 gives detailed information on the division. The table contains estimates for programs that take place (in full or in part) in one or more of our six regions. The use of services by illegal aliens may be somewhat higher than the general estimate in border towns, and somewhat lower in the northern part of the state. Percentages were extrapolated after obtaining estimates from the authorities concerned.

Conclusion. The major programs funded at the state level by the Department of Human Resources, and the five smaller agencies discussed, are frequently delivered at the local level by city or county governments or by contracted, nonprofit agencies. The next section of the paper will describe funding at the city and county level for social services.

Table F.10

Texas Department of Community Affairs

Children and Youth Services Division

Participating Contractors	Communities Impacted	Estimated State Cost for Providing Services to Illegal Aliens[1]
Regional Network for Children, Inc.	Austin	$133
San Antonio Coalition for Children, Youth, and Families	San Antonio	$270
Texas Coalition for Juvenile Justice	Dallas, San Antonio, and Houston	$160
Trinity Coalition, Inc.	El Paso	$308
Center for the Development of Non-Formal Education (CEDEN)	Austin	$350
Community Action Program – West	San Antonio	$100
Harlandale Independent School District	San Antonio	$305
Center for Battered Women	Austin	$165
Central East Austin Community Organ.	Austin	$145
Children's Heart Institute of South Tx.	Rio Grande Valley	$320
Mental Health and Mental Retardation Authority of Harris County	Houston	$290
Dallas Community College	Dallas	$220
Family Outreach of San Antonio	San Antonio	$ 90
Julia C. Hester House, Inc.	Houston	$160
Stoots' Learning Institute, Inc.	Houston	$150
Parents Anonymous of Texas, Inc.	El Paso, Austin	$250

(Table continued on next page)

(Table F.10, Continued)

Participating Contractors	Communities Impacted	Estimated State Cost for Providing Services to Illegal Aliens[1]
San Antonio Community College	San Antonio	$340
YWCA of El Paso	El Paso	$370
American Humanics, Inc.	Rio Grande Valley	$200
Total		$4,326

Source: Texas Department of Community Affairs, Children and Youth Services.

[1]Costs are based on a figure that is 2 percent of the entire TDCA grant to the contractor, and not 2 percent of the total costs for the given participating contractors. If a given participating contractor receives grants from other state agencies, then there is an additional cost burden imposed on the state for serving illegal aliens.

REGIONAL AND LOCAL FUNDING FOR SOCIAL SERVICES IN TEXAS

Overview of City-Sponsored Social Services. City governments sponsor social services through direct provision of programs as well as providing funding assistance to nonprofit agencies in the community.

1. Direct Services. Directly provided programs varied in each of the areas surveyed. Austin, for example, provides emergency food and clothing, job referrals, and assistance with applications and forms for other government services (income taxes, immigration papers, food stamp applications) at its multipurpose centers. San Antonio has an extensive city-operated and funded Youth Services Project that operates out of both multipurpose centers and other locations in the city. Dallas provides employment services for teenagers and adults. Some cities operate nutrition programs for the elderly. Eligibility for city services is generally based on need and not on citizenship status; however, if a program receives federal funds, federal eligibility requirements may be imposed.

Except for McAllen, the major cities in our study each operate one or more multipurpose and neighborhood centers that provide social services to the community. Multipurpose centers are built with federal funds but are operated with city funding. City expenditures are primarily for administrative and maintenance costs, but, as in Austin, direct services may be provided by center staff.

The centers can bring a variety of public and private agencies and social services into a single delivery system. They may house food stamp and AFDC intake offices, food pantries, counseling services, CETA program offices, senior luncheon programs, tutoring programs, youth services, energy assistance programs, information and referral services, and a variety of other community services. Eligibility requirements for programs at multipurpose centers depend upon each program's funding source; there may be strict standards, or only minimal eligibility requirements beyond the need for the services.

Dallas, Austin, Houston, and San Antonio all had functioning multipurpose centers in FY'82; El Paso had finished constructing their multipurpose centers, but the programs that were operating in FY'82 were primarily recreational and educational.

2. Contracted Services. Most of the cities in our study contract with nonprofit social service agencies that provide programs to respond to local needs. Included among the programs that receive city funds in several of our sites are battered women's shelters, rape crisis centers, day care centers, Big Brothers/Big Sisters, and services for the elderly and retarded. Some cities also fund unique programs, such as San Antonio's Centro del Barrio, which provides comprehensive social services for residents of a restricted geographic area. (This program also receives federal funds.)

The cities vary in the number of social service agencies supported through general revenues. The City of El Paso does not contract for social services (although the County of El Paso does); the City of Austin funded 40 agencies in 1982, more than any other city. The City of Dallas funds comparatively few social services agencies, possibly because there is extensive private support for programs.

County-Sponsored Social Services. Again, both direct and contracted services are in operation.

1. Direct Services. The county is often responsible for coordination and delivery of the state/federal AFDC, Food Stamp and Protective Services Programs. The county generally appropriates funds from general revenues for AFDC and Protective Services. In addition, counties operate emergency financial assistance programs which take the form of rent payments, payments of utility or medical bills, transportation and bus passes, food or clothing, and cash payments. It should be noted that eligibility for financial assistance is usually based on legal residency. Most counties are strict in their enforcement of this standard. The counties vary widely in their budgets for emergency assistance.

2. Contracted Services. The counties, like the cities, often fund community-based social service agencies. However, counties tend to have lower levels of contract expenditures than cities. Bexar County funds only the Bexar County Mental Health-Mental Retardation programs; El Paso County funds a battered women's shelter and a center for the deaf; in contrast, Travis County in FY'82 funded 34 different social service programs.

Survey Results of the Six Regions under Study.

Region: Austin and Travis County.

1. City of Austin. The City of Austin provides social services through neighborhood centers. There are seven city neighborhood centers. Three of these are part of a multiservice delivery system and share facilities with health clinics. The other centers house only social service programs.

Programs offered at each neighborhood center vary with neighborhood need. Programs are developed by the director of each center in conjunction with that center's advisory board and the city's Coordinator of Neighborhood Offices and Centers. There are no eligibility requirements for these social service programs. Information about services and client loads is included in Tables F.11 and F.12.

2. Travis County. In FY'82, Travis County provided social services through its Emergency Assistance Program, its Rural Centers Program, and its Family Self-Help Program. Travis County's emergency assistance program is unique in that it is the only program of this type which does not consider citizenship an eligibility requirement.

Table F.11

City of Austin and Travis County

Social Service Programs

Agency	Total Budget	Funding Sources				Per Client Cost	Total Clients	% Undocumented
		% City	% County	% Other Local	% State			
Community Action Neighborhood Centers	$ 652,300	64	-	-	36	$7.96	81,996[1]	Undetermined
Emergency Assistance Program	$1,165,300[1] Groceries: $ 113,400 Utilities: $ 90,000 Rent: $ 67,500 Medical: $ 4,061 Transport: $ 2,743	-	100	-	-	$36.00 Average grant	8,667[1]	17.3 Hispanic
Rural Centers Program	$ 322,044	-	50	16	33	Varies with service	8,400	<1

Source: Provider interviews.

[1] Includes rural health program.

Table F.12

City of Austin--Neighborhood Centers

Center	# of Clients	Major Services Provided
Clarksville Neighborhood Center	242, original opening Sept., 1982 80% Black 15% Anglo 5% Hispanic	Services for the elderly; meals and transportation assistance; emergency assistance--food and clothing; information and referrals
East First Neighborhood Center	2,552 1,947 are Hispanic, 2% of these undocumented	Emergency assistance--food and clothing; information and referrals; assistance with forms and applications--eligibility; housing and employment referrals
Montopolis Neighborhood Center	2,416 1,066 are Hispanic, 5% of these undocumented	Emergency assistance--food and clothing; housing referrals; information and referrals--city services; transportation assistance
Rosewood Neighborhood Center and Rosewood-Zaragosa Neighborhood Center (share Advisory Board)	40,690 12,066 are Hispanic, 0% undocumented reported	Housing referrals; community meeting facility; employment referrals; financial assistance--food and clothing
St. John's Neighborhood Center	5,598 1,074 are Hispanic, unknown percent undocumented	Senior Lunch Program; educational programs--tutoring; recreational programs; WIC; medical clinics; housing and employment referrals
South Austin Neighborhood Center	10,007	Emergency assistance--food and clothing; housing and employment assistance; transportation; assistance with forms and eligibility requirements

Source: Provider interviews.

The Rural Centers Program provides a variety of services in four rural centers. Services include social services--emergency food and clothing, housing and employment referrals, information and medical services.

The Family Self-Help program was designed to coordinate city and county services to decrease dependency on assistance programs. This program, which was funded only for FY'82, was primarily designed to decrease dependence on AFDC and Food Stamp programs.

Funding and client information for the Emergency Assistance and Rural Centers Programs is included in Table F.11.

3. City and County Contracts. Austin and Travis County provide more contracts to social service agencies than any other city or county in our survey. Services which receive city and county support through contracts include delinquency prevention programs, teenage parenting skills classes, assistance for the elderly programs, and employment programs. Agencies which met the funding guidelines stipulated for this study are described in Table F.13.

Region: Dallas and Dallas County.

1. City of Dallas. Direct social service programs sponsored by the City of Dallas focus on unemployment programs and the Martin Luther King, Jr. Community Center. The unemployment programs administered by the city receive federal funds and have Department of Labor eligibility criteria, which include citizenship. The city provides direct services and space for other governmental and nonprofit services at the King Community Center. Programs and funding information for the King Center are listed in Table F.14.

2. Dallas County. The Dallas County Department of Human Services has an emergency financial assistance program. This assistance program has citizenship eligibility requirements which are strictly enforced. However, assistance for illegal aliens is rendered through a private trust, the Orlean Fund. This fund is used to assist persons ineligible for county services and provides for food and clothing on a one-time basis. Table F.15 provides information on the Dallas city and county social service programs.

3. City and County Contracts. Although the City and County of Dallas do contract for a few social services, the majority of these contracts are state or federal grants which are administered locally. One example is the Dallas County Community Action Committee, Inc., which received 82 percent of its funds from state and federal allocations. The Community Development Division of the Dallas County Community Action Committee, Inc., supports five multipurpose centers and two community houses in the greater Dallas area. Services provided at the centers may include information and referral services, employment counseling, housing assistance, transportation services, recreational programs, and energy assistance programs. Three of the five directors of these multipurpose centers stated that their services were utilized by undocumented aliens. One director stated that possibly 10 percent

Table F.13

Austin and Travis County Social Service Contractors

Agency	Total Budget	Funding Sources % City	% County	Per Client Costs	Total Clients	% Undocumented
Big Brothers– Big Sisters	$145,291	24	14	$316.54	459	1% 0-5 clients
Caritas	$225,373	26	8	$ 15.99	12,000, 6,400 families	5%
Rape Crisis Center	$104,145	37	20	Contact, $ 34.00	300, 2,300 by phone	1%
Youth Employment Services	$ 84,911	70	12	$277.00	250	1%
Urban League	$639,130	5	0.8	Varies with service	800, 275 in job program	1%

Source: Provider interviews.

Table F.14

Programs at the Martin Luther King, Jr. Community Center

City of Dallas	Dallas County	Funding Sources			
		State and Federal	TEC	Nonprofit	Private
CETA Services	Dallas County Public Welfare	TDHR--includes food stamps, AFDC services, early periodic screening program, etc.	Children and Youth Project (youth svcs.)	Child Care Assoc. of Metropolitan Dallas	Warner Amex QUBE Cable of Dallas
General Intake-- Intake and Referrals					
City of Dallas Health Division				Dallas Alliance of Business	
Parks and Recreation				Dallas County Mental Health and Mental Retardation	
Dallas Public Library					
Senior Citizens Programs				WICS--Women in Community Svc.	
Utility Pay Station				Child Guidance	
Photocopying Services				Family Way	
Community Meeting Facilities					

Source: Provider interviews.

Table F.15

City of Dallas and Dallas County Programs

Agency	Total Budget	Funding Sources			Per Client Cost	Total Clients	% Undocumented
		% City	% County	% Federal			
Employment Programs	$234,262	45	-	55 CETA	Varies with service	3,795	0
Youth Employment Program (summer)	$234,627	58	-	42 CETA	Varies	1,638	0
King Community Ctr.	$470,000--includes some contract funds receipts				Unknown	Unknown	Unknown
Emergency Assistance Programs	$658,122	-	100	-	$222.86	2,953	0
Rape Crisis Center	$ 88,682	-	100	-	$ 56.05	1,582--includes direct & phone contacts	1

Source: Provider interviews.

of his client load of 3,000 for FY'82 were undocumented aliens. However, since no cost estimates were available per center, no estimates were made for the costs of services for undocumented aliens.

Region: El Paso and El Paso County.

1. City of El Paso. The City of El Paso's major social service programs are unemployment and training programs, and a large service program in the multipurpose centers. The unemployment program is cofunded by the federal government and carries citizenship eligibility requirements. (City personnel at all levels stressed that eligibility requirements in all programs were strictly enforced due to the proximity of the border.)

The multipurpose centers are administered by the Parks and Recreation Department of the City. In FY'82, although there were some information and referral services offered informally, the majority of the programs in these centers were recreational. Thus, client background information was not routinely collected and is not available.

2. El Paso County. El Paso County operates a general assistance program for legal residents with documented needs. This program provides assistance on a short-term basis only. Again, administrative personnel and caseworkers stated that eligibility requirements are strictly enforced.

Table F.16 presents information on the social service programs of El Paso City and County.

3. City and County Contracts. In FY'82, the City of El Paso funded eleven social service programs through its Community Development Block Grant. The County funded eight programs through its general revenues. Programs funded through the City include day care services, drug counseling and prevention programs, and some medical facilities. County-supported programs included the Battered Women's Center, child welfare programs, El Paso MH-MR, and some medical programs. Programs and funding information are included in Table F.17.

Region: Houston and Harris County.

1. Harris County. The Harris County Social Services Department has several programs designed to provide emergency assistance to the indigent. Financial assistance is available for those who are medically disabled and for those with extreme emergency needs such as eviction or utility cutoff notices. Other programs provide transportation for obtaining medical care, placement referral to community medical and social services, and burials for the indigent. Eligibility is based on legal residence in the county; undocumented aliens are referred to community agencies that do not have legal status requirements.

2. City of Houston. The City of Houston provides direct services

Table F.16

El Paso City and County Social Services

Agency	Budget	Funding Source		Client Cost	Total Clients	% Undocumented
		% City	% County			
Private Industry Council	_[1]	_[1]	_[1]	_[1]	_[1]	0
Community Recreation Centers	$1,090,531	100	0	_[1]	_[1]	_[1]
General Assistance	$ 402,500	0	100	$80.50	5,000	0

Source: Provider interviews.

[1]Information not available.

Table F.17

El Paso Area Social Service Contractors

Agency	Total Budget	Funding Source		Total Clients	% Undocumented
		% City	% County		
El Paso Youth Assistance:					
Counseling	$90,000	100 CDBG[2]	-[1]	102 families	0
Youth Employment	$130,000	100 CDBG[2]	-[1]	1,200	0
Child Guidance Center				1,140	
Rape Crisis Center	$36,830	100--all local funds; mix of city, co., & state--comes out of MH-MR funds		240	70% are Hispanic, 1% of these undocumented

Source: Provider interviews.

[1] Information not available.

[2] Community Development Block Grant.

through programs for the elderly, housing counseling, and neighborhood development. The city operates two multiservice centers, which serve as a physical base for city/county/state/private social services. Senior citizens are given special attention in multiservice center programs, and both centers have daycare programs. Each multiservice center has professional staff who administer and coordinate center programs, but do not have a direct service delivery role. Costs of providing services to undocumented aliens are not direct costs to this division, but are included in the costs of the agencies or programs that provide the direct services. Table F.18 lists the programs offered at the two multiservice centers.

The Community Development Division of the City of Houston Human Resources Department provides grants for private social service agencies in the community. The emphasis is on day care, services to the elderly, community development, and juvenile delinquency diversion. The city funds approximately ten private day care centers; seven programs for the aging; eight programs for youth, with emphasis on job training and development; and one social service program for AFDC recipients. Those private agencies with significant public funds are highlighted in Table F.19.

Private initiative in the social services area plays an important role in Houston. There are three major community centers operated by private and religious foundations that provide an array of services in response to the needs of neighborhoods. There is also an active Private Sector Initiatives group that stimulates and coordinates corporate involvement in job training and social services. These programs provide many of the direct services that in other cities are provided by public agencies. Their funding is primarily foundation money and donations, with minimum support from the city and state tax base.

Region: McAllen/Hidalgo County.

1. City of McAllen. The City of McAllen provides a limited amount of funding to private agencies for providing social services; however, no specific information on agencies funded was available to the public.

2. Hidalgo County. Hidalgo County budgeted $47,167.59 in 1982 for emergency assistance to indigent county residents. However, the services paid for are restricted to ambulance service and transportation to medical facilities outside the county for necessary medical care; $7,500 was budgeted for this purpose in 1982. As this service is not a social service, but rather medically related, and since the amount of direct cost is low, it is not included in our calculations.

Region: San Antonio and Bexar County.

1. Bexar County. Bexar County funds no social services other than the Child Welfare Program. The emergency assistance program in the area is operated by the City.

Table F.18

Programs Offered in the Houston Multiservice Centers

	FIFTH WARD	WEST END
City Operated	Civil Service Employment Information Housing Counseling Senior Nutrition	Neighborhood Services Nutrition Services
County Operated	Juvenile Probation	Juvenile Probation
State Operated	Rehabilitation Commission	
Privately Operated	Day Care	Day Care Comprehensive Services Vietnam Veterans Outreach

Source: Provider interviews.

Table F.19

Costs of Providing Social Services to Undocumented Aliens in Houston, Texas

Service	Funding			Total Budget	% Undocumented	Number Clients	Unit Cost
	% City	% County	% State				
Harris County Social Services:							
Emergency Assistance	-	100	-	$570,607	-[1]	6,463	$ 88.29
General Assistance	-	100	-	$677,000	-[1]	8,400	$ 80.60
City of Houston Community Development Grants Agencies:							
Big Brothers and Sisters[2]	16	-	16	$540,549	<1	600	$ 900.92
Cities in Schools	12	-	1	$600,000	-[1]	1,453	$1,238.82
Wesley Community Center[3]	-	-	-	-	40		$ 71.75[3]

Source: Provider interviews.

[1]No information available; administrators unable to estimate.

[2]32 percent of the funding is city and state money; breakdown is unknown, so 16% was assigned to each category.

[3]Specific budget data are unknown except for city grant.

2.   City of San Antonio.   The major direct service programs operated out of the Human Resources Department and funded out of general revenues of the City of San Antonio are: direct assistance payments to indigent city residents; juvenile delinquency diversion through the Youth Services Project; Family Care Providers, a home health service; and Senior Citizen Services.

The Community Centers Division operated two multiservice centers in 1982. Multiservice centers in San Antonio serve as a physical base for a variety of city/county/state/private social services.   The centers are each staffed with four city employees who serve in an administrative capacity.   Their role is to monitor the programs for which the multiservice centers have contracts; therefore, they do not provide direct services at any of the centers.   The staff occasionally will provide information and referral to walk-in clients, and may also get involved in special projects such as food distribution. Costs of providing services to undocumented aliens are not direct costs to this division, but are included in costs of the agencies that provide the direct services.   Table F.20 lists the programs offered at the two multiservice centers.

The City of San Antonio funds private agencies that provide social services to city residents.   The emphasis is on children, the aged, and special target groups, such as battered women and troubled youth.   The city funds eleven day care providers; one parent-child training program; several programs for the elderly; an alternative high school for students who have dropped out of public schools; Big Brothers and Sisters; a women's shelter; one general social services program for low-income residents of South San Antonio; a comprehensive mental health and counseling program in west and south San Antonio; and one juvenile prevention program that operates separately from the direct City Youth Services Project.   Private agencies with significant public funds are highlighted in Table F.21.

Table F.20

Programs Offered in the San Antonio Multiservice Centers

	<u>EASTSIDE</u>	<u>WEST END</u>
City Operated	Supportive Services for the Elderly Nutrition Program for the Elderly Family Resources Youth Services Project Community Action (federal grant)	Supportive Services for the Elderly Nutrition Program for the Elderly Family Resources Youth Services Project Parks and Recreation Community Action (federal grant)
County Operated	Juvenile Probation	Juvenile Probation
Privately Operated	Day Care Family Services	Day Care Avance Centro Cultural Aztlan

Source: Provider interviews.

Table F.21

Social Service Programs in San Antonio

| Program/Agency | Funding Sources | | | Total Budget | % Undocumented |
	% City	% State	% Federal		
San Antonio Dept. of Human Resources:					
Community Centers	97.5	1.2	1.3	$656,656	0
Family Resources	70.0	30.0	-	$756,963	0
Youth Services Project	90.5	9.5	-	$814,203	1
Family Care Providers	72.0	-	27.3	$392,290	0
Contracted Agencies:					
Avance	42.2	3.8	30.0	$237,410	4
Centro del Barrio	39.0	1.9	45.8	$744,309	0
Ella Austin Youth Advocacy	100.0	-	-	$153,000	0
Mexican American Unity Council	100.0	-	-	$368,798	Unknown
Big Brothers/Big Sisters	19.0	-	12.0	$120,000	0
Healy Murphy Learning Center	51.3	-	17.9	$433,271	1

Source: Provider interviews.

APPENDIX G

UNDOCUMENTED ALIEN STUDENTS IN TEXAS SCHOOLS

INTRODUCTION

There has been much debate over the past few years regarding the financial impact of the number of undocumented alien students in the public schools of Texas. The 1975 state provision forbidding the use of state funds to educate identifiable undocumented students contributed to the controversy. In September 1980, the U.S. District Court for the Southern District of Texas ("In Re: Alien Children Education Litigation") overruled this provision and ordered the school districts to admit all students living in their districts regardless of immigration status. The Supreme Court confirmed the District Court ruling. In light of these decisions, we seek here to make an estimate of the costs that each of our targeted districts, and the state as a whole, incur in providing educational services to undocumented students. The task is difficult, because the actual number of undocumented students is unknown. Since there is now no requirement for local school districts to ask for proper documentation of students at the time of enrollment, figures on the numbers of undocumented students are simply educated estimates by local school officials.

This report on the financial impact of undocumented students in Texas public schools is divided into four sections as follows:

I. Introduction (above). A presentation of the basic problems and the objectives of this appendix.

II. Background Information. An explanation of how school programs are funded in Texas as well as the methodology used in gathering the data on which our conclusions are based.

III. Program Breakdown. An exploration of the situation in each of the seven targeted cities, with the focus on estimates of numbers of undocumented students; funding sources; estimates of costs and benefits; and qualitative views of each district's unique circumstances drawn from local school officials' responses to the questionnaire sent to them.

IV. Conclusion. A summary of general impressions about the districts surveyed.

BACKGROUND INFORMATION

Our survey of undocumented alien students in Texas focuses on seven school districts: Austin, San Antonio, El Paso, McAllen, Brownsville,

Houston, and Dallas.   Each of these cities is assumed to contain
concentrations of undocumented aliens.

Revenues

Revenues for school districts come basically from three sources: (1)
state aid, (2) local ad valorem taxes, and (3) federal funds. The proportion
of these funds in past years for maintaining school programs in Texas is shown
in Table G.1.

Table G.1

Sources of Funding for Public Education in Texas

(percent)

Sources	School Year				
	1975–76	1976–77	1977–78	1978–79	1979–80
State Aid	47.9	44.8	47.8	48.2	48.8
Local Taxes	45.2	48.1	44.6	45.4	40.9
Federal Funds	6.9	7.1	7.6	6.4	10.3
TOTALS	100.0	100.0	100.0	100.0	100.0

Source: Billy Don Walker, Basics of Texas School Finance
        (Austin: Texas Association of School Boards, 1980), p. 20.

State Aid.   According to the 1949 Foundation School Program Act, the
Texas public school system has three objectives: (1) to provide a minimum
school program, (2) to maintain equality of education among school districts,
and (3) to ensure sufficient teachers.   The Foundation School Program (FSP)
allocation, comprising about 90 percent of all state aid, is based on the
number of students enrolled in school districts during the current school
year. Each school district, regardless of local property wealth, is entitled
to its share of this fund on a per capita basis.   In order to equalize funds
available to school districts, the state added equalization aid in 1975.
Under this program, additional funds are granted (up to $360 maximum per
child) to school districts whose property value per student is below the
statewide average plus 10 percent.

The state's resources for funding school programs come from three major
sources: (1) designated taxes, (2) interest on investments, and (3) general
revenues.

Revenues from Local Taxes. Local revenues are generated from uniform tax rates on the taxable value of property in the district. On the average, school districts levy $901 per student. Revenues from local taxes are allocated for three purposes: (1) local fund assignment (.0015 times the second index property value of the district as determined by the State Property Tax Board); (2) local enrichment; and (3) construction/indebtedness. Local school districts can levy additional property taxes to enrich the FSP in order to pay higher salaries and hire more personnel. Since federal and state funds are not used to finance capital outlays, school districts must issue bonds for school construction.

Federal Funds. Most of these funds are allocated for "target" programs, such as school lunch and breakfast programs, child nutrition, education for the handicapped, and occupational education.

Expenditures

School expenditures can be divided into five major categories: (1) general administration; (2) instructional services; (3) pupil services; (4) plant maintenance and operation; and (5) community services. Salaries and operating costs account for the lion's share of school expenditures. In 1981-82, spending by school districts for current operating expenses averaged $2,176 per student.

Methodology

In order to obtain the maximum information with which to make an estimate of the costs incurred by the State of Texas in dealing with undocumented alien children in its public schools, the various agencies involved in public education in Texas, as well as the school districts themselves, were contacted.

Initial research was based on data received from the Texas Research League, publisher of an annual compilation of educational statistics, Bench Marks for School District Budgets in Texas. The League uses information from the Texas Education Agency and Texas State Property Tax Board in compiling basic data, such as average daily attendance, student/teacher ratio, state and local funding for various programs, teacher salaries, and other information, for each district. Bench Marks* and the latest publication of the State Property Tax Board, which gives the property tax values for the targeted districts, provided basic data from which to develop further research.

----

*Texas Research League, Bench Marks for 1982-1983 School District Budgets in Texas (Austin, Texas, July, 1982).

Discussions with officials of the Texas Education Agency also provided details of total state aid, state aid per average daily attendance, state equalization aid, and the minimum cost of the educational program within the Foundation Program for each district. Data from the Texas Education Agency's own survey of estimated numbers of undocumented alien students in Texas public schools (completed October 1982) were also valuable.

The questionnaire sent to the school districts was designed to elicit the most relevant quantitative information (focusing on costs of minimum education programs, average costs of education per student, costs of special programs for Spanish-speaking students, amounts of aid received, and estimated numbers of undocumented alien students) as well as qualitative interpretations of the situation presented by the presence of undocumented alien students in the districts' schools. The questionnaires were sent to the school districts on January 27, 1983, along with copies of the authorizing letter from the Office of the Governor to expedite cooperation (see Annexes G.1 and G.2.)

PROGRAM BREAKDOWN

The following school district profiles are based on information from the responses to the questionnaires sent to the school districts. The monetary impact of the undocumented students is not calculated by every district, and when it has been calculated, monies coming into the district as a result of increased enrollment are not considered by the district in its response. In order to make an estimate of the financial impact of these students on each district, a formula was constructed which takes costs and benefits into consideration:

$$(A \times E) - ((S + F) \times E) = \text{Net Cost of Educating Undocumented Students}$$

Net Cost = Average Cost of Educating One Undocumented Student

A = Average cost of educating a child in the district
E = Estimated number of undocumented students in the district
S = Amount of state aid per average daily attendance (ADA) in the district
F = Amount of federal aid per ADA in the district

(See Table G.2 at end of this section.)

It should be remembered that the resulting costs are estimates, since the numbers of undocumented students given by the districts are estimates. When a district has not given an estimated number of undocumented students in its response to the questionnaire (as in the cases of El Paso, Dallas, and Brownsville), data from the Texas Education Agency's 1982 survey are used. Figures used for state and federal aid are the latest available (1981-82). Local fund assignment money which a district receives is not contingent upon the number of students in the district; rather, it is based on a percentage of the determined property value. Therefore, it is not included in the above formula.

The net cost figure calculated this way is an average cost per student. This may not reflect marginal costs, that is, the extra costs for meeting the needs of the undocumented students.

Austin

The Austin Independent School District estimates the number of undocumented alien students in its schools in 1982-83 to be 245 (up from its last estimate of 114 in 1980-81) out of an average daily attendance (ADA) of 50,175. This figure represents approximately 0.4 percent of the ADA. The number of undocumented students is obtained by combining the estimates from each local school. Information regarding the monetary impact of these students on the school, as well as their effect on the student/teacher ratio and general quality of education in Austin, is not given by the school district. However, when we use the formula of costs minus benefits, the net total cost of educating undocumented students in Austin is approximately $474,552. When this figure is divided by the estimated number of undocumented students, we estimate that the average cost of educating each of these students is $1,937 per year.

San Antonio

The estimated number of undocumented alien students in the San Antonio Independent School District in 1982-83 is 886 (estimates for previous years are not given) out of an ADA of 56,607. This figure represents approximately 1.5 percent of the ADA. The school district arrives at the number of such students by tabulating responses to its own School Survey Form. The monetary impact of undocumented students is estimated by the San Antonio I.S.D. to be $1,853,512. However, this figure does not consider benefits coming to the district due to increased enrollment. An adjusted average figure (using the formula above) is $919,446 total, or approximately $1,038 per undocumented student. Since this is an average and not a marginal figure, it does not imply that there would be savings of this amount if the undocumented children were not present. As to the impact of these students on the student/teacher ratio and general quality of education given in the San Antonio schools, the San Antonio I.S.D. states that there is no negative effect.

El Paso

The El Paso Independent School District does not give a current estimate of the number of undocumented students in its schools, and does not explain how the latest figure of 365, in 1980-81, was ascertained. However, in our calculations, we will use the number given in the TEA's 1982 survey, which was 627. This number represents approximately 1.03 percent of the current ADA of 60,431. The estimated net cost of educating such students is $378,288 total, or $603 per undocumented student. The district states that the number of undocumented students does contribute somewhat to its high student/teacher ratio of 23.1, although concrete supportive data are not given. In response to our questions about the transience of undocumented students, and the effect of this on the overall educational program, the El Paso I.S.D. replies that such information is not known. However, it is stated that the enrollment of undocumented students has no effect on the quality of education provided by the schools in El Paso.

McAllen

The McAllen Independent School District estimates the number of undocumented alien students in its schools in 1982-83 to be 1,100 (up from 1,050 in 1981-82, and 1,000 in 1980-81). This figure represents approximately 6.45 percent of the current ADA of 17,044, and was ascertained by counting the new undocumented students who register in the schools. The monetary impact of such students on the schools of McAllen is estimated to be $2,750,000 by the McAllen I.S.D., but possible monetary benefits from state aid due to increased enrollment are not taken into account. Our formula reveals that the net total cost of educating undocumented students is $751,531 total, or $683 per undocumented student. The presence of these students in the schools is believed by the McAllen I.S.D. to adversely affect the quality of education provided, because students arrive from Mexico throughout the school year with widely divergent educational backgrounds, and many are not adequately prepared to participate at their age level. This deficiency often affects the level of teaching in the classroom. McAllen has instituted a special Oral Language Program for non-English-speaking children which requires the services of twenty teachers. The McAllen I.S.D. states that undocumented alien children are highly transient. Of 824 students enrolled in the Language Development Program in 1981-82, 28.6 percent (236 students) moved out of the district during the school year.

Brownsville

According to the questionnaire response, the estimated number of undocumented alien students in the Brownsville Independent School District from August 23, 1982 to January 27, 1983 was 434 (compared to 791 for the school year 1981-82 and 833 for the school year 1980-81), as obtained from monthly reports of an attendance officer. However, the figure given in the 1982 TEA survey is 1,166, and we shall use that figure in the calculation. In terms of percentages, 1,166 is approximately 3.97 percent of the latest ADA of 29,336. The Brownsville I.S.D. does not estimate the monetary impact of such students on the schools, but the formula shows that the net cost of educating undocumented students is -$544,895 total, or -$467 per student (the minus sign is correct). If our formula is a realistic way of figuring costs, it seems that in Brownsville, monetary benefits outrun costs and that it is to the district's financial advantage to have such students in the schools.

The district states that local money that could be used for educational enrichment is currently obligated for the immediate construction of portable classrooms and other facilities. It is stated that the presence of undocumented students has a detrimental effect on the quality of education provided in that classrooms become more crowded (higher student/teacher ratios), decreasing the possibility of small group or individual instructional situations. In some classes, a morale problem often exists when teachers perceive that language and other skill deficiencies of undocumented students are insurmountable. The transience of these students is not a major problem, as the undocumented population in Brownsville is relatively stable. Only recently have more families become mobile (due to the peso devaluation).

Houston

The Houston Independent School District estimates the number of undocumented alien students in its schools in 1982-83 to be 5,202 (up from 4,078 in 1981-82, and 3,118 in 1980-81), which is approximately 2.96 percent of the current ADA of 175,700. This figure was ascertained by counting the number of students at each school lacking proper documentation. The monetary impact of these students is estimated by the Houston I.S.D. to be $14,000,000, but our formula makes it to be $9,787,147 total, or $1,881 per undocumented student. The presence of these students in the Houston schools is believed by the Houston I.S.D. to lower the quality of education provided. Undocumented students are highly transient; many move to and from different schools (both within the Houston I.S.D. and inter-district) during a given school year. According to the Houston I.S.D., this mobility often disturbs the stability of educational programs, and detrimentally affects the other children enrolled. The presence of such a large number of undocumented students (most of whom cannot speak much English) also necessitates the existence of special programs and instruction at a lower student/teacher ratio. As competent bilingual teachers are increasingly difficult to find, the problems are exacerbated.

Dallas

A large number of Hispanic students attend Dallas public schools, but their legal status is not determined by the Dallas Independent School District. Therefore, the Dallas I.S.D. response to our questionnaire makes no estimate of the number of undocumented alien students in the district. However, their response to the 1982 TEA survey puts the estimate at 1,515 undocumented students. This is approximately 1.31 percent of the latest

Dallas ADA of 115,246. The monetary impact of undocumented students is also not estimated by the Dallas I.S.D., but we estimate it to be $2,221,187 total, or $1,466 per undocumented student. It is stated that undocumented students tend to live in the same geographical area of the district (although this is true for many other low-income students as well). The presence of undocumented students is said to have no effect on the student/teacher ratio, or the quality of the overall educational program. A Baseline Curriculum, used throughout the district, helps to ensure continuity for all students.

CONCLUSION

It should be repeated that it is difficult to estimate how many undocumented alien students there are in the public schools of Texas. Schools are not under any obligation to ask for proper documentation when students enroll, and they must provide an education to all who are present. Most school districts admit that their estimates are rough indications of the real numbers, and that it would not be practicable to make more systematic counts.

It appears that there has not been a large increase in the number of undocumented alien students in Texas public schools in the wake of the 1980 U.S. District Court ruling. Most districts experienced slight yearly increases. Not surprisingly, the greatest concentrations of undocumented alien students are in the larger cities, where their parents are most likely to find employment. Houston has by far the most undocumented students (by their own estimation), followed by Dallas, Brownsville, McAllen, San Antonio, El Paso and Austin. The figures for San Antonio and El Paso seem to be on the low side, but there is no way to double check. Looking at percentages, undocumented students seem to comprise rather insignificant portions of the total student populations. McAllen leads our districts with 6.45 percent, and percentages for the other districts are much less. McAllen is followed by Brownsville, Houston, San Antonio, Dallas, El Paso and Austin.

The cost of education per undocumented alien student is greater in the large cities because the large cities generally have a greater local fund assignment (through having a greater index property value), and tend to have more of a commitment to providing above-average education. These more affluent districts do not qualify for as much state aid (especially equalization aid), and therefore must pay more than the small districts for the education of their undocumented students (as well as their native students). A burden is also placed upon the border districts as their property values tend to be low and therefore do not allow them to receive much local fund assignment money.

The average cost of providing educational services to undocumented alien students (using statistics from the targeted districts) is $1,020 per student, but this figure reflects a range of from -$467 in Brownsville to $1,937 in Austin. This average cost of education for undocumented students is significantly less than the statewide average of $2,176 (1981-82). The average total net cost to the districts is $1,998,179, but this is misleading because it takes Houston's huge net total cost of $9,787,147 into account.

Table G.2

Estimating Net Average Costs of Providing Education

to Undocumented Alien Children, by Independent School District

Formula: (Average cost per ADA (average daily attendance)
           x estimated undocumented students) -
           ((State aid per ADA + Federal aid per ADA)
           x estimated undocumented students)

School District	Calculations
Austin	(2,889 x 245) - ((832 + 120.05) x 245)= $474,552.75 (Net) 474,552.75/245 = $1,936.95 (Average Cost per Undocumented Student)
San Antonio	(2,092 x 886) - ((1,026 + 28.25) x 886) = $919,446.50 (Net) 919,446.50/886 = $1,037.75 (Average Cost)
El Paso	(1,867 x 627) - ((1,007 + 256.67) x 627) = $378,287.91 (Net) 378,287.91/627 = $603.33 (Average Cost)
McAllen	(1,966.16 x 1,100) - ((1,064 + 218.95) x 1,100) = $751,531 (Net) 751,531/1,100 = $683.21 (Average Cost)
Brownsville	(1,268.18 x 1,166) - ((1,420 + 315.50) x 1,166) = -$544,895.10[1] (Net) -544,895.10/1,166 = -$467.31[1] (Average Cost)
Houston	(2,691 x 5,202) - ((716 + 93.58) x 5,202) = $9,787,146.80 (Net) 9,787,146.80/5,202 = $1,881.42 (Average Cost)
Dallas	(2,433 x 1,515) - ((787 + 179.87) x 1,515) = $2,221,186.90 (Net) 2,221,186.90/1,515 = $1,466.13 (Average Cost)

Source: See text.

[1]The minus figures are correct.

With the exception of Dallas, all the other districts have total net costs of
under $1,000,000 (with Brownsville registering a negative net total cost).

The districts in general believe that the presence of undocumented alien children in the schools adversely affects the quality of education given (through increased student/teacher ratios in the regular classes, necessary individual attention in the bilingual and remedial classes, and deflection of educational enrichment money from qualitative program improvements towards the building and renting of additional classrooms and the hiring of additional teachers). Also, the comparative transience of undocumented children often disturbs the stability of established programs. However, there are financial offsets from state funds that come to the districts as a result of increased enrollment.

Annex G.1
Authorization Letter from Governor's Office

OFFICE OF THE GOVERNOR

WILLIAM P. CLEMENTS, JR.
GOVERNOR

November 30, 1982

Dr. Sidney Weintraub   Dr. Gilberto Cardenas
Dean Rusk Professor   Assistant Professor
L.B.J. School of Public Affairs   Sociology Department
Sid Richardson Hall 3.226B   Burdine Hall 458
University of Texas   University of Texas
Austin, Texas 78712   Austin, Texas 78712

Dear Dr. Weintraub and Dr. Cardenas:

I wish to confirm the support of the Office of the Governor for the
research which you are directing on the cost to the State of Texas to
provide services for undocumented aliens.

Under the agreement between the University of Texas and the State, the
research will seek to develop information both from the side of the
providers of public services at the state level and at various localities
in the state, and from the undocumented aliens who use these services. I
am confident that state and local officials responsible for providing
public services will give the researchers their full cooperation.

Sincerely,

Jarvis E. Miller

Jarvis E. Miller, Director
Governor's Budget and Planning Office

jc

Annex G.2
School District Questionnaire

10/25/82

Education--providers of services

I.   General

1.   What is the ADA for your district currently (1982-83)?

2.   What was the ADA for your district in:

a) 1981-82 _____

b) 1980-81 _____

c) 1979-80 _____

3.   What is the student/teacher ratio currently (1982-83)?

4.   What was the student/teacher ratio in:

a) 1981-82 _____

b) 1980-81 _____

c) 1979-80 _____

II. Funding

1.   What is the property value of your district? (assessed value used by district)

_____

2.   What was the property value in:

1981-82 _____

1980-81 _____

3.   What is the cost of the minimum program (within the Foundation Program) for your district?

_____

4.   Has this cost increased over the last three school years? By how much?

1981-82 _____   increase? _____

1980-81 _____   increase? _____

1979-80 _____   increase? _____

5.   Do you receive equalization aid from the state government?

How much? _____

6. Did you receive equalization aid from the state government in?

                                amount

    1981-82   _____

    1980-81   _____

    1979-80   _____

7. Indicate the dollar amount coming to your district:

	1982-83	1981-82	1980-81	1979-80
Federal government	_____	_____	_____	_____
State government	_____	_____	_____	_____

8. Are these funds restricted? Please explain.

9. What is the average cost of education per student in your district?

10. What is included in this cost?

11. Do you spend all of the funds that you receive? (Include all sources of government aid.)

III. Special Programs

1. What types of special programs do you have that are geared specifically to Spanish speaking students?

    Bilingual
    ESL
    Remedial Reading
    Others

2. How much do these programs cost?
    Bilingual
    Total   _____

    Per student   _____

    ESL
    Total   _____

    Per student   _____

    Remedial Reading
    Total   _____

    Per student   _____

Other

Total _____

Per student _____

3. Where do the funds for these programs come from? How much?

	Federal	State	Local
Bilingual	_____	_____	_____
ESL	_____	_____	_____
Remedial Reading	_____	_____	_____
Other	_____	_____	_____

4. Do you participate in the School Lunch, School Breakfast program?

	Yes	No
School Lunch		
School Breakfast		

5. Where do the funds for these programs come from? How much?

	Federal	State	Local
School Lunch.	_____	_____	_____
School Breakfast	_____	_____	_____

6. Have illegal alien students participated in any of these programs? How many?

Bilingual	_____
ESL	_____
Remedial Reading	_____
School Breakfast	_____
School Lunch	_____
Others	_____

7. Has their participation forced you to hire additional staff? Please explain.

8. Have you ever applied for the above programs and been refused? Which ones and why?

9. Have you never applied to any of these programs even though your district is eligible? Which ones and why?

IV. Space

1. Has there been a shortage of classroom space for the district in the last few years?

2. Is there currently a shortage of space? Why?

3. Do the illegal alien students contribute to the existing shortage of space?

4. How have you handled this problem and at what cost?

   portable/temporary classrooms _____

   rental of church buildings _____

   new construction _____

   other _____ _____

V. Subjective questions

1. How many illegal alien students enrolled in your district in:

   1982-83 _____

   1981-82 _____

   1980-81 _____

2. How do you estimate this figure?

3. Do the illegal alien students contribute to the high student/teacher ratio?

4. Are illegal alien students very transient? What has been your experience in the past? If they are transient, how does this affect the overall educational program?

5. Estimate the monetary impact on your schools of educating the illegal alien student. How do you figure this?

6. Does the enrollment of illegal alien students affect the quality of education that you are able to provide? If yes, how?

APPENDIX H

POLICE SERVICE UTILIZATION AND PRISON OCCUPANCY BY
UNDOCUMENTED PERSONS IN TEXAS

INTRODUCTION

In order to determine the cost to the six localities studied and make statewide assessments of the impact of the undocumented population on police services, one must consider three factors: (1) the percentage of the total population which is undocumented; (2) the amount of contact that police officers have with undocumented persons; and (3) the types of crimes in which undocumented persons are involved either as victims or suspects, and the cost of reacting to those crimes. Since a person's legal status is not a consideration in determining eligibility for the use of police services (as a victim or suspect), police departments do not normally keep records of such status. Thus, it is difficult to accurately gauge the impact of undocumented persons on the cost of police services.

To determine the cost to state and local governments of undocumented person occupancy of city and county jails, as well as state prisons, one must consider three other factors: (1) the number of undocumented persons who are inmates at each of these facilities; (2) the average duration per inmate; and (3) the average cost per inmate per unit of time. The unavailability of information on inmate legal status in all areas other than San Antonio and Bexar County makes it difficult to accurately gauge the impact of undocumented persons on the jail and prison systems.

This appendix provides a summary of the methodology used in data collection, and an overview of how the undocumented population is believed to affect the police services of the localities considered. It also provides an estimate of the occupancy level of city and county jails and state prisons by undocumented persons, and an estimate of the cost of occupancy at each governmental unit level.

BACKGROUND INFORMATION

Census Data

All census data are taken from the U.S. Department of Commerce's 1980 Census of Population. Undocumented population approximations are based on the techniques discussed in Chapter 3. The approximations are summarized in Tables H.1 and H.2.

Table H.1

Undocumented Population by City, 1982

City	Hispanic Pop.	/	Tot. Texas Hisp. Pop.	X	Bean & King Range Est.	=	Undoc. Pop. Est.[1]	Percentage Tot. Pop.[2]
Austin	64,766	/	2,985,824	X	568,900	=	12,340	3.6 to
					918,400	=	19,921	5.8
Dallas	111,083	/	2,985,824	X	568,900	=	21,165	2.3 to
					918,400	=	34,168	3.8
El Paso	265,819[3]	/	2,985,824	X	568,900	=	50,647	11.9 to
					918,400	=	81,762	19.2
Houston	281,331	/	2,985,824	X	568,900	=	53,603	3.4 to
					918,400	=	86,534	5.4
McAllen	47,361	/	2,985,824	X	568,900	=	9,024	13.6 to
					918,400	=	14,568	22.0
San Antonio	421,954	/	2,985,824	X	568,900	=	80,396	10.2 to
					918,400	=	129,787	16.5

Source: Frank D. Bean, et al., Estimates of the Number of Illegal Migrants in the State of Texas, Texas Population Research Center, Paper No. 4.001 (Austin: University of Texas, 1982).

[1] Undocumented Population Estimate =

$$\frac{\text{Total City Hispanic Population}}{\text{Total State Hispanic Population}} \text{ X Bean \& King State Estimates.}$$

[2] Percentage Total Population =

$$\frac{\text{Undocumented Population Estimate.}}{\text{Total City Population}}$$

[3] This figure derived from Table 25 in Census Publication PC 80-1-B45. Table 31 in the same publication gives a slightly lower total of 265,762.

Table H.2

Undocumented Population by County, 1982

County	Hispanic Population	/	Tot. Tex. Hisp. Population	X	Bean & King Range Est.[1]	=	Undoc. Pop. Est.[2]
Travis	72,228	/	2,985,824	X	568,900	=	13,762 to
					918,400	=	22,216
Dallas	154,561	/	2,985,824	X	568,900	=	29,449 to
					918,400	=	47,541
El Paso	297,001	/	2,985,824	X	568,900	=	56,587 to
					918,400	=	91,354
Harris	369,077	/	2,985,824	X	568,900	=	70,322 to
					918,400	=	113,523
Hidalgo	230,212	/	2,985,824	X	568,900	=	43,863 to
					918,400	=	70,810
Bexar	460,911	/	2,985,824	X	568,900	=	87,819 to
					918,400	=	141,770

Source: Frank D. Bean, et al., Estimates of the Number of Illegal Migrants in the State of Texas, Texas Population Research Center Paper No. 4.001 (Austin: University of Texas, 1982).

[1]Undocumented Population Estimate =

$$\frac{\text{Total County Hispanic Population}}{\text{Total State Hispanic Population}} \text{ X Bean \& King State Estimates.}$$

[2]Percentage Total Population =

$$\frac{\text{Undocumented Population Estimate.}}{\text{Total County Population}}$$

Methodology

Police Services. Three approaches were used to collect data: document research, interviews, and questionnaires. Individual police department budgets and organization charts were reviewed to determine whether or not there were costs and programs directly attributable to the undocumented population. Interviews were conducted, primarily with research and planning division personnel, to clarify the costs and nature of programs. Research and planning division personnel were also used as the access point for each department. The "General Police Department Questionnaire" (see Annex H.1) was submitted to each department, and the information returned formed the basis for department level impact projections. "Questionnaire for Police Officers" (see Annex H.2) was distributed evenly to patrol officers and their supervisors in Austin and San Antonio to assess the level and type of contact which undocumented persons have with the police force. Below are more details on the two questionnaires.

1. General Police Department Questionnaire (Annex H.1). This questionnaire was completed in detail by the research and planning divisions of the Austin and San Antonio Police Departments. General information was supplied by telephone from the Houston, Dallas, El Paso, and McAllen Police Departments.

This questionnaire was designed to gain and clarify information on police department organization and budget figures, percentage Hispanic population by city sector, resource allocation by sector and crime, crime statistics, cooperation with other jurisdictions and agencies, impact of undocumented population on patrol officer tasks, and trends in the use of police services by undocumented persons.

2. Questionnaire for Police Officers (Annex H.2). Copies of this questionnaire, 300 in Austin and 450 in San Antonio, were distributed to patrol persons through their respective research and planning divisions. The Houston, Dallas, El Paso, and McAllen Police Departments chose not to participate in the survey, citing manpower limitations.

The following conditions were agreed to for the administration of the officer questionnaires:

1. The survey was completely anonymous. A participant's name would in no way be connected with his/her responses.

2. Participation in the survey was to be completely voluntary.

3. None of the participants' jobs were to be jeopardized as a result of their participation or nonparticipation in the survey.

4. No press release or other announcement of the study or its results was to be made prior to the submission of the final

report to the Governor's Office.

These conditions helped insure that responses were candid and honest, with a minimum of outside influence. This is especially important, as these questionnaires are the basis on which undocumented persons' contact with police officers, and thus their use of police services, is measured.

The officer questionnaire distributed in Austin did not include instructions to return the survey form even if there was no contact with undocumented persons. This may be responsible for the relatively low return rate of these questionnaires compared to the return rate in San Antonio.

The number of questionnaires completed and returned in San Antonio may have been affected by two factors: first, on February 1, 1983, all shifts rotated hours; and second, two other survey forms--one of which was mandatory and took approximately two hours to complete--were being circulated during the same period as this questionnaire.

While in many cases the results of this survey indicated that legal status was either not a concern or not conclusively determined, the responses do give an indication of the level and nature of contact with suspected undocumented persons, the types of crimes in which they are involved as victims and/or suspects, seasonal fluctuations, and trends. The questionnaires permitted the insertion of personal information to qualify individual responses.

Jail and Prison Occupancy. All information on average cost, average duration of imprisonment, and total inmate population for 1982 was supplied by telephone from each city and county jail office. Texas state prison inmate statistics for 1982 were provided by the Texas Department of Corrections (TDC) in Huntsville, also by telephone.

POLICE SERVICE UTILIZATION ASSESSMENT

Overview

Of the six localities studied, none of the police departments has special procedures or reports for dealing with undocumented persons. Only El Paso, McAllen, and San Antonio cited notification of the INS as a cost, which they all consider negligible. Without exception, police departments estimated that the absence of undocumented persons would not result in any down-scaling of services, personnel, or equipment. In other words, the marginal cost of the presence of undocumented persons to the localities' police departments is estimated to be zero.

All localities also noted that the highest cost crimes, regardless of the legal status of the persons committing them, are normally murder, rape, and robbery.

Results from Police Officer Questionnaire

Our assessment of police service utilization was based on the "Questionnaire for Police Officers" distributed in San Antonio and Austin; 400 questionnaires were distributed in San Antonio with a 44 percent completion and return rate; 300 questionnaires were distributed in Austin with a 37 percent completion and return rate. The results of the questionnaires are summarized as follows:

Question Number:

2. Total number of valid surveys returned:
   175 San Antonio
   112 Austin

3. Percentage of patrol persons who believe that they dealt with undocumented persons in an official capacity during the last year:
   83.6%

4. Method of determining whether or not a person was undocumented (multiple responses account for the percentages not summing to 100%):
   66.9% asked them directly
   49.1% information surfaced during the normal course of procedure
   40.8% undocumented person volunteered information
   40.4% by the person's appearance (dress/behavior)
   39.7% because the person could not speak English
   30.3% information from a third party
   23.7% examined documents
    1.4% location of suspect
    0.3% style of language spoken

5a. Total number of officers who believe that they encountered undocumented persons over the past week:
    148 (51.6%)

5a1. Average number of undocumented persons believed to have been encountered by these officers over the past week:
    7

5b. Total number of officers who believe that they encountered undocumented persons over the past month:
    196 (68.3%)

5b1. Average number of undocumented persons believed to have been encountered by these officers over the past month:
    22

6. Total number of undocumented persons believed to be

encountered over the past year by category of offense:
186 (64.8%) stopped for traffic violation (other than DWI)
175 (61.0%) suspects in a crime (other than DWI)
147 (51.2%) misdemeanor
143 (49.8%) involved in a traffic accident
142 (49.5%) felony
132 (45.6%) suspected of DWI
119 (41.5%) victims of a crime
    29 (10.1%) assault
    24 (8.4%) robbery
    13 (4.5%) theft
     8 (2.8%) burglary
     2 (0.7%) hired, but not paid
     1 (0.3%) family disturbance
     1 (0.3%) other disturbance
     1 (0.3%) murder/homicide
     1 (0.3%) rape
     3 (1.0%) other crime

Suspect of other specified crime
9 (3.1%) assault
8 (2.8%) other disturbance
6 (2.1%) suspicious activity
5 (1.7%) other crime
3 (1.0%) murder/homicide
3 (1.0%) family disturbance
3 (1.0%) public intoxication
2 (0.7%) loitering
1 (0.3%) burglary
1 (0.3%) shoplifting
1 (0.3%) homosexual activity
1 (0.3%) picked up by INS

7. Total number of officers who responded positively to
question six whose encounter resulted in:
178 (62.0%) an arrest
163 (56.8%) a citation
140 (48.8%) questioning and release
 55 (19.2%) aid to victim
  7 (2.4%) legal advice
  5 (1.7%) EMS/medical
  2 (0.7%) referral
  1 (0.3%) settle dispute
  1 (0.3%) notification of INS

8. Total number of officers who believed that they responded
to a call for assistance by an undocumented person over
the past year:
151 (52.6%)

8a. Total number of reported calls for assistance by
undocumented persons by category:
 61 (21.3%) family disturbance
 44 (15.3%) other disturbance

```
33 (11.5%) assault
16  (5.6%) robbery
12  (4.2%) burglary
 9  (3.1%) theft
 7  (2.4%) traffic accident
 5  (1.7%) public intoxication
 3  (1.0%) murder/homicide
 2  (0.7%) suicide
 1  (0.3%) suspicious activity
 1  (0.3%) other accident
 1  (0.3%) criminal trespass
 1  (0.3%) runaway
 1  (0.3%) hitch-hiker
 1  (0.3%) legal aid
11  (3.8%) other calls
```

9. Total number of officers who believe that there is a
    seasonal fluctuation in the number of undocumented persons
    encountered:
    73 (25.4%)

    Of these, the following months were designated as those
    when most undocumented were encountered (most officers
    designated 2-3 months and this multiple response
    accounts for the numbers not totaling to 73):
    ```
    64 (22.3%) Jun
    62 (21.6%) Jul
    54 (18.8%) Aug
    22  (7.7%) May
    16  (5.6%) Sep
    13  (4.5%) Apr
    ```

    The following months were designated as those when
    least undocumenteds were encountered:
    ```
    45 (15.7%) Jan
    44 (15.3%) Dec
    41 (14.3%) Feb
    11  (3.8%) Nov
     9  (3.1%) Mar
    ```

10. Total number of officers who believe that there has been
    a trend over the past two years in the number of incidents
    involving undocumented persons:
    150 (52.3%) increasing
     71 (24.7%) constant
      8 (2.8%) decreasing

11,12,13. There was no significant correlation between the numbers
    of undocumented persons reportedly encountered by an officer
    and that officer's Spanish language ability or racial/ethnic
    status.

The questionnaires indicate highest incidences of encounters in San

Antonio's Sector One (downtown) and Austin's Charlie South (southeast) sector. This is consistent with census data of Hispanic residence and police department estimations. Both of these sectors are considered to be "high crime areas."

The questionnaires also indicate that many officers suspect that a large percentage of undocumented persons do not file against a suspect, report a crime, call for assistance, or accept police assistance for fear of detection and/or deportation. This may be an indication of a higher than reported incidence of crimes with undocumented persons as victims.

PRISON OCCUPANCY ASSESSMENT

San Antonio and Bexar County

Detailed information on undocumented persons in city and county jails was available only for San Antonio and Bexar County. This jail system is somewhat unusual in that the city and county share the same facility. Of the six localities studied, only El Paso and El Paso County have a similar arrangement.

The 1982 budget for the San Antonio-Bexar County Jail was $6,100,000. The average cost per inmate per day is estimated at $21, and the average duration of detention, for all prisoners, is estimated at two days.

Legal status is normally determined by INS review, either in person or by reviewing booking slips for the place of birth. In 1982, of 40,439 total city prisoners apprehended, 522 were undocumented, and of 20,914 total county prisoners apprehended, 407 were undocumented. Thus, there was an estimated $21,924 cost to the City of San Antonio and $17,094 cost to Bexar County, or 0.006 percent of their combined budget. These estimates included all nationalities of undocumented persons, of which approximately 85 percent were Mexican citizens, approximately 8 percent were El Salvadoran citizens, and approximately 5 percent were Canadian citizens.

The types of crimes for which undocumented persons in San Antonio and Bexar County were arrested in 1982 are summarized in Table H.3. Those crimes reported to be the highest cost crimes--murder, rape, and robbery--account for 6.5 percent of the total crimes committed by undocumented offenders.

Upon completion of jail stay, undocumented persons who are convicted of felonies normally go to the Texas Department of Corrections to serve their sentence, after which they are deported. Non-felony offenders face voluntary departure if the crime is not serious, or deportation, or prosecution for illegal entry, or a formal request for voluntary departure at a later date (in the event that the spouse is legal and the crime is not a serious one).

Table H.3

Incidence of Crimes for Which Undocumented Persons

Were Arrested in San Antonio and Bexar County, 1982

Category	Frequency
Felony	223
Murder, voluntary manslaughter, other murder	9
Aggravated robbery with dangerous weapon and other robbery	30
Rape and other sex related	21
Burglary and felony theft	137
Crimes involving narcotics and marijuana	12
Aggravated assault	6
Repeat DWI, carrying weapon	8
Misdemeanor	706
Theft	125
Possession of less than two ounces of marijuana	18
Prostitution or other sex related	3
DWI, simple assault, not involving moral turpitude	195
Drunks and other misdemeanors	365
Total (522 city and 407 county arrests)	929

Source: San Antonio INS.

Other Cities

If it is assumed that the same percentage of undocumented persons is arrested in each city as in San Antonio,* then by using median figures for estimated populations of undocumented persons in each city, average costs per city can be computed as shown in Table H.4. However, one should be cautious about drawing conclusions from this data, given San Antonio's long history as a migrant-receiving community--a history which is not easily comparable to other cities in the sample. Also, both the City of San Antonio and Bexar County, in which it is located, represent the areas with the highest estimated undocumented populations of the six cities and counties treated here. Using these percentages to estimate the other five city and county jail populations represents, therefore, an upward bias in the number of inmates and consequently in the costs.

Other Counties

If the percentage of undocumented persons arrested in each county is assumed to be similar to Bexar County's,** then average costs per county can be computed as shown in Table H.5.

---

*Note on computation:
Percent Undocumented Persons Arrested =

$$\frac{\text{Number Undocumented Persons Arrested}[1]}{\text{Estimated Undocumented Population}[2]}$$

For San Antonio: (upper range) $\frac{522}{80,396} = 0.65\%$

(lower range) $\frac{522}{129,787} = 0.40\%$

[1]See Table H.3.
[2]See Table H.1 estimates.

**Note on computation:
Percent Undocumented Persons Arrested =

$$\frac{\text{Number Undocumented Persons Arrested}[1]}{\text{Estimated Undocumented Population}[2]}$$

(**continued on p. 243)

Table H.4

Average City Jail Cost Estimates Due to Occupancy by Undocumented Persons, 1982

City	Estimated Undoc. Population[1]	X	Percent in Jail[2]	X	Average Stay (in days)	X	Average Cost Per Day[3]	=	Estimated Cost for 1982 Attributable to Undocumented (in dollars)
Austin	16,131		.0040	X	1.5	X	$30.00	=	$ 2,904 to
		X	.0065	X	1.5	X	$30.00	=	$ 4,718
Dallas	27,667		.0040	X	1.0	X	$39.69	=	$ 4,392 to
		X	.0065	X	1.0	X	$39.69	=	$ 7,138
El Paso	66,205		.0040	X	1.5	X	$17.61	=	$ 6,995 to
		X	.0065	X	1.5	X	$17.61	=	$11,367
Houston	70,069		.0040	X	1.0	X	$50.00	=	$14,014 to
		X	.0065	X	1.0	X	$50.00	=	$22,772
McAllen	11,796		.0040	X	1.0	X	$17.50	=	$ 826 to
		X	.0065	X	1.0	X	$17.50	=	$ 1,342
San Antonio	105,092		.0040	X	2.0	X	$21.00	=	$17,655 to
		X	.0065	X	2.0	X	$21.00	=	$28,690[4]

Total $46,786 to $76,027

Source: Computations based on Bean and King and the 1980 Census.

[1] Average computed from Table 1.1.
[2] Based on percent in San Antonio City Jail.
[3] City jails compute average costs differently. Some use the total budget, while others use only part of the budget.
[4] Using this formula to estimate gives us an average of $23,173, slightly above the $21,924 cost estimated more accurately from San Antonio direct data. This gives us some confidence that our figures are conservative.

Table H.5

Average County Jail Cost Estimates Due to Occupancy by Undocumented Persons, 1982

County	Estimated Undoc. Population[1]	X	Percent in Jail[2]	X	Average Stay (in days)	X	Average Cost Per Day[3]	=	Estimated Cost for 1982 Attributable to Undocumented (in dollars)
Bexar	114,795	X	.0029	X	30	X	$21.00	=	$209,731 to
		X	.0046	X	30	X	$21.00	=	$332,676
Dallas	38,495	X	.0029	X	30	X	$23.95	=	$ 80,210 to
		X	.0046	X	30	X	$23.95	=	$127,230
El Paso	73,971	X	.0029	X	30	X	$17.61	=	$113,329 to
		X	.0046	X	30	X	$17.61	=	$179,763
Harris	91,923	X	.0029	X	30	X	$22.72	=	$181,699 to
		X	.0046	X	30	X	$22.72	=	$288,212
Hidalgo	57,337	X	.0029	X	30	X	$17.50	=	$ 87,296 to
		X	.0046	X	30	X	$17.50	=	$138,469
Travis	17,989	X	.0029	X	30	X	$29.00	=	$ 45,386 to
		X	.0046	X	30	X	$29.00	=	$ 71,992

Total $717,651 to $1,138,342

Source: Computations based on Census and Jail Supervisor Estimates.

[1]Median figures calculated from estimates in Table 1.2.
[2]Using percentages from Bexar County.
[3]County jails compute average costs differently. Some include the total budget in the computations, while others exclude certain items as overhead.

Texas Department of Corrections

The Public Affairs Office of TDC in Huntsville reports that in a count of inmates on April 30, 1983, 501 were found to be non-U.S. citizens. Assuming that all of these were undocumented aliens, and that 501 represents an average daily total, then the yearly average cost of undocumented aliens can be estimated (see Table H.6).

Table H.6

TDC Yearly Average Cost of Undocumented Persons

Number of Undocumented Inmates in TDC Facilities Per Day--- 501

Average Cost of Each Inmate Per Day-----------------------$12.11[1]
    Daily Cost of Undocumented Inmates-----------------$6,067.11
                                                      X 365

Yearly Average Cost of Undocumented Aliens-----$2,214,495.15

Note: The yearly average cost figures, although less than one percent of the total 1982 TDC budget of $254,980,778,[2] are still biased upward because some of the non-citizens are legal resident aliens.

[1]This figure was reported by the Public Affairs Department of TDC in Huntsville--(409) 295-6371, Ext. 419.

[2]The TDC actually operates on a two-year budget. The state allocated a total of $516,972,186 for fiscal years 1982-1983. J. Byrd of the TDC Public Affairs Office reports that all of this is state money; TDC gets no federal money.

CONCLUSIONS

Any conclusions drawn from the above information on police services and jail/prison occupancy must be qualified with a recognition of the limitations

---

(**continued)

For Bexar County: (upper range) $\frac{407}{87,819} = 0.46\%$

                  (lower range) $\frac{407}{141,770} = 0.29\%$

[1]See Table H.3.
[2]See Table H.2 estimates

of data collection, non-standard computation formulas, and the overall incompleteness of data. Still with these limitations in mind, some conclusions can be drawn.

From Police Department and Jail/Prison Data

The total cost for the operation of local police departments, city/county jails, and the state prison system would not change in the absence of undocumented persons. In other words, the marginal cost (in dollars) to the taxpayer is zero.

The average costs to local and state government, while quantifiable, are low when compared to total police department, city/county jail, and state prison system budgets. As suspects, undocumented persons are considerably more likely to be involved in misdemeanor than felony offenses.

It should also be noted that indirect impacts occur on medical and health services such as hospital costs; social services such as the Family Violence Program and Protective Services for Children; and legal services such as Legal Aid.

If impact were based on one-half or twice the Bean and King estimates, the marginal cost (in dollars) to the taxpayer would still be zero, and the average cost to local and state governments would still be low when compared to total budgets.

From Police Officer Data

A large majority of police patrol officers believe that they have contact with undocumented persons at least monthly.

The incidence of contact with undocumented persons is highest in city sectors with proportionately large Hispanic residency.

The incidence of contact with undocumented persons is highest during warm weather months and lowest during cold weather months.

Undocumented persons are at least as likely to be victims as they are to be suspects in reported crimes.

Annex H.1

GENERAL POLICE DEPARTMENT QUESTIONNAIRE

1. Please provide a map or diagram indicating the sectors into which the Police Department divides the city.

2. What sectors of the city are suspected to have the greatest concentrations of undocumented persons? Why these sectors?

3. To which sectors of the city were the Police Officer Questionnaires distributed? How many were distributed in each sector?

4. Describe the method of distribution and collection of the surveys.

5. What is the total city population? What is your source of information?

6. What is the population of each sector? Source of information?

7. What is the city's total Hispanic population? Source of information?

8. What is the total Hispanic population by sector? Source of information?

9. What is the total size of the city police force and how is that broken down by job (example: total number of patrolmen ____)?

10. What is the total size of the police force by sector?

11. What is your total budget and how is it broken down by activity and/or division?

12. If possible, please estimate total budget per sector.

13. Within your city, what sectors require the most resources?

14. Within your city, what crimes require the most resources?

15. List total city crime statistics.

16. List crime statistics by sector.

17. List statistics by suspect's race (most notably, Hispanic).

18. List statistics by victim's race (most notably, Hispanic).

19. Does your Police Department have any special programs and/or personnel for dealing with Hispanic and/or undocumented persons? If so, please list and describe each, including total budget.

20. Are there any other special costs involved with undocumented suspects and/or victims? If so, please specify and quantify.

21. Do federal or state agencies ever request your assistance in matters involving undocumented persons? If so, please specify.

22. Does the Mexican government or its law enforcement agencies ever ask your Department for assistance in dealing with undocumented persons or do you maintain reciprocal agreements? If so, please specify.

23. If there were no undocumented persons in your city, could you downscale your Department? If so, please specify how.

24. Has your Department noted any trends (seasonal or otherwise) in the frequency of undocumented persons as suspects and/or victims? If so, please specify.

24. How many officers on your force are bilingual? How many are patrolmen and to which sectors are they assigned?

26. What percentage of your investigations are estimated to involve undocumented persons as victims and/or suspects?

27. What percentage of the cases for which your officers make court appearances are estimated to involve undocumented persons as victims and/or suspects?

28. What percentage of these cases' convictions are undocumented persons? How is status determined?

Annex H.2

QUESTIONNAIRE FOR POLICE OFFICERS

As part of a study on the use of public services by the undocumented population of Texas being conducted by the LBJ School of Public Affairs, the following questionnaire is being circulated among police officers in various cities. Your participation is totally voluntary and all responses are anonymous and confidential.

The purpose of these questions is to help determine what additional costs, if any, are incurred by this agency in dealing with undocumented persons during the performance of the agency's normal functions. We would appreciate your answering the questions with as much candor and accuracy as possible. All questions refer only to your experiences with undocumented persons during the last year, and only to those encounters which were directly related to your official duties.

1. Date: _____

2. Sector/Area of the City:_____

3. In your official capacity during the last year have you dealt with any persons whom you knew to be undocumented?

    _____No (if no, please indicate here and turn in questionnaire)

    _____Yes (if yes, continue)

4. How did you determine whether or not a person was undocumented?

    _____examined their documents

    _____asked them directly

    _____they volunteered the information

    _____information surfaced during the normal course of procedure

    _____information from a third party

    _____by the person's appearance (dress/behavior)

    _____because the person couldn't speak English

    _____other (specify)_____

5. Over the past week how many undocumented persons do you think you encountered? _____

    Over the past month? _____

6. Of those you encountered during the last year, about how many

were: (enter the number, if none, enter zero)

____stopped for traffic violation (other than DWI)

____suspected of DWI

____suspects in a crime (other than DWI) ____felony

____misdemeanor

____involved in a traffic accident

____victims of a crime (specify)_____

____other (specify)_____

7. Of those in question 6, how many resulted in:

____an arrest

____a citation

____questioning and release

____aid to victim (specify) _____

____other (specify) _____

8. In the last year have you responded to a call for assistance made by an undocumented person?

____No

____Yes (specify number and types of calls)_____

_____

9. Do there seem to be seasonal fluctuations in the numbers of undocumented persons you encounter?

____No

____Yes (specify) Months with most _____

Months with least _____

10. Over the past two years, has the number of incidents involving undocumented persons been:

____Increasing

____Decreasing

____More or less constant

Personal Information:

11. Do you speak Spanish?

_____Not at all

_____Very little

_____Some

_____Fluently

12. Do you understand Spanish?

_____Not at all

_____Very little

_____Some

_____Very well

13. Would you identify yourself as:

_____White, not of Hispanic origin

_____Chicano/Mexican American/other Hispanic

_____Black

_____Other

THANK YOU very much for your cooperation!

SELECTED ANNOTATED BIBLIOGRAPHY

Arnold, Fred. "Providing Medical Services to Undocumented Immigrants: Costs and Public Policy." International Migration Review 13 (Winter 1979): 706-715.
     This paper reviews some of the cost estimates that have been made by hospitals and county governments, examines methodological problems in arriving at such estimates, and discusses the progress (or lack of progress) of proposed legislative programs that address this issue.

Avante Systems, Inc. and Cultural Research Associates. A Survey of the Undocumented Population In Two Texas Border Areas. San Antonio: Cultural Research Associates, September, 1978.
     The information for this study was based on interviews with 600 apprehended and unapprehended illegal aliens in El Paso and the Lower Rio Grande Valley. It was determined that many of the aliens interviewed paid social security and federal income taxes. However, few utilized public services such as unemployment insurance and welfare. The study concludes that rather than seek public assistance, illegal aliens rely on an informal network of friends and relatives.

Bean, Frank D., Allan G. King and Jeffrey S. Passel. "The Number of Illegal Migrants of Mexican Origin in the United States: Sex Ratio-Based Estimates for 1980." Demography 20, No. 1 (February, 1983): 99.
     This article reports the results of applying a sex ratio-based method to estimate the number of undocumented Mexicans residing in the United States in 1980. The approach centers on a comparison between the hypothetical sex ratio one would expect to find in Mexico in the absence of emigration to the United States and the sex ratio that is in fact reported in preliminary results from the 1980 Mexican Census. The procedure involves, inter alia, assuming a range of values for the sex ratio at birth and for census coverage differentials by sex in Mexico. Even the combinations of these values most likely to result in large estimates suggest that no more than 4 million illegal migrants of Mexican origin were residing in the United States in 1980.

Bustamante, Jorge A. "Undocumented Immigration from Mexico: Research Report." International Migration Review 11 (Summer, 1977): 140-77.
     This report is based on 919 interviews with illegal aliens recently deported from the United States. The interviews were conducted in eight border cities in Mexico. The report indicates that the majority of the illegal aliens paid social security and federal income taxes while working in the United States. Only a few of the respondents utilized public services such as welfare, schools, or free medical care. The author concludes that the illegal aliens contribute more to the public coffers via taxes than they receive in public services.

Cardenas, Gilbert and Estevan T. Flores. "Social, Economic and Demographic Characteristics of Undocumented Mexicans in the Houston Labor Market: A Preliminary Report" (report submitted to Gulf Coast Legal Foundation, 2601 Main, Houston, TX 77002, 1980).

Based on a sample of 138 undocumented Mexican immigrants residing in Houston, Texas, this report examines the following broad range of topics: demographic and household characteristics of the population; employment and income information; wage deductions; income tax payments; consumption characteristics; length of residency and residency intentions; hospital and public and private social service usage; union participation; and children's attendance or non-attendance in public and private schools. The findings relevant to this study include that 80 percent of those employed had income taxes deducted from their wages, 84 percent had social security deducted, and 49 percent had hospital insurance deducted. A little over half (52 percent) of the sample had filed income tax returns. The mean total monthly expenditure made for such items as rent, food, clothing, transportation, child care, and other living expenses was $655. Over half (55 percent) of the respondents remitted no money to relatives in Mexico. About a third (39 percent) of the sample had never been to a hospital or clinic, and of those who had been, 58 percent paid for the services out of pocket, with an additional 24 percent paying with private insurance. Other findings were: 7 percent of the sample owned land in the U.S.; less than 1 percent of the sample were receiving welfare, unemployment compensation, social security benefits, AFDC, Catholic charities, or migrant health services; and 21 percent of the families interviewed had children in U.S. schools.

Cohen, Lucy M. "Gifts to Strangers: Public Policy and the Delivery of Health Services to Illegal Aliens." Anthropological Quarterly 46, no. 3 (July, 1973): 183-95.

This paper examines policy problems of providing health care to illegal aliens. The author argues that policy makers are reluctant to extend government-sponsored medical care to illegal aliens because they view the aliens as "outsiders," and consider medical coverage for these people as "gifts for which there is no return."

Conner, Roger. Breaking Down the Barriers: The Changing Relationship between Illegal Immigration and Welfare. Washington, D.C.: Federation for American Immigration Reform, Immigration Paper IV, September, 1982.

This monograph challenges the assumption that illegal aliens pay more in taxes than they receive in public services. Focusing on the utilization of welfare services by illegal aliens, the author cites recent studies which indicate that a number of illegal aliens do receive AFDC and unemployment benefits. He dismisses earlier studies (North and Houstoun, 1976; Cornelius, 1977; and Bustamante, 1977) because of their small and "unrepresentative samples." The author asserts that today's illegal immigrant is urban, educated, permanent, and "more aggressive" in dealing with the government. He concludes that the high utilization of public services by illegal aliens is another reason to oppose illegal immigration.

Conrad, Jane Reister. "Health Care for Indigent Illegal Aliens: Whose

Responsibility?" <u>University of California, Davis Law Review</u> 8 (1975): 107-26.

The author argues that the current system for providing health care to illegal aliens is inadequate and potentially dangerous. The illegal aliens pose a potential health hazard because of their low rates of immunization and general reluctance to seek medical attention for fear of being detected or being unable to pay. The fundamental problem is that neither the local, county, state, nor federal government is willing to bear the financial burden of providing medical services to these people. The author proposes policy recommendations, and calls for comprehensive legislation which would clarify government responsibility and insure that the illegal aliens receive proper health care.

Cornelius, Wayne A. <u>Illegal Mexican Migration to the United States: Recent Research Findings, Policy Implications and Research Priorities.</u> Cambridge: Massachusetts Institute of Technology, 1977.

This is an important study which deals only tangentially with costs for providing services to undocumented migrants compared with revenues received from such persons. The conclusion is that revenues exceed costs.

Cross, Harry E. and James E. Sandos. <u>The Impact of Undocumented Mexican Workers on the United States: A Critical Assessment.</u> Battelle Population and Development Policy Program, Working Paper No. 15. Washington, D.C.: Battelle Human Affairs Research Centers, 1979.

This paper provides a good summary and analysis of what has been found about undocumented persons from various studies. The data compared include that from referenced studies by Robinson, Lancaster and Scheuren, Heer, Lesko Associates, Flores and Cardenas, Van Arsdol, Villalpando, North and Houstoun, Cardenas, Bustamante, Cornelius, CENIET, Orange County Task Force, Avante Systems, Mines, Reichert and Massey, Shadow, Stoddard, Dagodag, Kelly, Johnson and Ogle, Canedo, Kearney and Stuart, Chiswick, Liner, Maram, Massey, Piore, Warren, Williams, and Reyes Associates as well as work of their own. Data about tax payments and service utilization are compared with the findings that wages are paid differently along the border than elsewhere; Texas employers make fewer paycheck deductions than do their Californian counterparts; and long-term migrants pay in more taxes and have more opportunity to use tax-funded services than short-term migrants. Data about use of social services vary widely among the various studies, and it is stressed that different groups within the undocumented population have different service utilization rates, with long-term settlers being the highest user group.

Elwell, P.J. et al. "Haitian and Dominican Undocumented Aliens in New York City: A Preliminary Report." <u>Migration Today</u> 5 (December 1977): 5-9.

This study was based on data generated from 54 interviews with unapprehended Haitians and Dominicans. The authors discovered that the majority of the aliens interviewed were paying social security and federal income taxes. By and large there was a low rate of utilization of public services by these undocumented aliens. However, in comparison with undocumented aliens from other countries, the Haitians and Dominicans had a higher rate of utilization of schools, hospitals, and unemployment insurance. The authors conclude that in view of their contributions to the government in terms of taxes, and their relatively low utilization of public services, the undocumented Haitians and Dominicans are not a drain on public coffers.

Moore, Joan W. "Mexican Americans and Cities: A Study in Migration and the Use of Formal Resources." International Migration Review,   5 (Fall 1971): 292-308.

   Based on a probability sample of household heads and their spouses for Mexican Americans living in Los Angeles County in 1965-66, Moore explores the tendency of researchers to overlook use of informal resources in explaining the low utilization of formal resources by Mexican Americans. She discusses the influence of historic patterns of discrimination and current U.S. living conditions in shaping the resource-use patterns of Mexican Americans. She finds that there is a tendency by Mexican Americans to use informal (kin and friends) resources rather than formal (government, professionals, institutions) resources, and that this tendency is more pronounced for women than men, and for those born in rural places than those born in urban places. Additionally, choice of formal or informal sources of aid is influenced by the nature of the problem for which help is being sought. The more bureaucratized the problem, the more likely a person is to seek formal aid.

North, David S. and Marion F. Houstoun. The Characteristics and Role of Illegal Aliens in the U.S. Labor Market: An Exploratory Study. Washington, D.C.: Linton and Co., Inc., 1976.

   This study is based on interviews with 793 apprehended aliens. The authors found that the majority of the illegal aliens paid social security and federal income taxes. With the exception of hospitals, the illegal aliens utilized few social services and income transfer programs, e.g., unemployment insurance, education, food stamps, and welfare. The authors conclude that the illegal aliens are not a drain on the public coffers; however, they suggest that more research needs to be done in this area.

Orange County Task Force on Medical Care for Illegal Aliens. The Economic Impact of Undocumented Immigrants on Public Health Services in Orange County: A Study of Medical Costs, Tax Contributions, and Health Needs of Undocumented Immigrants.   County of Orange, California, Board of Supervisors, 1978.

   This report is based on data from 177 interviews of illegal aliens and on information collected from Orange County schools and hospitals. The results indicate a low rate of utilization of public services by illegal aliens. The only exception was health care. However, the study indicates that most of the aliens paid their bills and few received free medical care. The study concludes that illegal aliens are not a burden on the County because they are contributing more in taxes than they are receiving in public services.

Simon, Julian L. "What Immigrants Take from and Give to the Public Coffers." Champaign-Urbana: University of Illinois, 1980. (Mimeographed)

Using the 1976 Survey of Income and Education, Simon compares 15,000 immigrant families to 135,000 non-immigrant families. The immigrants are legal immigrants. Simon finds that until about 12 years after arrival, immigrants use substantially less of such public services as welfare, unemployment compensation, food stamps, medicare-medicaid, and schooling for children than do native families, largely due to less use of social security because of their youthful age. After 12 years, the immigrant families show usage patterns similar to those of natives. With respect to payments, Simon finds that after 2 to 6 years, immigrant families come to pay as much in taxes as do native families, and after this they pay substantially more. The net balance of the two forces is positive in every year for the natives, such that immigrants contribute more to the public coffers than they take from them.

Texas Department of Human Resources. Final Report on the Study of Illegal Food Stamp Participation by Mexican Nationals. Austin, July, 1982.
This study was conducted by the Texas Department of Human Resources and the U.S. Department of Agriculture. Examining the utilization of food stamps by Mexican nationals along the Texas-Mexican border, the study indicated that few Mexican nationals were actually receiving food stamps.

U.S. Congress, House of Representatives. Medical Treatment of Illegal Aliens. Hearings before the Subcommittee on Health and the Environment. Washington, D.C.: U.S. Government Printing Office, 1977.

U.S. General Accounting Office. Impact of Illegal Aliens on Public Assistance Programs: Too Little Is Known. Washington, D.C.: U.S. General Accounting Office, December, 1977.

------------. Issues Concerning Social Security Benefits. Report to the Congress by the Comptroller General of the United States. Washington, D.C.: U.S. General Accounting Office, 1983.
This report analyzes the rapid growth of social security payments to aliens living abroad. The data indicate that by and large these beneficiaries worked in the U.S. less time, paid fewer social security taxes, and have more dependents than the average social security beneficiary. The report outlines measures for curtailing future social security benefits to aliens living abroad and estimates the potential impacts of implementing these changes.

Valverde, Leonard A. and Albert Cortez. The Impact of Mandated Enrollment of Undocumented Students in Selected Texas Public Schools. Report for the Office of Advanced Research in Hispanic Education, College of Education, University of Texas at Austin, 1983.
Information gathered from a sample (N=49) of Texas school districts with relatively high counts or percentages of undocumented students revealed that large concentrations of such students result in a need for more bilingual teachers, more facilities, and/or more specialized support personnel. To assess the accuracy of the perceptions of those completing the survey, a question was asked about increase or decrease in enrollment

of undocumented students from the previous year, and this information was then compared to actual counts. There was about 80 percent accuracy in reporting, with the greatest error occurring when the count had actually declined. Most of those interviewed favored a per pupil funding for undocumented impact of over $500. Those surveyed noted unique needs they felt undocumented students brought to the schools as well as contributions they thought such children made to the educational process.

Van Arsdol, Maurice D., Jr., Joan W. Moore, David M. Heer, and Susan Paulvir Haynie. Non-Apprehended and Apprehended Undocumented Residents in the Los Angeles Labor Market: An Exploratory Study. Report prepared for the Employment and Training Administration of the U.S. Department of Labor, 1979. (Available from National Technical Information Service, Springfield, Virginia, 22151.)

Using an immigration service as a source of interviews, information was gathered about social, labor force and earnings experiences of non-apprehended undocumented immigrants to Los Angeles from Mexico and other Latin American countries. This was compared to previously described apprehended migrants, with the result that those oriented towards staying longer in the U.S. were found to include more females and to have lower labor force participation rates and more kin ties. Of the sample, 11 percent reported that they were currently receiving some transfer payments in the form of welfare, earned social security, pensions or other sources; 12 percent, including those now receiving welfare, reported that they had received welfare at some time; 37 percent owed bills to the county hospital, and 21 percent had children in U.S. schools.

Villalpando, Manuel V. A Study of the Socio-Economic Impact of Illegal Aliens, County of San Diego. San Diego: Human Resources Agency, County of San Diego, 1977.

This study was conducted for the San Diego County Immigration Council. The Council examined the utilization of public services such as education, welfare, hospitals, and law enforcement by illegal aliens and estimated the cost to the County of providing these services. It was determined that although there was a low rate of utilization of public services by illegal aliens, the County does incur costs. However, the study concludes that the revenue received from taxes paid by the illegal aliens far exceeds the cost of providing these services.